THE WAR OF THE
RUNNING DOGS

THE WAR OF THE
RUNNING DOGS

How Malaya Defeated the
Communist Guerrillas 1948–60

Noel Barber

'The Revolution was effected before the war commenced. The Revolution was in the minds and hearts of the people'

John Adams, USA, 1818

'The answer lies not in pouring more troops into the jungle, but in the hearts and minds of the people'

General Templer, Malaya, 1952

CASSELL

Cassell Military Paperbacks

Cassell
Wellington House, 125 Strand
London WC2R 0BB

First published in 1971 by William Collins
This Cassell Military Paperbacks edition 2004

British Library Cataloguing-in-Publication Data.

A catalogue record for this book is
available from the British Library.

ISBN 0 304 36671 4

Printed and bound in Great Britain by
Cox & Wyman Ltd, Reading, Berkshire

www.orionbooks.co.uk

FOR SIMONETTA WITH LOVE

CONTENTS

LIST OF ILLUSTRATIONS

War in Malaya (Popperfoto)

Malayan village burned by bandits (Popperfoto)

Malaya repeals Emergency (Associated Press Ltd)

Sir Henry Gurney, British High Commissioner in Malaya (Popperfoto)

Sir Henry Gurney assassinated – thirty-seven bullet holes in his Rolls-Royce (Popperfoto)

Tapping rubber, whilst a guard stands by, alert (Popperfoto)

Malaya's unhappy neutrals (Popperfoto)

Members of the Scots Guards clearing an area suspected to be the hiding place of Communist bandits (Radio Times Hulton Picture Library)

British fighters landing by helicopter (Popperfoto)

Evacuation of casualties from the Malayan jungle (Radio Times Hulton Picture Library)

Evacuation of casualties by helicopter (Radio Times Hulton Picture Library)

Troops searching the Malayan jungle for Chinese squatters (Radio Times Hulton Picture Library)

Troops ford a jungle stream near Kuala Lumpur (Associated Press Ltd)

A member of the Malay Special Police checking the identity card of a suspect (Radio Times Hulton Picture Library)

Harry Hopkins touring Malaya meets the fighting planters (Popperfoto)

General Sir Gerald Templer, British High Commissioner in guerrilla–harried Malaya, congratulates a platoon of Gurkhas (Associated Press Ltd)

Dyaks in action against the Communists in the Malayan jungle (Radio Times Hulton Picture Library)

A Gurkha stands guard on a Malayan rubber estate (Popperfoto)

Suspected Communists rounded up from the dense jungle (Associated Press Ltd)

Chin Peng, Chen Tien, Abdul Maidin and John Davis who served with the Communists during Japanese occupation (Popperfoto)

The Chief Minister of the Federation of Malaya, Tunku Abdul Rahman (Popperfoto)

Their Majesties outside the front entrance of Istana Negara (Popperfoto)

CAST OF PRINCIPAL CHARACTERS

The Government
SIR EDWARD GENT High Commissioner
SIR HENRY GURNEY High Commissioner
GEN. SIR HAROLD BRIGGS First Director of Operations
GEN. SIR GERALD TEMPLER First 'Supremo'
SIR ROBERT THOMPSON Malayan Civil Service, later Secretary
    for Defence
MALCOLM MACDONALD Commissioner-General for South-
    East Asia

The Police
NICOL GRAY Commissioner, 1948–52
COL. ARTHUR YOUNG his successor
IRENE LEE
DAVID STORRIER Special Branch
EVAN DAVIES
'TWO-GUN' BILL STAFFORD Officer in charge of Detectives,
    Kuala Lumpur

The Malayans
TUNKU ABDUL RAHMAN Malaya's first Prime Minister
YEOP MAHIDIN leader of 26,000 kampong guards
C. C. TOO Psychological Warfare Expert

Planters and Miners
PETER LUCY rubber planter
ROBERT PUCKERIDGE rubber planter
IRA PHELPS tin miner
NORMAN CLEAVELAND tin miner

The Communists
CHIN PENG leader of the Malayan Communist Party
LAU YEW head of the armed forces
LAM SWEE Political Commissar
LEE MENG leading girl courier
'SHORTY' KUK leader of Johore Communists
OSMAN CHINA key propaganda expert
GOH PENG TUN
HOR LUNG
ABDULLAH CD leading Malay Communist

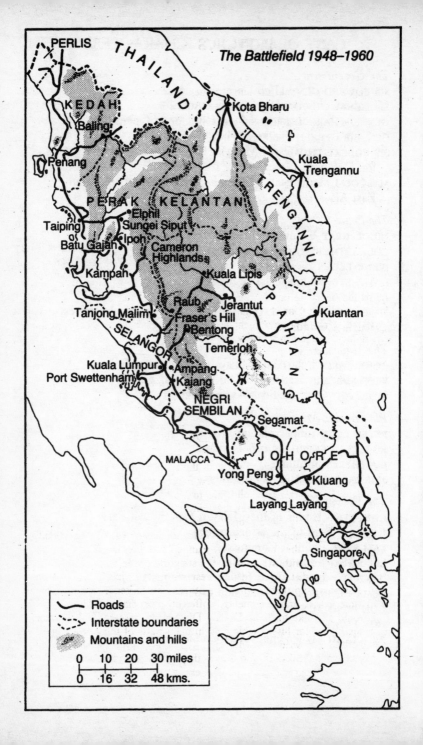

The Battlefield 1948–1960

PERLIS
THAILAND
KEDAH
Baling
Penang
PERAK
KELANTAN
Kota Bharu
Kuala Trengannu
TRENGANNU
Taiping
Elphil
Sungei Siput
Ipoh
Batu Gajah
Cameron Highlands
Kampah
Kuala Lipis
PAHANG
Tanjong Malim
Raub
Jerantut
Fraser's Hill
Bentong
Kuantan
SELANGOR
Temerloh
Kuala Lumpur
Ampang
Port Swettenham
Kajang
NEGRI SEMBILAN
Segamat
MALACCA
JOHORE
Yong Peng
Kluang
Layang Layang
Singapore

Roads
Interstate boundaries
Mountains and hills

0   10   20   30 miles
0   16   32   48 kms.

AUTHOR'S NOTE

CTs

Throughout this book Communist guerrilla fighters are referred to as CTs, short for Communist Terrorists. At first they were officially labelled 'bandits' – until the British discovered that this word had unfortunate connotations. 'Bandits' had been the identical term used by the Japanese and Chiang Kai-shek to describe Communists; since neither of these powers had been successful, the use of 'bandits' by the British put them on a similar level in the eyes of Malayan Chinese. The British therefore changed 'bandit' to 'Communist Terrorist' or CT. In order to make for easier reading, I have used the term throughout.

A War or an Emergency?

It *was* a war but there was a curious reason why it was never called one. As the author John Gullick, an authority on Malaya and one-time member of the Malayan Civil Service, points out, 'It was a war – though out of regard for the London insurance market, on which the Malayan economy relied for cover, no one ever used the word.' This misnomer continued for twelve years, for the simple reason that insurance rates covered losses of stocks and equipment through riot and civil commotion in an emergency, but not in a civil war.

Straits Dollars

During the war there were eight Straits dollars to the £ sterling, and all computations have been made at this rate.

ACKNOWLEDGMENTS

So many people have helped me with the research for this book, that it would be invidious to single out a few names, ranging as they do from high-ranking generals and politicians to Malay policemen and ex-Communists. There is also another more intriguing reason why it would be unfair to name only these people: a great deal of my information came from Special Branch leaders who could not in any case by identified. This is, after all, the story of a war planned and won largely by civilian and police effort with the military in a supporting role, and many of the anonymous Special Branch chiefs responsible for victory are still on 'active service'. To them and all the others who so generously gave me their time, advice and documents, I offer my most sincere thanks.

I would also like to thank Donald Dinsley, my research collaborator in many books, for his valuable help in many parts of the world while I was working and writing in Malaysia.

My grateful thanks are also due to those authors and publishers who kindly gave me permission to publish extracts from their books.

N.B. *Kuala Lumpur*, 1969–70

Phase One
THE COMMUNIST OFFENSIVE
1948–51

1 THE BATTLEFIELD

Above all else, and from the earliest moments of history, one primordial force has dominated the life of every man, woman and child in Malaya – the gentle Malays themselves, the industrious Chinese, the listless Indians, the perspiring British alike. It is the jungle; the jungle which none can escape, the jungle which reaches to the back of every compound, to the back of every mind; the jungle which blots out the sun over four-fifths of Malaya's 50,850 square miles. Harsh and elemental, implacable to all who dare to trifle with its suffocating heat or hissing rains, the jungle alone has remained untamed and unchanged.

Here the tall trees with their barks of a dozen hues, ranging from marble white to scaly greens and reds, thrust their way up to a hundred feet or even double that height, straight as symmetrical cathedral pillars, until they find the sun and burst into a green carpet far, far above; trees covered with tortuous vines and creepers, some hanging like the crazy rigging of a wrecked schooner, some born in the fork of a tree, branching out in great tufts of fat green leaves or flowers; others twisting and curling round the massive trunks, throwing out arms like clothes-lines from tree to tree. In places the jungle stretches for miles at sea level – and then it often degenerates into marsh, into thick mangrove swamp that can suck a man out of sight in a matter of minutes. In the heart of the country the giant trees cover the great north-south mountain range that rises to 7,000 feet, virtually bisecting Malaya from north to south.

In an evergreen world of its own that will never know the stripped black branches of winter, elephants, tigers, bears and deer roam the thick undergrowth; flying foxes, monkeys and parrots chatter and screech in its high places; crocodiles lie motionless in the swamp; a hundred and thirty varieties of snake slither across the dead leaves on wet ground; the air is alive with the hum of mosquitoes ferocious enough to bite through most clothing; and on the saplings and ferns struggling to burst out of the under-growth thousands of fat, black, bloodsucking leeches wait patiently for human beings to brush against them. Only on the jungle fringe is there colour and light and a beauty unmarred by fear. Here, when the sun comes out after a tropical shower, thousands of butterflies hang across the heat-hazed paths in iridescent curtains.* Brightly coloured tropical birds dart like jewels between clumps of bamboo, giant ferns, ground orchids, flame of the forest trees, bou-gainvillaea, wild hibiscus, in a countryside heavy with the scent of waxen-like frangipani blossoms, where the occa-sional monkey watches suspiciously from the heights of a tulip tree with its clusters of poppy-red flowers.

This is the jungle and this was, for twelve years, to be the battlefield for a strange and terrible war, as relentless and as cruel as the jungle itself; one in which Communism for the first time in history launched an all-out guerrilla war with the avowed aim of conquering Malaya for the disciples of Mao Tse-tung.

Malaya is one of the most beautiful countries on earth. Pear-shaped, hanging like a five-hundred-mile-long pen-dant below the narrow Kra isthmus which links it to Thai-land – its only land frontier – it is a little larger than England without Wales, a little smaller than the State of

---

* There are eight hundred species of butterfly and two hundred species of dragonfly in Malaya.

Florida. To the south lies Singapore and, below the equator, the scattered spice islands of Indonesia; to the west the still, hot waters of the Indian Ocean stretch to Africa; to the east the China Sea swirls westwards to the Philippines and the Pacific, northwards until its breakers dash against the shores of countries whose very names are evocative of blood spilled in racial wars – Cambodia, Vietnam, Hong Kong, China, Japan, Korea.

In 1948 Malaya was not only beautiful; it had achieved a rare distinction: it was a contented paradise in which men of many skins and creeds lived in harmony, enjoying the highest standard of living in all Asia as the country moved quietly but firmly – and without any strife – to the day when it would be granted independence from the British who had ruled it for nearly a century.

Perhaps it was the prosperity brought about by the booming rubber and tin markets that made it easier for people of many races to live cheek by jowl; perhaps it was the catalytic qualities of the British, who (whatever their faults) loved the country passionately and on the whole ruled it wisely. Perhaps the reasons went deeper – to the fundamental differences in outlook and aspirations of each race, so markedly different that no one was likely to tread on anyone else's toes; to religions and cultures so widely divergent that Malays, Chinese and Indians – whether politicians, businessmen or rubber tappers – could work together by day and then return each evening to their separate communities, to their own ways of life.

The Mohammedan Malays, whose country this was, numbered just over half the population of 5,300,000 and were distinguished by qualities of dignity rare in this world, by impeccable manners, by love of an easy-going life and consequently a lack of interest in making money. To the ordinary Malay, life revolved round his kampong, preferably near the sea or the brown rivers that laced the countryside, where all a man needed was a plot of land. Palms produced oil, roofing, coconuts – and even strong drink, for when the juice of the coconut bark was squeezed out, the fermenting toddy became as lethal as whisky. A paddy field provided enough rice; breadfruit, golden breast-shaped papayas clustering beneath parasol-shaped tree-tops, the evil-smelling but nutritious durian, grew in every kampong. On the roadside wild ginger, cinnamon, figs waited to be picked. A dazzling array of tropical fruits – mango, rambutan, dikku, pomelo, starfruit – flourished in every compound, while the waving green wands of sago formed a fence – if such a thing were needed – to mark off one man's property from his neighbours. Fish was so abundant in the sea or rivers that the simplest traps enabled a household to eat well without the chore of actually fishing. And if a man wanted a little pocket money, then a few rubber trees provided him with enough strips of latex, for which there was always a ready demand.

For the most part the Malays accepted British authority with polite indifference and reserved their reverence – and that is not too strong a word – for their Sultans. These were the rulers of the nine Malay States which formed the basis of the Federation of Malaya* and though they were 'assisted' by British Advisers, each Sultan, despite his limited powers, still maintained a royal court magnificent in its oriental splendour. For all formal occasions, the Sultan sat under a giant state umbrella (a royal monopoly), immobile since immobility was a sign of divinity, his person so sacred that it was forbidden to touch him. Around him lay his insignia of office handed down over the centuries – the jewel-studded kris, or dagger, the seal of state, the sceptre, the betel box; while in front of him at formal levees, vast throngs gathered to see the chiefs of his state arrive to make their formal submission of loyalty, each

* Johore, Pahang, Negri Sembilan, Selangor, Perak, Kedah, Perlis, Kelantan, Trengganu.

chief approaching the dais, sitting cross-legged, laying his hands on the earth in front of him, and drawing his body forward painfully until he reached the throne.

Of course the Sultans with their panoply had no more political significance than the Queen making her ceremonial speech at the Opening of Parliament, but the Sultans took good care that their subjects should not forget this was *their* country. In private, however, they were very different. Educated, sophisticated, they were also fun-loving. Indeed, the Sultan of Johore,* the most southerly state in Malaya, was so wealthy that he dined off gold plate, gave £500,000 to the British in World War Two – and was so fond of the ladies that the Governor once had to ask him to limit his 'raids' on the taxi-girls of the local Great World dance hall.

Only one indigenous race in Malaya refused to bow to the power of the Sultans: the Aborigines. They had never been counted but by 1948 they were estimated at between fifty and a hundred thousand. Anthropologists believe that some tribes were descended from Indo-Chinese who migrated southwards a thousand years ago. Shy and gentle, they dwelt in unexplored areas, a pale brown race of long-haired people left alone to live; the men naked but for a loincloth, the women dressed in sarongs of bark. Expert with their bamboo blowpipes, they hunted small game, often lived in communal houses built on piles driven into the edge of a river near their plots of land. Once they had worked out the soil – on which they grew rice, vegetables, sugar-cane – they moved on.

Mostly animists who believed that every object from a stone to a stick had its own living spirit, they were more advanced than the Aborigines in Australia and New Guinea and could on occasion be quite hard-headed. Despite the fact that they never ate any of the pigs,

* He died in May 1959 aged 85.

chickens or dogs reared in their village (because they believed it would be like eating a member of their own family), they happily traded their dogs, pigs or chickens for those raised in a neighbouring village, so that each settlement could have a feast without a twinge of conscience. But all attempts to 'civilize' them had failed.

No contrast could have been more extravagant than the regal splendour or the simple lives of the Malays with the lives of the two million industrious Chinese, many born in Malaya but still aliens, their deepest loyalties being rooted in China, which they had never seen but from which they had brought their women, religion and customs. Certainly it was the Chinese (who had come to Malaya in the sixth century) who provided the industry and wealth to make Malaya prosper.

Every city, almost every village in Malaya, had its Chinatown, and as one turned a corner from the prim British government buildings or a padang with Malays playing their favourite sport of badminton, it was like turning into another country, another world. The easygoing walk of the Malays gave way to the bustle of Chinese hawkers loping along, their food containers dangling from bamboo poles arched across bony shoulders. Whole families – the men in vests and shorts – pecked at their meals with chopsticks on the street kerbs under canopies of coloured laundry hanging from poles jutting out of the windows above. Black-haired, black-eyed children, like exquisite dolls, played ball on the roadside, dodging the taxis, trishaws, bicycles and the large American air-conditioned cars of their richer compatriots. In the shops, lacquered ducks as flat as boards, birds' nests, sharks' fins, hung from every window, while the cheaper restaurants blared with neon signs and music. Even the smells changed. In 'Malayan' Malaya, they had seemed to be of the earth, of fruits, in Chinatown they were compounded of spices and the continual frying of assorted lumps of scraggy meat which had hung, covered by flies, for days in the oppressive heat. This was the hectic frenzy of every Chinatown in every settlement in Malaya. They were foreign enclaves living entirely separate lives from the Malays, rarely inter-marrying, but each race tolerating the foibles and whims of the other – for while the Mohammedans were horrified at the thought of eating pork, never worked on Fridays, and fasted at Ramadan, the Chinese reared and ate pigs, worked seven days a week if necessary, and celebrated every festival by guzzling all they could eat – those who could afford it, for 600,000 of the Chinese in Malaya belonged to a rather different category.

These were the squatters, families who lived in ram-shackle home-made huts on the jungle fringe, on land to which they had no title, diligently toiling on plots where they raised pigs, ducks, chickens, and grew vegetables. The number of squatters had increased alarmingly during the Japanese Occupation as starving Chinese fled the cities to try and eke out a living as far removed from the Japanese as possible.

They had nothing in common with the West's idea of squatters. They were not migrants, nor were they motiv-ated by antipathy to the government. They had just lived there for so many years – and now numbered one out of every ten in Malaya – that no government had even dared to consider ordering them to move.

In the suburbs of some cities the scene abruptly changed. The poles of washing vanished, the bustle, the noise, the frenetic pace of Chinatown gave way to the languid world of the Indian, for half a million Indians lived in Malaya, providing a floating labour force, mostly on the rubber estates. They came mainly from the Madras area, spoke Tamil (and were therefore usually called Tamils), and earned twice as much as they could have done in their own impoverished country. They worked, they saved until they had enough to return home and buy a plot of land,

and meanwhile they were absorbed into the polyglot fusion
of races that made up the country, living quietly in areas
where the streets were filled with men in flapping shirt
tails, often squatting on their hams as they talked, the
women sauntering by in vivid saris, the pavements daubed
with the scarlet stains of betel nut, the air choked with the
scent of chillies and hot curries cooking.

And then there were the British, whose influence had
started when Raffles of the East India Company took over
a trading post in Penang in 1805, and who 'acquired'
the vital island of Singapore in 1824. After that, British
influence spread rapidly across the country of Malaya,
and though the Sultans always retained certain rights and
privileges, the country was in effect British by 1874.

Now, the British numbered 12,000 – members of the
Malayan Civil Service, policemen, rubber planters, tin
miners, doctors, businessmen – all with a prestige slowly
declining in the postwar resurgence of Asia; but each one
of them in love with a wondrous country as diverse as its
people, and, to the best of their ability, putting Malaya on
its feet after the Japanese Occupation. By 1948 tin was
booming and so was rubber – natural rubber which had
been grown originally from seedlings smuggled out of
Brazil, germinated at Kew Gardens, and which now supplied more than half the world's needs – of which ironically
Communist Russia was in 1948 Malaya's largest customer.

This was Malaya in 1948, a country in the distant mar-
ches of the Commonwealth, so beautiful that no man could
wish to live in a better one; and this was the country to
which violence, terrorism and war came at twenty-five
minutes past eight on the morning of June 16.

Sungei Siput, with its main street of shophouses, coffee
shops and one cinema was typical of the tin-mining towns
of northern Malaya. Eighteen miles north of Ipoh, the
main city in the State of Perak, it lay to the west of the

north-south mountain range, straddling the main trunk road leading from Ipoh to the north, the heart of a thriving mining industry which provided more than a third of the world's tin. The ridge of mountains that bisected Malaya not only split the country geographically, but economically, so that almost all the country's seven hundred tin mines and most of its three million acres of rubber lay on the highly developed sector west of the mountains.

The town was small, surrounded by the pale ochre moonscapes of worked tin mines, the dredging ponds, the lifeless, metallic-coloured water sprouting with tall, straight lilies; and always in the background the grotesque-looking dredges, like half-finished Meccano constructions. To the east, as the flat country merged into the foothills of the mountain range, the tin mines gave way to rubber plantations, many isolated like the Elphil Estate, which lay twenty miles east of Sungei Siput at the end of one of the loneliest roads in Malaya, a road which only ended when it reached the main office building of Elphil, with its corrugated iron roof, whose manager was Arthur Walker, a man of fifty who had spent twenty years in the country.

Just before eight o'clock on June 16 Mrs Walker drove into town (early to escape the heat) for some last-minute shopping before she and her husband sailed for England and home leave. Like all planters, Arthur Walker made the rounds of the estate before breakfast and shortly after eight o'clock he returned to the office to see his estate clerk, Kumarin, an Indian, and to clear up a few papers. Kumarin went back to his own office which had a window overlooking the main gate.

Shortly before 8.30 three young Chinese rode up to the office on bicycles. Carefully they leaned them up against the building and in no apparent hurry walked towards the door of the office. Walker's dog started barking and he tried to quieten it as the men walked in. Kumarin heard one Chinese say to Walker, '*Tabek, Tuan!*' ('Salutations, sir!') Walker returned the greeting cheerfully, with apparently no thought that anything was amiss. Within seconds two shots shattered the morning stillness. Through the window, Kumarin saw the three Chinese walk leisurely to their bicycles. For one second, as he peered, terrified, Kumarin's eyes met those of one of the men. The Chinese returned the stare with a cold unsmiling face devoid of emotion. With a touch of arrogance the man, who seemed to be the leader, stared unblinkingly, obviously to show that he was quite unafraid of being identified by a vital witness. Then, with a gesture that bordered on insolence, he spat once, turned away, and the three men mounted their cycles and calmly rode off down the road.

Kumarin rushed through the communicating door into Walker's office. The estate manager's body lay slumped by the office safe. He had been shot twice through the heart and chest. The key to the safe lay by his side, and the safe, containing $2,000, was untouched.

Within half an hour, and ten miles away, twelve armed Chinese surrounded the main building of Sungei Siput estate; inside, John Allison, the 55-year-old manager, was in his office, while in an adjoining room Ian Christian, his 21-year-old assistant, was discussing the day's work with two Chinese clerks.

Christian's office had a separate outside door. Two Chinese with revolvers kicked it open, told Christian and the clerks to put their hands above their heads. As at Elphil, the clerks' most haunting memories are of the cold-blooded, almost casual attitude of the men – 'as though they were soldiers obeying orders and weren't even very interested.'

In English one Chinese coldly asked Christian for his revolver. 'I haven't got one,' Christian replied.

No one spoke, and in a silence almost uncanny, the man took a length of cord from his pocket and tied Christian's hands behind his back. As this was happening, three

Chinese had burst into Allison's office next door, while the others remained on guard outside. Allison's arms were also pinioned and he too was asked for his revolver. 'It's in the bungalow,' he answered.

The man motioned Allison to stand up. Another man brought in Christian and the two clerks. All were then marched to the bungalow, sited on a rise about a hundred yards distant. With cold efficiency, with no show of emotion, no shouts, no prodding of guns, Allison and Christian were ordered into the bungalow. The two clerks were left outside under guard. Ten minutes later the British were brought out, and with revolvers stuck into their backs, were marched to the office. One Chinese turned to the two terrified clerks and reassured them in Malay: 'Don't be afraid. We're only out for Europeans and the running dogs' – 'running dogs' being the Communist epithet for British supporters, though later it was generally for most anti-Communists, particularly the police.

As they reached the door, another Chinese motioned with his gun to the clerks to wait outside. Casually he remarked, 'These men will surely die today. We are going to shoot all Europeans.'

Within a few minutes, Allison and Christian had been bound to chairs in Allison's office. They were shot sitting in them. The Chinese, completely disregarding the cowed and terrified estate clerks, calmly opened the door, walked out – and disappeared. As at Elphil – as in countless estates in the years to come – no one made any attempt to stop the murderers. Only when they were certain the Chinese had gone did one of the clerks telephone the police.

A third Briton, Donald Wise, who planted at Kamuning, a few miles out of Sungei Siput, escaped with his life because his jeep broke down while he was on his rounds. Three Chinese who had ridden up to the office on bicycles became suspicious at the delay and decided to leave.

Eighteen miles to the south, in Ipoh, the Chinese Affairs Officer was at his desk patiently listening to an old woman who had travelled eighty miles to air a minor grievance. The man was Robert Thompson – Bob Thompson to everybody – one of the most remarkable men in Malaya, a man who worked his way through the war until eventually he became Secretary of Defence, was knighted (and later asked by President Nixon to visit Vietnam on his behalf).

Bob Thompson, son of an English clergyman who had spent forty years in the same Surrey parish, was a fluent Chinese scholar who had joined the Malayan Civil Service in 1938. He spoke excellent Cantonese, understood several other dialects. When the Japanese attacked in the Far East in 1941 he had been caught in Hong Kong, had walked across part of China to escape, then joined an RAF unit supporting the famous Wingate Chindits. Thompson had a brilliant war record and was decorated with the DSO and MC, the latter partly for (according to the citation) 'always being to the fore with his tommy-gun'.

Now thirty-two, he bore a startling resemblance to the late Herbert Marshall, the actor, and was a passionate lover of Malaya and a fervent believer that Communism could never be beaten by force of arms alone, but only by showing men and women a better way of life. A dashing, handsome, highly intelligent bachelor, with a ready chuckle, he was far removed from the generally accepted image of the stuffy Colonial administrator.

The Chinese Affairs office was housed on the ground floor of a two-storey building near Ipoh's ornate railway station. It had been built in 1880 of hard, tough chengai, a kind of ironwood, indeed the only wood in Malaya through which voracious white ants could never eat their way. The top storey housed the headquarters of the Perak State Police, and on the ground floor Bob Thompson worked in one corner of a room over forty feet long. It was an open-plan office, with no private cubicles where government officials could escape. Everybody was on view to anyone coming in with a problem, and to Bob Thompson it was the modern equivalent of the open meetings that in early days had always been held under the village banyan tree. Bob was listening to the dignified old Chinese lady who insisted that her son-in-law kept insulting her. As Chinese Affairs Officer, he tried to settle scores of problems a week, ranging from this old lady's to labour disputes – all brought by the thrifty Chinese who hated wasting money on legal battles.

Thompson will never forget that morning – the lazy fans providing barely enough movement of hot air, the clerks in their white duck suits, the sunlight filtering in bands through the rattan curtains. As he listened, a plain-clothes officer from upstairs almost ran across the big desk-cluttered office – and one *never* ran in Malaya – and as he reached Thompson's desk, simply said, 'Bob – it's started!' Briefly he told him of the murders and Thompson jumped out of his chair ready to leave, though (and it is typical of the man) he spared a few minutes to tell the old lady that he would write a severe letter warning the son-in-law to behave. Then he called an interpreter, his Malay driver, and set off in his Chevrolet for Elphil Estate.

As he raced north, Thompson was thinking of a sinister incident that had occurred only three weeks previously. He had stopped at Sungei Siput for a drink with a police officer friend and asked why there seemed to be such a crowd milling in the town. Bitterly the police officer replied, 'Bob – you and I *know* there's going to be a bust-up before long. Tonight all the top Communists are meeting here in Sungei Siput – and I can't do a damn thing about it. If I were allowed to, I could pick up every top Communist in Malaya tonight.'

Like almost every European in Malaya, Thompson was deeply concerned at the increasing violence and industrial strife. In 1947 over three hundred Communist-dominated

strikes had paralysed rubber plantations or tin mines. In
the last month two labourers had been shot on a tin mine,
while police in one town had opened fire on a rioting band
of labourers armed with spears, stones, bottles and lead
piping, killing seven after they refused to disperse. On
rubber estates posters tacked to the trees cried, 'Destroy
the Running Dogs'. And outside the country, as though
in harmony, Communists were harrying the Burmese
government and fighting in the streets of Indonesia.

By the very nature of his work, Thompson was able to
see what was coming. It was part of his job to know all
the important Chinese, including unsavoury characters,
and for some time he had remarked on the absence of
several top agitators and Communists. He was under no
delusions about these latest outrages. They were no ordinary murders, and, as he drove along the Lintang Road
towards Elphil, he knew that his first priority must be to
prevent panic. Half a dozen rubber estates in the area
employed a total of twelve thousand men and it needed
only one spark to start them streaming in their hundreds
to Sungei Siput. Tearing along, he passed a military
convoy. A company of Gurkhas was on the way to Elphil
and Thompson knew that these tough, squat, fearless
Nepalese troops who had fought with the British army for
decades would provide the finest tonic for bewildered,
terrified labourers. Their courage was a legend over all
Asia.

As he reached Elphil, he stopped the car in dismay.
The office – separated from the roadway by an ornamental
box hedge barely two feet high – was surrounded by a
throng of workers, their excited high-pitched talk drown-
ing every other noise, as they ignored a couple of Malay
policemen begging them to calm down and leave. Forcing
a way through the crowd, Thompson managed to reach
the office where Walker's body still lay between the safe
and the big two-pillar desk in the L-shaped room.

Thompson needed only one glance at the imposing safe – still unopened so that robbery was out of the question – before turning to his interpreter and saying, 'This is the start – the start of a war.'

There was little Thompson could do until the Gurkhas arrived when, as though by magic, their very presence caused the crowd to melt away. Thompson and the company commander arranged that the Gurkhas should be split up into small groups and posted – for the next few days, anyway – on all the estates in the area. 'The Communists may be tough enough to murder lonely planters like Walker,' Thompson told the officer, 'but there's not one Communist in Malaya with the guts to take on the Gurkhas.'

Thompson now drove to Sungei Siput Estate where Allison and Christian had been murdered. It was reasonably calm, but just to be sure nothing happened later, Thompson – who had not bothered to arm himself – decided to spend the night alone in Christian's bungalow. 'I ate poor Christian's supper,' he remembers, 'but I didn't like to sleep in his bed.' He dossed down on a sofa, and after a bad night's rest decided to return to Ipoh. His office had telephoned him that angry planters were 'on the march'.

As he was about to leave, he saw a typical example of the British eccentricity that so often seemed to thrive in 'the Empire'.

The half-dozen Gurkhas and a police officer at the gate stiffened to attention as an imposing Humber car approached. Two flags fluttered on its front wings – the Union Jack and the Perak State flag – and that meant that the British Adviser to the Sultan had arrived.

The police officer saluted and then said anxiously, 'Don't you think, sir, you should have an escort?'

'Escort? Good God!' snorted the Adviser. 'Why on earth

should I need an escort? I've got my walking stick and my wife.'

While Thompson was speeding back to Ipoh, more and more reports of murders and atrocities were reaching police stations up and down the country. On the Senai Estate near Johore Bahru – within easy driving distance of the palace belonging to the Sultan who so enjoyed his dancing girls – ten men lay in wait for a Chinese head labourer and pumped fifteen bullets into him. In Pahang, a family was burned alive in a house. At Taiping, not far from Sungei Siput, a Chinese contractor was murdered. There seemed no pattern – except perhaps one: to make sure that the people of Malaya realized from the start that this was a war of terror none could escape. Nowhere was this major Communist theme demonstrated with more horror than on the edge of Voules Estate, also in Johore, where five terrorists in jungle green with red stars on their hats openly walked into a kampong and knocked on the door of the headman, a Chinese rubber tapper called Ah Fung. Coldly, impersonally, with Sten guns nonchalantly cradled in their arms, and regardless of the crowd that quickly gathered, the CT leader told him, 'We need subscriptions. You will collect fifty cents a week from every tapper on the estate.'

Ah Fung pleaded that it was impossible, nobody would obey him. 'Are you the headman or are you not a man?' the CT asked him scornfully. Still Ah Fung wailed that he could not, that he had a police record, so was suspect.

The CT looked at him impassively. 'My name is Goh Peng Tun,' he said, 'and this is a war against the hated British. Perhaps your colleagues will co-operate if I show them how we deal with traitors.' Then, with a nod to another CT, 'Tie him up.'

A terrified Ah Fung now shrieked, 'I'll do it.' But the CT retorted, 'Too late.' On the edge of the estate, Ah

Fung was tied to a tree, still protesting that he was no traitor. His wife and eight-year-old daughter were brought and tied to nearby trees. Then Goh Peng Tun beckoned to a CT to lend him a parang, the deadly flat-bladed Malay jungle knife. Looking at the woman and girl, he shouted, 'Make them keep their eyes open!' and as CTs forced their heads in the right direction, Goh Peng Tun wielded the parang. With the first stroke he cut off the man's right arm above the elbow, and as the blood spurted, he hacked off the left one.

The wailing and screaming mother and daughter begged for mercy. Goh Peng Tun turned to them and said, 'I am in a benevolent mood today. I will spare his life.' Before the CTs left, one tacked a leaflet on the tree above the sagging, bleeding body of Ah Fung. It read simply: 'Death to the Running Dogs'.

While the labour forces were being intimidated CT jungle units were also starting to attack lonely estate bungalows up and down Malaya, and the next day, as Thompson reached Ipoh, the planters called a meeting in the Perak Club, not far from Thompson's office. In twos and threes they arrived and dumped their revolvers in the mahogany-lined entrance hall with its notice-board giving the latest rubber and tin prices.

The planters had good cause to be angry, for as tension mounted they had watched with impotent frustration the complete lack of any action by the Federal Government in Kuala Lumpur, led by Sir Edward Gent, the High Commissioner. All demands by planters and miners' for arms and protection had been pooh-poohed by Gent, who considered them 'alarmist'. The planters would have been even more angry had they known the real extent to which Gent disliked them. At one planters' deputation to the High Commissioner, W. F. N. Churchill, a member of the Malayan Civil Service, had been present. He noted in his diary that evening: 'Sir Edward told me, "Planters make me sick. Do they want me to put a bloody guard on every estate bungalow?" '

That was just what the planters did want – that or an issue of arms so they could raise their own forces of guards. For these outrages were, in the words of Donald Wise, 'the last straw – a bloody disgrace. We all knew it was going to happen, and Gent hasn't done a damn thing.' Another planter shouted sarcastically, 'Why don't we recommend Gent for a bar to his OBE?'

Donald Wise was in a delegation which demanded to see Gent in Kuala Lumpur the next day, where the planters gave him such an uncomfortable half-hour that he declared a State of Emergency in the Ipoh and Sungei Siput areas of Perak and in part of Johore. Incredibly, he refused point blank to declare a nationwide emergency – until the following day when the *Straits Times* echoed the thoughts of every planter in Malaya by printing an editorial headed simply, 'Govern or Get Out'.

Within twenty-four hours public opinion forced Gent to extend the Emergency to cover the entire country. He cancelled all police leave, even recalled police on leave in Britain. He asked the Army to 'assist the civil power', and they immediately issued Sten guns to police and (while the supply lasted) planters and miners who knew how to use them. The government was given stringent powers of search, detention and curfew, and plans were made to form a Special Constabulary armed with rifles to guard the lonely estates and mines. Donald Wise and others who had been in the army were detailed to train many of them – though without any target practice, for bullets were rationed to five a month (and government red tape demanded a strict accounting of every bullet fired).

Within days, the streets of the major cities had changed. Police on traffic duty wore revolvers. Planters stumping into the Coliseum, their favourite bar in Kuala Lumpur, put their rifles or revolvers on racks before ordering their stengahs. Everywhere there was talk of 'war' – yet there was a curious omission in their gossip. There might be vague talk of Chinese infiltration across the Thai border, of the hidden hand of Mao Tse-tung, but nobody seemed at first to realize just who had upset the happy routine of Malayan life, who was putting them under attack. 'We'll beat these bloody Commies in a couple of weeks,' was the general summing up.

Bob Thompson was not so sanguine. He knew that this was war to the bitter end, and moreover a war in which the Communists were led, ironically, by brave and resolute Chinese who had fought with British officers behind the Japanese lines after the fall of Singapore in 1942, men whose courage had been sufficiently recognized for them to have taken part in the Victory march through London.

2 THE PROTAGONISTS

The final, irrevocable Communist decision to launch an all-out war had been taken little more than two weeks prior to June 16 at the end of a secret meeting of the Party Politburo, held during the last half of May in the jungles of Pahang, the largest state in Malaya, a vast area of mountain and rain forest, of riverine villages with fragile wooden boathouses clinging like molluscs to the banks of the yellow waters under their canopy of giant fern trees, bamboo, nipah palms and the occasional mangrove, whose sinister, twisting roots sprang like giant spiders round the lapping edges of still waters.

Here, the Communist Party Politburo staged its last meeting of peace to plot war. Pahang had been chosen because it lay midway down the five hundred miles between Thailand and Singapore, and so was accessible. It also had the advantage for a secret meeting of being sparsely populated. Pahang lay east of the mountain range, and on that side great tracts lay undisturbed except for apes, monkeys, the occasional wild bison and Malaya's famous barking deer.

Nearly fifty Malayan Communist Party leaders arrived at a large camp hidden in thick jungle between the towns of Bentong and Raub, and as they made their way up the main road to Raub – some walking, some cycling, some having caught the local bus at Bentong – they were met at the seventh milestone by sentries disguised as tappers.

Among the early arrivals was a good-looking man of twenty-four called Osman China, whose parents had been Chinese, but who had been adopted as a boy by Malays. He was an intellectual rather than a fighter, for he had passed his Senior Cambridge Examination at Singapore's Victoria School and if his first love was Communism, his second was intriguingly different. As he reached the seventh milestone he clutched under one arm a tattered, well-thumbed volume of Shakespeare's plays.*

A sentry, so well 'disguised' that his black tapper's clothes were stiff with the spilled latex of years, led Osman China round the edges of a rubber plantation, through rows of identical trees with their cups fastened to mottled trunks. The rubber thinned out. Underfoot the soft, brown, weeded earth ceased. The light filtering through the regularly spaced trees faded, for they had reached the jungle fringe, and soon the sun vanished as they walked through the jungle. A path had been hacked along the three-mile route to the camp, and along it a succession of sentries waited for the men who had been summoned and who now had to make the two-hour journey, dripping with sweat which refused to evaporate in the saturated air. Visibility, Osman China remembers, was down to fifteen yards as they penetrated into the jungle, until without

* Osman China many years later described this meeting to David Storrier of Special Branch.

warning two armed men rose from the undergrowth barely two yards ahead of him.

The first sentry set off back towards the main road, the new ones guided him to the camp. And to Osman China, a city man at heart, it must have been a staggering sight, for this was no collection of hastily erected 'bashas'.†
Before him solidly-built huts encircled a parade ground with the Red Flag hanging limply from a pole. At one end were administrative offices, latrines, kitchens, and a command post, from which (much to his bewilderment) lengths of thick twine ran across the beaten ground. They led, he later discovered, to sentries a quarter of a mile away, who could tug the string to give an alarm.

Several top-ranking Communists had already arrived, but the man whom Osman China greeted first was Chin Peng, Secretary-General of the Party, a remarkable Malayan Chinese aged twenty-six, born in Sitiawan, where his father ran a small bicycle repair shop. Pleasant-faced, though inclined to pimples on his fair skin, he was five feet seven inches tall and walked with a slight limp. He had a quiet, gentle manner, reflected in the soft voice he used to speak six languages, including English. He had joined the Party at eighteen, cutting stencils for the prop-aganda department, and though some historians believe Chin Peng, who had visited China in 1945 and 1946, was a puppet of Mao Tse-tung, nothing could be further from the truth. This strange, courteous, bookish man was a product of Malayan soil, of his own times, as individualistic as Ho Chi-minh.

Chin Peng was the undisputed leader of the Malayan Communist Party. By a strange and curious twist of fate, which he shared with many of his top commanders, to say nothing of the rank and file, he had learned the art of jungle guerrilla warfare from, of all people, the British.

† A basha is a temporary shelter made of attap.

It had happened quite simply. After the Fall of Singapore in 1942 several British officers, including Colonel Spencer Chapman (author of the magnificent *The Jungle is Neutral*) remained behind in the jungle to harass the Japanese, and eventually to prepare for the British liberating forces, which in the event were never needed after the atom bombs had been dropped on Japan. Chapman and his colleagues were known as 'Force 136'. Soon other British officers were being parachuted into Malaya or landed secretly by submarine, and it was the most natural thing in the world for the Chinese – who had hated the Japanese since their invasion of China – to help Force 136. Over the years their number rose to about five thousand. They called themselves 'The Malayan Peoples' Anti-Japanese Army'. They were trained in jungle warfare by the British, and in the use of modern weapons which were parachuted regularly into Malaya. The British officers of Force 136 operating behind the Japanese lines had had no illusions about the Communist activities of men like Chin Peng, but as in Jugoslavia, where Britain gave Tito, an avowed Communist, all the support possible, Britain believed the risk was worth taking, and Spencer Chapman regarded Chin Peng as 'Britain's most trusted guerilla'.

After the war it had been easy for Chin Peng and his army to pose as the sole victors over a foe against which the white man had been powerless. Ironically, it had needed a Japanese victory (and subsequent defeat) to promote Malayan Communists from a political party into one of organized resistance.

Now in the jungle Chin Peng was dressed in a white shirt and khaki shorts. He had put on a little weight, but Osman China felt that 'his brain was ticking over all the time we talked. He insisted that if the Communists could succeed in Greece and China against big armed resistance, they were bound to succeed in Malaya where all the Chinese were in sympathy.'

All that first day the delegates dribbled into the camp – men with strange names. There was Ah Kuk, known as Shorty Kuk because he was barely four feet nine inches tall. Shorty Kuk had fought with Force 136, and so had Hor Lung, at thirty-two a ruthless, dedicated Communist, who had once infiltrated through the Japanese lines, killing five of the enemy before retracing his steps to the neutral jungle. Lau Yew, who had led the Malay delegation to London for the Victory Parade, was – in contrast to Chin Peng – a fighter rather than a politician. For all these men who had shared the perils of the jungle for so long, the meeting must have had something of the atmosphere of an Old Comrades' reunion, and they talked far into the night as they lay side by side on the mat-covered planks of a shelf that was their communal bed.

We cannot, of course, know the full details of all that occurred at this momentous jungle meeting, but we know the main points. Chin Peng's aim was to establish a Communist Republic in Malaya, and he had already laid most of his plans. The dedicated Communists and sympathizers (for not all were card carriers) had to be split into two groups, each with vitally different functions. One would be a small, deadly striking force operating from secret jungle bases. The other would be large, dispersed and consist of ordinary citizens responsible for supplying the striking force with money, food – and information.

The striking force presented no problems. Five thousand members of the 'Malayan Peoples' Anti-Japanese Army' which had worked with Force 136 would, by the convenient change of only one word, become the 'Malayan Peoples' Anti-British Army'. Their arms had been hidden in hundreds of jungle caches, still in the canisters in which they had been parachuted down during the Japanese Occupation – and concealed from the British. They would be the real fighters, and would be paid $30 a month out of subscriptions to be raised by extortion from innocent citizens. They would use many of the old jungle bases in which they had lived with Force 136. Other bases had been newly prepared – some capable of holding five hundred men, some for 'killer units' of half a dozen CTs. They would operate independently when necessary, but would receive political directions by courier from Chin Peng.

Their main objective, however, needed no directive, for that had been supplied years previously by the dictum of Lenin: that by the infliction of terror, a well-organized minority can conquer a nation. The army, which was issued with khaki uniforms, would operate from their secret jungle bases in the form of eight regiments posted in strategic parts of the country. To this day no one knows the exact strength of each regiment. Some were large, some consisted of only three hundred men. But one thing was certain – fanning out from these regimental bases, the units would wage war on the classic pattern of Mao Tse-tung,* a type of war that Mao had dreamed about, and which would now be unleashed for the first time across the length and breadth of a country. Chin Peng might not have realized it, but he was initiating on a nationwide-scale a type of guerrilla warfare that would become a new and terrible force in the wars of Asian countries like Vietnam, Laos, Cambodia.

All the CTs had to do was to strike swiftly with murder and terror – then melt back to the jungle before the police arrived. And this was easy, for no police force, however efficient, could cover the whole country, could watch, night after night, the lonely rubber plantations, the isolated

---

* While Lenin believed in urban revolution, i.e. seizing a radio station and key points in a *city*, Mao Tse-tung believed in rural revolution – leaving the cities alone, concentrating on the peaceful area until the city was helpless in the centre.

villages. The CTs would always have the element of surprise on their side.

The second, dispersed force was totally different. It wore no uniform. It received no salary. Called the Min Yuen (which means 'Masses Movement'), it consisted of ostensibly normal, innocent citizens who would in fact back up the army. Already the Min Yuen was operating on virtually every level of Malayan life. Communists worked as waiters in British clubs, as clerks in government offices, as schoolteachers, newspaper reporters. Others operated among the squatters on the jungle fringe, tappers on the estates, in the rabbit warrens of big cities. Invaluable part-timers, they would supply the army with food, money or information, screen it, warn it of impending trouble. Chin Peng was convinced that, as his successes mounted, the Min Yuen would grow even larger and that the bulk of Chinese peasants would support an uprising, would be eager to help as couriers, spies, saboteurs, or in the collection of subscriptions.

The two branches of the army were linked by the Party itself, which was so thoroughly organized that Chin Peng's Central Executive had a chain of command reaching down through the regiments to the smallest CT group, with strict Party discipline enforced by political cells in every jungle camp, often with political commissars who had the power to countermand local military instructions if politically necessary. The chain of command that reached every military unit worked just as effectively with the civilians of the Min Yuen. Instead of regiments, platoons, units, Chin Peng had organized, in descending order, State Committees, District Committees, and then small cells – the civil equivalent of a small jungle unit. Since a State member could also be a political commissar, there was at first a considerable measure of integration.

On the fourth day of the conference Chin Peng explained

for the first time just how he proposed to conquer Malaya – a war which he envisaged as falling into three distinct phases.

In Phase One guerrillas who had proved their mettle against the Japanese would attack lonely estates and mines, police and government officials in small towns and villages, forcing the British to evacuate rural areas and make for the bigger towns. This was the classic Mao Tse-tung approach.

This done – and Chin Peng does not seem to have doubted that it *could* be done – Phase Two would start. Areas evacuated by the British would be re-named 'Liberated Areas'; in them guerrilla bases would be set up, the army would be expanded with recruits from the Min Yuen who would train and prepare for Phase Three. This was to be the climax, one of territorial expansion fanning out from the Liberated Areas, with the army attacking towns, villages, railways, while the Min Yuen destroyed the economy and security. Then the guerrilla army would take the field against the British, backed by the might of China if necessary, and by the moral weight of Soviet Russia.

It was as simple as that; and if with hindsight it seems incredible that intelligent men like Chin Peng and Osman China – to say nothing of many others – firmly believed they could overthrow the might of Britain, then one must remember that in other parts of Asia other Communists entertained similar dreams – and some of those dreams came true. And if their army of five thousand seems woefully small, it must not be forgotten that the insurrection in Vietnam was to start with an armed force of Communists almost exactly equal to that of Malaya.

It also seems strange, looking back at that conference, that nobody seems even vaguely to have considered the possibility of losing. Nobody (according to Osman China) thought to raise the question of what would happen if the British hit back, if Whitehall hurled in reinforcements.

And nobody seems to have considered one other point. Ostensibly this was a war to free Malaya from the yoke of 'Imperialist Britain', to throw out 'the running dogs' so that Malaya could become independent. But already the British had virtually given Malaya a promise of independence.

And so, ironically, a savage war was joined in which British and Chinese, who for years had shared the hardships of the jungle while fighting as comrades, now became bitter enemies dedicated to each other's deaths. The irony cut even deeper. On the one hand, the Communists, instead of waiting, would be fighting for 'independence' which was already in the offing; on the other hand, British planters, miners, policemen, would stay and fight in Malaya, knowing that with independence there would inevitably be Malayanization, resulting in lost jobs for Britons who had spent half a lifetime in the country they had come to love as much as their own.

Only one point had not been made clear to the delegates: why had this particular time been chosen – and had any orders been received from Moscow or Peking? To this day many British – as well as many dedicated Communists – believe that the insurrection was part of a major plot to disrupt South-East Asia. They based this hypothesis on an impressive array of related facts. Malayan Communist Party chiefs had attended three important conferences – one in Prague in 1947; the first conference of Commonwealth Communist parties in London in January, 1948, and the Russian-sponsored conference of Asian and Australian Communists in Calcutta in the same year. Then, too, at the first meeting of the Cominform in Moscow in 1947 Zhadanov had stressed that national liberation movements in South Asian countries were now to operate 'as an important adjunct of the International

Communist movement'. It was only too easy to believe that these conference decisions had inspired Malaya.

The basic reason for the insurrection was, however, significantly different: when Chin Peng called his jungle conference, the Malayan Communist Party was on the verge of disintegration. All legal attempts by the 'masses' to bring Malaya to its knees had resulted in fiasco. Despite labour disruption, the Communists had been incapable of organizing positive long-term political activity, and since few of the heroes from the jungle could speak English, the Party had failed to make any real headway in subverting the government service. The trade unions, under a brilliant Communist called Lam Swee, were protesting against the Central Bureau's use of Union funds. There were rumours of high spending and dissolute living in the Politburo. Chin Peng's problem was to find an answer to the rumours circulating about his predecessor, Loi Tek, a man whose origin had been clouded in mystery, though it was firmly believed by many that the Third International had sent him to Malaya. He was Vietnamese and his movements had been so secretive when he was head of Malaya's Communist Party that few of the Central Committee members had ever been able to approach him directly. He had, in short, become a legend, and when he had absconded with the Party funds on March 6, 1947, Chin Peng had not dared to tell his comrades, but had kept the news secret for nearly a year while he established his leadership. Only now, as the rumours multiplied, as a scapegoat was needed, did Chin Peng decide to tell Party members of Loi Tek's disloyalty.

With an irony that would be hard to match even in the most far-fetched work of fiction, Chin Peng was absolutely right in his attack on Loi Tek. Loi Tek *had* absconded, he *had* been directly responsible for the failure of Communism in Malaya. But what Chin Peng did *not* know when he decided to make Loi Tek a scapegoat was that the most brilliant party leader in Malaya's Communist history was no Communist. He was a British secret agent who had previously worked in Indo-China until he had been 'blown' there, whereupon the French had sent him down to the British in Singapore with a note saying, almost in these words: 'This is a very useful chap. You might find him handy.' The British had planted him in Singapore – which meant that for a long time Britain had run the Malayan Communist Party. Loi Tek had only been spirited away (never to be heard of to this day) when it became clear that he was about to be 'blown'.

This was the internal crisis which partly forced Chin Peng to go underground and catapult the Communists into a war. The survival of his party depended on it. The fact that external factors were favourable was excellent, but one wonders if the hard-pressed Chin Peng had time to take more than a cursory look into the future as he tried to sort out his problems. Thus the decision was taken, and 'Plan For Struggle' – a directive for launching an 'armed struggle' – was born.*

Almost as soon as Bob Thompson reached Kuala Lumpur, he went to see Major-General Boucher, Commander-in-Chief of the armed forces in Malaya. Boucher was a tough fighting man who had seen action against Greek guerrillas, but he was not the equal of Chin Peng. It was one thing to attack isolated bands of Greek Communists. It was quite different to deal with the carefully co-ordinated plan of nation-wide terror which Malaya now faced. But at least Boucher was prepared to listen, and he listened now as men like Bob Thompson and others with experience of the country warned him that this was no 'Empire skirmish', in which a few rabble-rousers could

---

* In order to denigrate Loi Tek, Chin Peng issued at this time the 'Manifesto of the Loi Tek Incident' – which did not, of course, reveal that he was a British spy.

be stamped out. Thompson was perhaps thinking of an incredibly naïve statement Boucher had made: 'I can tell you this is by far the easiest problem I have ever tackled,' Boucher had said. 'In spite of the appalling country, the enemy is far weaker in technique and courage than either the Greek or Indian Reds.'

Apart from the fact that this did not say much for the British officers who had trained the enemy, Thompson also felt that this was probably the general impression in much of Malaya – and even at home in Britain, for the London newspapers arriving in Malaya hardly mentioned the Emergency. Yet Thompson and a few others knew that this was a war which could last many years; a new kind of war, one on which the fate of all Asia hinged, for with Singapore the gateway between East and West, the security not only of South-East Asia but of Australia was at stake. In its way, the war now facing Malaya was more critical than that against the French which was already beginning to rumble in Indo-China (and would later consume Vietnam), for Thompson knew that ports like Hanoi and Saigon had none of the geopolitical importance of Singapore. He knew, too, that if Britain did not stand fast, if they underrated the enemy, Indonesia and probably Thailand would turn Communist, and then anything could – and probably would – happen. The trouble was – how many people would realize this? And how could they be convinced of the facts, particularly abroad where, in the spring of 1948, Russia and America were slithering towards the brink of total war. The Berlin Airlift was only a few weeks away. In Greece the Communists held four-fifths of the country. In the Middle East, the end of the Palestine Mandate meant that Jew and Arab were poised at each other's throats. In Indo-China Ho Chi-minh was training the men who would win the battle of Dien Bien-phu in 1954 and end a century of French influence in Asia. In Manchuria, Mao Tse-tung was on the march, gathering the momentum that would finally topple the regime of Chiang Kai-shek, or at least confine it to the ignominy of a government-in-exile. The Korean war was barely two years distant. No wonder the West had little time to think of Malaya.

Together the army chiefs and civilian leaders took stock of the military situation. On paper Malaya seemed to have an overwhelming advantage. Against Chin Peng's army of 5,000 CTs, the security forces could muster 10,223 police officers and men (though with no armour) and eleven battalions of troops, three from the Malaya Regiment, six Gurkha, two British – the Seaforth Highlanders and the 1st King's Own Yorkshire Light Infantry. The apparent superiority was, however, an illusion, for when the war started the guerrillas outnumbered the actual fighting men of the army in Malaya; each of the eleven understrength battalions numbered approximately nine hundred men, of which five hundred were required to put the other four hundred with rifles into the jungle; so that Chin Peng's 5,000 battle-trained CTs faced about 4,000 British and Malay fighting men, few with any jungle experience.

Even worse, however, was the government's political machine – one so outmoded that only Whitehall could have devised it. At a time demanding urgent decisions in the face of insurrection, Malaya had eleven separate governments. They were linked by the Federal Government in Kuala Lumpur, a hotch-potch city with a red mosque, one of the world's most ornate railway stations, the 'Spotted Dog' (as the Selangor Club was called) facing the padang with its cricket, football, tennis or hockey matches, and the striped Moorish-looking government buildings with their cupolas and towers in the background.

Each of the nine states had their Sultan assisted by his Malay 'Prime Minister' and a British Adviser. But in addition there were two other territories – the Settlements of Penang and Province Wellesley and of Malacca – which were headed by British officers of the Malayan Civil Service. These eleven states all came under the authority of the Federal Government, led by the British High Commissioner. (The island of Singapore, connected to the mainland by a causeway, was a separately administered Crown Colony.)

Out in the countryside in times of peace, where men like Thompson were given enough authority to make many decisions on the spot, this archaic form of government had worked well enough, but it was hardly capable of retaliating vigorously against the fanatical onslaught of Communism, particularly as Sir Edward Gent, the High Commissioner, was quite unequal to the task now facing him, however brilliant he might have been in theory. At Oxford he had gained a double first, and a rugger Blue (perhaps more important in the eyes of the selection board).* In the war he had won a DSO and MC. During twenty-five years at the Colonial Office he had specialized in Asian countries, always looking ahead to the independence. Yet when he descended on Malaya in March 1946, after its liberation, his high-minded zeal for reform was such that he took an instant dislike to those members of the Malayan Civil Service returning after nearly four years of internment. Gent snubbed what he called the 'old brigade' – and they hated him. Many British Advisers to the Sultans warned him of Communist preparations in 1947 but he brushed them aside. Of course, the High Commissioner, representative of the Crown, was a man who governed, but did not administer. Others offered him information and advice, but it was unfortunate that Gent preferred not to accept

---

* For many years four out of five successful men recruited by the Colonial Office had been to Oxford or Cambridge, and generally had gained a Blue in some sport. They were advised not to flaunt their scholastic records if they had achieved any academic success.

the advice of those who knew the country better than he did.

It was also true that Gent worked on such an exalted level that he could have no real contact with the Malay Sultans whose country this was, or the Chinese who controlled great wealth. On no account could the High Commissioner be seen to favour one more than another, for with the prospect of independence in the not-too-distant future, each one was in competition, and most of those invited to a quiet dinner at King's House, the official residence in Kuala Lumpur, arrived ready for battle. No wonder that nothing was done as, in the words of John Gullick of the Malayan Civil Service, 'the round of official consultation and formal entertainment between Gent and community leaders took its course, courteous, stiff, and not very friendly.'

The Commissioner of Police at this time was H. B. Langworthy, a sick man trying to reorganize his shattered police force, and if Gent listened to anyone, it was probably to him. But Langworthy also refused to accept advice, though several high officials warned him. John Barnard, one brilliant police executive, sent in detailed reports of secret arms dumps and jungle training camps. W. F. N. Churchill, Adviser to the Sultan of Kelantan, noted in his diaries: 'The Special Branch of the Police Force had a good idea of what was brewing but Gent did not heed the warnings; he remained obstinately of the opinion that no danger really existed. Langworthy also preferred not to listen to his Special Branch.'

Langworthy was symptomatic of a police force which at this moment (and in spite of many brave men) was woefully inefficient. There was a fundamental and tragic reason for this. The force was split right down the middle so bitterly that many policemen on one side refused to speak to their comrades on the other.

The bitterness was a hangover from the fall of Singapore when Sir Shenton Thomas, the governor, had exhorted the police 'to stay at your posts until the flag has been hauled down'. With defeat inevitable, many had felt it would serve Britain better to run away and live to fight another day. But those who did remain at their posts, and consequently spent nearly four years in Changi jail, never forgave those who got away, even though many had joined Force 136 and had been parachuted back to fight behind the Japanese lines.

When Donald Wise, manager of Kamuning rubber estate, went to a reception at King's House in 1948, he had barely finished chatting with one police officer before he was approached by another who whispered confidentially, 'I wouldn't talk to him if I were you. He's one of the seventeen.'

Wise – an ex-parachutist – was nonplussed until the second police officer explained that 'the seventeen' were police officers from different parts of Malaya who had 'run away from Malaya in 1942'. The rift was now so deep that if one of the seventeen came into a police mess, those who had been in Changi would often walk out without a word.

One senior police officer was above this – and above being overawed by Gent. This was the outspoken Colonel John Dalley, on the point of retirement, who had gained fame before the fall of Singapore by leading 'Dalley's Desperadoes' in a last-minute effort to stem the Japanese advance.

In 1947 Dalley had written to Gent 'urging action against uniformed armed Communists training and encamped in the jungle'. He had sent a copy to Langworthy, who had retorted flatly that there were no uniformed men in the jungle.

Dalley did not let the matter rest. He sent a three-page memorandum to Gent showing what should be done. He wrote to Malcolm MacDonald, Commissioner-General for

South-East Asia, whose co-ordinating functions over all British interests in the area did not extend to participating in the actual work of government. This son of Ramsay MacDonald, the Labour Leader, was something of a 'character' and over the years had developed a public image of the shirt-sleeved, approachable democrat (in contrast to the uniformed bureaucrats of the territorial government), and had the ear of the Socialist government in Whitehall. He lived in some style in Bukit Serene, a palace lent to him by the fun-loving Sultan of Johore, where MacDonald entertained all manner of people, often casually inviting Aborigines to remain for the night (until the incensed Sultan, who was something of a snob, threatened to cut off the water supply to Bukit Serene's swimming pool). MacDonald was also a keen bird-watcher and when he wanted to study the habits of the sunbird, which rarely flies below tree-top level, he managed to acquire an ancient fire-engine, and could at times be seen precariously perched at the very top of its swaying, extended ladder.

On the other hand, MacDonald had his feet on the ground when there was work to be done, for, as Lord Acton put it, in history the man with the sword is already followed by the man with the sponge – and MacDonald was extremely skilful at mopping up any mess. He was also one of the few men to realize the root causes of upheavals taking place all over his area; that, as he put it, 'it was a positive, not a negative movement, not only anti-Western, but pro-Asian, as the new Asia tried to overthrow the economic and political feudalism of the past.' And because he understood this, he was always prepared to act on the Churchillian precept that 'jaw-jaw is better than war-war.'

He was so impressed with Dalley's report that he sent it to London, for Dalley had produced a remarkably accurate estimate of CT strength, telling Gent that there were five thousand active fighters and 250,000 Min Yuen supporters in the towns and villages, 'but [as Dalley wrote later] Gent ridiculed the figures . . . MacDonald accepted them.'

'Gent grossly underestimated the signs of danger,' MacDonald recalls, and decided to fly up to see the High Commissioner in his private plane. (Despite protests from Whitehall, MacDonald always flew in a two-seated Auster without radio contact, 'but my pilot was a VC.')

Gent refused to change his opinions and that evening in King's House MacDonald told him bluntly, 'I'm sorry but I think you're wrong. I've the highest regard for you as a civil servant but this is a war, and I'm going to telegraph Whitehall that we must have a new High Commissioner.'

Late into the night MacDonald drafted his cables, and long after bed-time he showed them to Gent, asking the High Commissioner to add any comments he liked. Gent felt there was nothing to say.

It is a measure of MacDonald's power behind the scenes that a few days later Whitehall cabled him privately telling him that Gent was to be sacked. Indeed, Whitehall asked MacDonald to break the news to the High Commissioner. On June 29, Gent was recalled to London.

On the night before Gent left (for what were ostensibly called 'consultations') he attended a conference with Mac-Donald which lasted until two in the morning. Dalley was present, though only Gent and MacDonald knew what had happened, and Gent was 'very subdued'. As the conference broke up, however, he made an extraordinary request: would MacDonald mind if he borrowed his private office for a few minutes, as he wanted to talk to Dalley.

Dalley entered the room. Out of his attaché case Gent produced Dalley's three-page critical memorandum, went through it carefully paragraph by paragraph, and then admitted to Dalley that everything in it was true. Too late did Gent realize how wrong he had been to regard Chin Peng's army as little more than a rabble to be routed when the first shock had been absorbed. He had been unable to see that Chin Peng's army might be partly illiterate, but it was highly trained and efficient. To one critic he had dismissed the events scornfully as 'a war of nerves by the forces of disorder'.

Now, in MacDonald's private office, Gent turned to Dalley and asked, 'Can we still be friends?' The two men solemnly shook hands, and Dalley remembered later that (not knowing of Gent's fate) 'my main feeling was one of relief, feeling that when we reached London we would give full support to all-out action.'

Four days later the aircraft in which Gent was travelling collided with another over London and he was killed. He was, as John Gullick, who worked with him, put it, 'like the hero of a Greek tragedy [who] failed by a flaw of his own character and was ruined by the dangerous excess of his own virtue, his dedication to the preparation of Malaya for its independence.'

3 THE PLANTERS

Almost overnight Malaya was transformed into a country at war as thousands of miles of barbed wire criss-crossed the land like a voracious new jungle creeper with tentacles no one could check. The first helicopters hovered overhead, road blocks cluttered the main highways, police posts were reinforced, soldiers jumped out of army trucks bearing regimental arms on khaki backgrounds – many of them fresh-faced conscripts hardly brown from their first tan, their khaki shirts stained with dark patches of sweat under the arms. Soon they were taking their first elementary lessons in jungle warfare. True there was not a great deal that troops or police could do in those early days except speed, as new reached them, to the scene of some lonely outrage; and indeed the attacks were so sporadic and often so hidden that a visitor to Malaya might have been excused for wondering if this *were* an organized war, and not just an outburst of civil strife. This was particularly so in cities like Kuala Lumpur where the slogan was 'business as usual', where the government clerks sorted out their papers unhurriedly under the four-bladed fans, where the tuans gathered each evening, as they had always done, at the 'Spotted Dog', lolling on the veranda, a stengah in hand, as they watched the younger men sweating at tennis or cricket on the padang in front of them.

It was a very different story in the rural areas, for here the old happy-go-lucky atmosphere of Malaya at peace had vanished. Chin Peng was losing no time. Thirteen days after the Emergency was declared, as Gent was preparing to leave for London, forty CTs captured the isolated village of Jerantut in central Pahang. After cutting the telephone wires, they fired blindly into the wooden police station, then set fire to it. The first villager who ventured into the streets was 'arrested', tied to a telegraph pole and formally executed with a shotgun at close range. After that every shutter in Jerantut remained closed. A few miles to the north CTs attacked the labourers' quarters on the edge of a rubber estate near Lipis, rounded up a hundred men and women, and demanded food and subscriptions. Silently the woman handed over rice and the men fifty cents each – all except one man. Darting from behind a hut swinging his deadly parang like a meat cleaver, he sliced open a CT down the back. Mercifully for him he was shot dead. His wife and two daughters, however, did not escape so painlessly. They were tied up and bundled into an old wooden hut, which was then set on fire. Twenty-six miles north-west of Kuala Lumpur, CTs attacked the country's only coal mine at Batu Arang. Occupying it for nearly an hour, they killed five men, burned the police station, smashed up three giant dragline excavators and eight trailers.

The objective was simple – to brand innocent, frightened people with the trademark of terror. It did not matter whether the attacks were large or small – like wildfire the news sped along the Asian grapevine that if ordinary men and women wanted to stay alive they must do only one thing: obey. The alternative was death – and only if one were lucky would the killing be swift. That was why in the Johore village of Layang Layang, a silent crowd watched a Malay policeman fighting desperately for his life against three Chinese CTs. No one stirred to help. No one dared later to name the murderers.

The worst sufferers in those early days were not only isolated police stations, but the planters, by the very nature of their isolation. There were a thousand European planters – almost all British – in Malaya when the war broke out, running estates of varying sizes belonging to giant rubber companies like Dunlop or Goodyear, or smaller ones frequently owned by rich Chinese. The planters received a salary and bonus, plus a bungalow for their families, and could be changed from one estate to another owned by the same firm, or even switch from one firm to another. Some estates – such as Dunlop's Ladang Geddes – covered 14,000 acres. Others were barely a thousand acres. But whatever the size, the planter lived in the heart of his estate. In the days of peace it had been a glorious life, with visits to the club in the nearest township, tennis, good shooting, cheap drink, a rubber of bridge, regular leaves at home, with the family boat fares paid by the company. Now, in a twinkling, it had all changed, and planters with only a few arms faced hit-and-run tactics as they hastily started training squads to defend the estate perimeters.

Isolation, of course, is a comparative term. Some estates – like Elphil where the first murders were committed – were twenty miles from the nearest town. Others were much closer – but once *on* the estate, surrounded by jungle, a planter was just as isolated even if he were only a few miles from a big city.

One estate that came in for heavy punishment was Amherst Estate, which was attacked day after day, though it was barely eight miles along the Bentong Road from Kuala Lumpur. Amherst was planted by a tall, lean, tanned, handsome Englishman of forty, a crack shot and outdoor sportsman. His name was H. F. de C. Lucy, but he was known throughout Malaya as Peter Lucy. He was married to 'Tommy', who had been born in Shanghai, a fifth daughter on whom her father had bestowed a male nickname. She was a beautiful woman who loved Asia but hated Communism so bitterly that after the first attack on Amherst she presented her husband with an ice-bucket inscribed 'Death to the Communists' and placed it on the semi-circular bar in the corner of their bungalow living-room.

From Tommy we have perhaps the most complete picture of the day-to-day life on a rubber plantation in those early days, for she typed regular long circular letters to family and friends – and kept copies. 'The old war-time feeling of insecurity is back again,' she wrote as early as June 1948. 'We have to make up our minds that guns, ammunition and guards are the order of the day. We are building a small sandbagged room round the store cupboard (the site needless to say chosen by me in case of hunger should we be besieged!) so that we could hold out until help arrived if we are attacked.'

After six years of marriage (of which Peter spent nearly four in a Japanese prison) Tommy was expecting her first child; for the moment it was referred to in her letters as Jemima-Jim, 'the name being both masculine and feminine until we know what it's going to be, though Peter is convinced it's going to be both.'

Like every planter's wife, Tommy faced one daily fear – the moment when Peter set off on his early morning rounds before breakfast, for this was zero hour, this was the time when a wife could never be sure that her husband would return. 'That's when my worries start,' Tommy wrote, 'and I know Peter is praying the Communists won't attack the bungalow while he's away. It's quite a touching reunion when each finds the other is safe.'

Tommy Lucy's philosophy was simple: 'We're not going to be slaves of the situation. We're going to carry on with our jobs in the home and in the district despite the Communists. It's very important that we shouldn't be useless parts of the machine against the bandits. Our biggest value is from the point of view of morale. I'm quite sure it makes a great difference to the labourers and the other people in the district to see that we're carrying on normal lives.'

It took a great deal of quiet courage to live a 'normal life' – particularly as people like Peter and Tommy must have realized that while they were staying and fighting, everything would change with independence and Malayanization. The estate would go on, of course. The same firm would continue to own it. But inevitably (and understandably) European planters would gradually be replaced by Malayan.

Amherst was a small bungalow, so a heavily-protected room had to be built for the expected baby. And with the prospect of having to make a sudden dash to hospital in Kuala Lumpur, Peter had to provide suitable transport. He bought a Ford V8 and decided to armour it, replacing the windows with steel plates, erecting a metal shield with eye slits which could be lowered over the windscreen by pulling a cord. Under the bonnet the engine had its own armour plating, and finally he fitted the car (immediately christened 'The Monster' by Tommy) with 'Lifeguard' tyres which would not deflate for three miles if pierced by a bullet.

Then he set about preparing the defences of the bungalow. One barbed wire fence protected the workers' lines, with its small school and crèche for children of the hundred and eighty Tamil tappers. At the end of the laterite road leading to their bungalow up a curving hill through the rubber, a triple barbed-wire fence surrounded the bungalow lawns and gardens. Three fortified posts were guarded night and day. Peter laid on a phone to the bungalow, four searchlights (each with its own battery in case one was knocked out) and at a dozen points gongs which had to be struck once an hour, day and night, by guards whom he trained as best he could.

Their bungalow, with its bar in one corner, and a rack of guns in the hall, was not, as on so many estates, crowded in by the rubber. Standing on a rise, it had plenty of air, for all the old rubber trees which had finished their useful span of forty years had been replaced with seedlings, so that as Tommy remarked, 'It gives us an excellent field of fire.' Like Peter, she was a crack shot, and when the CTs attacked, she operated a Bren gun which Peter had managed to acquire. Tommy Lucy was an enthusiastic gardener, specializing in hibiscus, and their garden was filled with exotic plants; soon, however, the summer house was turned into a guard post, and parapets with sand-filled double walls (sandbags rotted too quickly) marred the perfect lawn sloping down from the bungalow.

Peter had armed his Ford just in time. At six o'clock one morning he buckled on his revolver and set off, his three dogs at his heels, on his rounds at Amherst. Tommy's baby was due any time and he was early because he wanted to return to the bungalow in time for breakfast with her.

This was the moment of the day Peter Lucy loved most. The humming of thousands of insects still mingled with the croaking of frogs and the cries of a nightjar. He could hear a cock crowing in the tappers' lines and the discordant voice of a hornbill which had awakened him several times during the night. Before him lay the cavernous aisles of the estate, thousands and thousands of trees uniform in height, in leaves, in colour, where already the heat of the day was beginning to press down like an insidious damp blanket with hardly a breath of air to fan the sweating faces of the tappers under the unchanging arches that stretched from one end of the estate to the other.

He had almost reached his jeep when the dogs stiffened. Four cracks shattered the hum of insects and started a flapping of frightened birds. By the lines, Tamils, formed up in a square as the overseer called out their names in the daily muster, broke ranks. Peter saw one stumble, drop his latex bucket on its shoulder-pole and sprawl bloodily across the parade ground.

The firing came from the jungle and was followed by a fusillade from Peter's guards. Peter raced to the sand-bagged summer-house on the lawn and as he joined one of the guards, he heard the staccato burst of a Bren gun from inside the bungalow. That would be Tommy at her post.

As with so many CT attacks, there was sporadic fighting for a few minutes, followed by silence. Peter wanted to chase the CTs, but at that moment Ah Tin, the houseboy, in his neat starched white jacket, came running across the lawn and gasped, 'Tuan come quickly. Mem not well.'

Tommy was sitting on the floor by the Bren. She tried to smile as she whispered, 'Peter, get the Monster out – get me to Kuala Lumpur – quickly.'

Peter and the boy helped Tommy into the Ford. Her pains could not have started at a more dangerous time, for the estate road passed by the jungle fringe and CTs might still be lurking there. Nor could Peter make a dash for it, for the Ford, lumbered with it heavy armour, could only do thirty miles an hour. There was only one thing to do. Peter wound up the iron windows, lowered the bullet-proof windscreen and started to sweat it out in a metal box. He gave Tommy a revolver and left his by his side on the seat.

It was as well he did. Less than two hundred yards from the bungalow perimeter the CTs opened fire. He could only try and get the ancient Ford up to her maximum speed while listening to the ping of bullets hitting the armour. Tommy opened the nearside 'window' to a crack, lifted her revolver and though unable to take aim emptied it into the roadside. 'It made me feel better,' she remembers.

It took them nearly an hour to reach Kuala Lumpur Hospital where on the following morning, Peter was proved right, though it wasn't Jemima-Jim. Two fine boys, to be named William and John, were born to Tommy Lucy. Two weeks later she was back at Amherst – and manning the Bren again.

The godmother to one of the twins was Mollie Puckridge, wife of a rubber planter, and the Lucys' best friend. Their estate could not have been more different from the Lucys'.

Robert Puckridge planted Jenderak Estate in Pahang, a lonely 5,000 acres between the towns of Jerantut and Temerloh, yet with no road linking the twenty miles separating these towns. The Puckridges could only reach their estate by river or by the ancient one-track railway known as the Sakai Express, which consisted now of square bullet-proof metal boxes without seats. This would stop 'on request' at Jenderak Halt – a small wooden hut on the estate reminiscent of nothing so much as an old-fashioned privy at the bottom of the garden. Despite the dangers, the Puckridges revelled in this isolation, with *The Times* arriving three weeks late (always to be opened, one a day, in strict date order) and food supplies kept as fresh as

possible by melting ice; and there was also a weekly supply
of fifteen books from Mrs Nixon (who ran the library in
Kuala Lumpur).

'Puck' – an ex-RAF officer who had shot five elephants
at Jenderak in a matter of months – loved the estate, which
abounded in game. But he was determined to be 'British'
with a capital 'B' and as the CTs stepped up their attacks
he decided it was time to show the flag – literally. Every
evening at sundown he lined up his squad of home-trained
guards beside the flagstaff. Ceremoniously, the Union Jack
was hauled down for the night while 'Puck' blew his own
home-made trumpet.

Even when a CT surrendered one Sunday – a rare
occurrence in those early days – 'Puck' had trained his
houseboys so well that none dared to wake the tuan during
his siesta, and the CT had to wait, kicking his heels, until
tea-time, when 'Puck' politely accepted his surrender and
wrote a poetic account of the event for the *Straits Times*,
of which the first verse read:

> *On Sundays on Jenderak*
> *The bandits all surrender;*
> *They know it really is a piece of cake,*
> *When they bring their guns and rifles,*
> *Grenades and other trifles,*
> *And wait outside the fence till I'm awake.*

Apart from the driver of the Sakai Express, that CT
was the only visitor the Puckridges had for the next seven
months, during which the CTs fired on the bungalow
almost every night. Each morning Mollie insisted on going
on the rounds with 'Puck', for she hated the idea of being
left alone. She held the gun, Puck drove the Land-Rover
– with his hat on the seat filled with grenades. Yet Mollie
remembers it now as 'a wonderful life, though the CTs
fired guns every night and there were so many bullet holes

in the room that when it rained it was like sleeping in a colander.'

In the first few weeks, four more British planters were murdered in widely separated areas, and in Perak the planters meeting in the FMS Bar – their favourite haunt in Ipoh – ran a sweepstake on who would be killed next. The winner was the one who guessed where and when.

Yet it never seems to have entered the heads of planters to pack up and get out. Or rather if it did – and obviously it must have crossed their minds – it was rejected. For though the planters were bitterly disillusioned at the lack of government protection (not that the government *could* give them much protection), it was not only their families they were worried about, but also their tappers. Matters came to a head after a particularly grisly attack on the labour force at the 1,700-acre Galloway Estate near Kajang, fifteen miles south of Kuala Lumpur, where David Trevaldwyn, a tough all-Malayan rugby forward, and his wife Lynn lived in a bungalow surrounded by rubber, which in turn was surrounded either by jungle or swamp. The local CT platoon was led by the notorious 'Bearded Terror of Kajang',* who was not only a cold-blooded killer, but an audacious fighter. Already troops acting on a tip-off had tried to catch him at Galloway. At one stage a soldier at a check-point saw four 'tappers' walking nonchalantly towards him. Thinking it was a police sweeping party, he nodded and the men – including the Bearded Terror – smiled back and walked on.

The Bearded Terror knew that the tappers were the key force in the rubber business, and their job, though menial, needed a certain skill. Every morning, sometimes seven days a week, the tappers set off around six o'clock, dressed in their oldest clothes, to earn between two and

---

* Though always known by his nickname because of his wispy beard, his real name was Liew Kon Kim.

three dollars a day. Sometimes wives worked side by side with husbands to double the family income. Tapping was a simple but delicate operation, for too large a cut could ruin a tree. Working swiftly through a hundred rubber trees to an acre – and tapping each tree on alternate days – a tapper removed a thin shaving of bark, the cut sloping downwards, barely a sixteenth of an inch below the previous cut. Along this tiny ledge the milky white latex dripped – more strongly in the mornings than later in the days – into a small cup fastened below the end of the cut. Six hours later the tapper returned to empty the cup into a pail and take it to the factory for processing. The Bearded Terror knew full well how important it was to terrorize the tappers in order to extort food and money and his CTs set about the prospect with brutal determination. The endless rows of tress backed by swamp offered them perfect conditions for attack, for no European, let alone a local overseer, could hope to keep watch over thousands of acres of woodland.

In the last week of June he appeared with thirty CTs out of the shadows on David Trevaldwyn's plantation. A hundred or so tappers were working quietly. Two Chinese caught hold of the nearest man and, stifling his screams, quickly and efficiently slit his throat. The others, paralysed with fear, started to flee – but significantly made no noise, never screamed for help. No shots were fired, though several CTs had Sten guns. They knew the tappers realized that their only hope of escape, of living, lay in silence. Within three minutes the CTs had caught four more struggling men and one woman – all protesting their innocence – and slit their throats in the same workmanlike manner. The others got away.

There seemed no reason for it – except the obvious one of striking terror into the hearts of simple people. Not one of the survivors talked, and indeed Trevaldwyn knew nothing of what had happened until he was making his second round and almost crashed his jeep into a tree as he caught sight of the open throats, the staring eyes, the bodies already crawling with ants. He raced back to his office, assembled his men, tried to find out what had happened – only to be met with a stony silence. (Not until many years later was he able to persuade one or two survivors to talk.)

The reaction of men like Trevaldwyn and Peter Lucy was one of cold fury – and an increased determination to 'stick it out'. Tommy Lucy remembers that when they heard the news from Trevaldwyn (the details were censored in the Press) they were sitting on the veranda and Tommy said to Peter suddenly, 'Do you ever think of packing it up – getting out of this?'

The firing over their bungalow had been particularly heavy that night and Peter was drinking a stengah, his shotgun still across his knees. He took a long drink and then replied simply, 'Of course not. This is our home – why should we be driven out of it? And what about the people on the estate?'

'I knew you'd feel like that,' said Tommy, also thinking of the Asians who worked for them at Amherst.

Within days of this outrage a deputation of planters descended on Kuala Lumpur, demanding action. The police, who certainly did not have the men or weapons to protect entire estates, suggested that planters would be safer if they lived in group headquarters and went to their plantations each morning. That, said the planters, scornfully in an official statement, 'offered no protection for the Asian staff and labourers and any form of discrimination is regarded as deplorable.' The safety of the European planters, the deputation added, was 'of little significance when compared with the protection and safety of the great numbers of Asians, staff and labourers alike, who are just as much entitled to this protection as the Europeans.'

At least Bob Thompson, though he could not produce arms out of a hat, had a brainwave for improving the morale of lonely planters, especially the many bachelors living by themselves in isolated bungalows and whom 'I could picture looking out from the veranda into the rubber trees in the darkness of the night.' He organized a 'sleep with planters' plan, ('It's not what you think!') whereby groups of men in the nearby towns volunteered to drive out around six o'clock – just before the swift tropical night blacked out the countryside – and spend the night with planters. In those earliest days it was a great success.

Thompson also had another idea. One day Puck Puckridge watched a Land-Rover drive up and was astounded to see a grimy unshaven Thompson jump out. He was in uniform. As he cried, 'Bob!' Thompson said, with mock severity, 'Colonel Thompson, if you please.'

And he *was* a colonel. Thompson of course had a magnificent record as a guerrilla fighter in Burma, so he and three officers from Force 136 formed 'Ferret Force' in which they led small platoons of the regular army troops into deep jungle to try and harass the CTs. No one expected Ferret Force to beat the CTs. It was a temporary measure, but it helped to close the gap until the army was better deployed. The only trouble was that Thompson had to have an army rank and it was impossible to ask the War Office to gazette him – it would have taken far too long. So he joined the FMS Volunteers with the rank of 'Second Lieutenant, acting Lieutenant-Colonel', and made only one stipulation. 'I wasn't going to have everyone thinking I was an army bloke,' he says. 'So I put up my RAF wings on my tunic.'

The eight hundred European miners – 'European' being a polite term for non-Asians so that it included Americans – faced many similar problems, though with some differences. By the nature of things the miners operated in more compact areas nearer settlements; they also had an engineering turn of mind, so were able to improvise more quickly, more instinctively perhaps, than the planters.

At the Pacific Tin mine at Kampar, north of Ipoh, the manager, Ira Phelps, – a tall, freckled, raw-boned Mormon who came from Oregon – set off for the jungle fringe with oxyacetylene equipment to dismantle rusted Japanese tanks and British scout cars which had lain there since 1942. In a matter of days Phelps had salvaged enough armour plates to cover all his vehicles. Phelps and his middle-aged wife Elsie lived in a sprawling bungalow on some stilts on a hill behind the town, and from their large living-room, with its rattan furniture, American rugs on the stained wooden floor and the square-bladed fans whirring lazily above, Ira could keep an eye on the mine spread out before him – three ungainly dredges, the pale scars of new clay, the ochre ponds, and most of all, the mile-long road leading to the mine – a stretch of silvery-white sand, flanked by workers' houses, wild bananas and coconuts, and, as Phelps described it gloomily, a perfect ambush alley.

Behind the Phelpses' bungalow, the jungle crept to within fifty feet of their back door, and from the first day of hostilities, Chinese CTs came down the hill behind, leaving a sentry to guard their line of retreat, while they moved into Kampar to collect food, extort money and kill waverers.

Elsie, a placid, motherly woman from Salt Lake City, had no time to be worried. She was working on a serious culinary problem; a new cook had joined her, Mrs Ah Ping, and because Ira had a voracious appetite. Elsie was teaching the slightly bewildered Chinese the intricacies of preparing coleslaw, Thousand Island dressing, hamburgers, corned beef hash and other American dishes which she offered to twenty guests every Sunday, as soon as they had left their guns – now as indispensable as women's handbags – in the rack in the hall. Almost every Sunday the CTs attacked Kampar and British troops replied, but as the guests nervously listened to the shells whining in the jungle behind, Mrs Phelps would say calmly, 'Those British boys are very nice and wouldn't think of hitting us.'

Ira's most pressing problem was arms for his nineteen British and American engineers thrashing tin out of the pale mud of the Kinta Valley. He went to Kampar to ask if any were available – when to his astonishment the local police officer said that in fact he had a thousand M1 repeater carbines, and plenty of ammunition.

'A thousand!' spluttered Ira. 'Well, for God's sake – you can let me buy a *few* for my men.'

The policemen looked unhappy. 'I said I'd got the *guns*,' he admitted, 'but we've only got one clip magazine.'

Which meant, of course, that he might just as well have had only one carbine.

'Will you let me borrow it?' Ira asked. 'I reckon I can copy it.'

And even though the police said it was impossible, Ira Phelps did. He got his tool shop to cast dies, made a perfect duplicate clip magazine – and then he struck a bargain with the police: he would make them all the clip magazines they wanted if they sold him one carbine for every three magazines. In a few days every man at Kampar was armed.

Ira's precautions quickly paid off. Within the week fifty CTs crept down the hill and launched an all-out attack on Kampar. In an orgy of destruction, one group concentrated on the railway station. They shot three guards, burned down the station, together with stocks of rubber in the sidings valued at $40,000. Every shutter in Kampar was closed, but while half a dozen CTs kept the small police station busy with harassing fire, another group broke down the doors of one of the town's biggest Chinese

restaurants, found the owner and his family cowering in a
cellar and ordered a Chinese dinner for fifty. Their hunger
satisfied, they rampaged round the town in Wild West
fashions, shooting street lights, cutting telephone wires,
smashing windows. In all five people were killed – but the
CTs did not dare to attack Ira's well-armed mine.

Kampar was the most northerly of Pacific Tin's Amer-
ican-owned mines, but the headquarters was at Ampang,
barely six miles out of Kuala Lumpur, yet a hotbed of
Communism. Norman Cleaveland was in charge of all his
company's operations in Malaya, and while Ira was looking
after his mine in the north, Cleaveland, a 47-year-old
bachelor educated at Stamford University, was fighting a
battle on the diplomatic level to get arms for Americans.

He persuaded a doubtful Chamber of Mines to cable
Whitehall demanding arms urgently. The reply was dis-
concerting. 'There are plenty of arms in Malaya,' cabled
the Colonial Office loftily. 'I know there are,' exploded
Cleaveland, 'but they're in the wrong hands.'

Cleaveland next cabled his office in New York asking
for arms to be airlifted. Back came a reply: 'If we sent
you arms, wouldn't you be making yourself a target for
reprisals?' Norman's return cable – which he believes clin-
ched his demands – was a classic of laconic insult. It
consisted of only four words: 'I am a target.' The next day
New York agreed to everything Cleaveland asked for – a
Pan-American charter plane carrying three hundred
revolvers, five hundred sawn-off heavy buckshot shotguns,
sixty riot guns, some sub-machine guns and 70,000 rounds
of ammunition.

The arms did not, alas, arrive before Cleaveland had a
narrow escape when twenty CTs attacked the Tuck Onn
tin mine which adjoined his. They smashed all the
machinery, fired the homes of the workers and Cleaveland
was horrified to learn that the attack had been launched
from a large camp six hundred feet above Ampang valley.

It had bamboo huts, tables, chairs, a good water supply, and – as Cleaveland noted – even latrines and bamboo seats. It had obviously been built before the war, and it was just three miles from Cleaveland's bungalow.

As planters and miners all over Malaya settled down to what promised to be a long, long war, Norman Cleaveland, who had a flair for colourful adventure, soon found himself with a new, spare-time job. A member of Kuala Lumpur Flying Club, he was the first man to start aerial pay drops to lonely plantations – a move which later became routine over the whole of Malaya, for despite military protection, the weekly pay convoys, carrying the tapper's wages from the nearest towns, were always glittering prizes for CTs. Every Friday Cleaveland climbed into a single-engined Tiger Moth, loaded it up with burlap bags stuffed with notes, and dived low over the lawns flanking every planter's bungalow. Only once did he misjudge the drop zone – and $30,000 went hurling through the planter's tin roof.

There were, of course, lighter moments, and even an error could cause a laugh. The island of Penang was suddenly flooded with what appeared to be violently anti-British leaflets. Presumably the Communists had distributed them – but not until one had been translated did the police discover what had happened. The date was July 4, and a young woman in the US Information Service had thought it a good idea to commemorate this important day in American history by translating into Chinese the American Declaration of Independence.

In Johore, Jack Masefield, the Chief Police Officer, was escorting a group of civilian 'boffins' from the War Office, showing them all they asked to see in his area. One professor was fascinated to learn that CTs invariably camped at the heads of small rivers. 'And I suppose,' he asked Masefield, 'that they don't only use the rivers for drinking and washing, but for *everything*.' The sinister accent on the word 'everything' made it clear to Masefield that he should reply, 'Certainly. All Chinese are very clean, and they always defecate in a river if possible.'

'Capital,' said the boffin, and then offered his plan which had all the merits of simplicity. Troops would leak quantities of mildly radio-active food in places where the CTs were known to get their supplies. The CTs would carry the food to their camps at the river head, eat it, defecate in the rivers, after which it would be easy for troops with Geiger counters to follow the radio-active waters to the camps. Fortunately no more was heard of the idea.

A month to the day after the declaration of Emergency, the security forces had a stroke of luck. A policeman killed Chin Peng's only real military adviser – 34-year-old Lau Yew, who had been at the original jungle meeting, had organized the disposition of the eight regiments, and who was a keen student of Mao Tse-tung's works, particularly his theories of rural revolution. Lau Yew had been such a brilliant guerrilla fighter behind the Japanese lines with Force 136 that Chin Peng had never hesitated to charge him with the military conduct of the war.

The man who killed Lau Yew was Police-Superintendent 'Two-Gun' Bill Stafford, a stocky, broad-shouldered, barrel-chested, aggressive man with grey-green eyes, who had been a 'crime-buster' before the Emergency, and was already something of a legend in Malaya. Born in Margate, he had been a stoker with the Royal Navy in the Far East. At Hankow in China he had pulled the Lindbergs out of the Yangtze river when their plane collapsed in 1931 ('The proudest moment of my life'.) He had drifted into the Navy police in Hong Kong, then Singapore, from which he had escaped during the Japanese invasion. Later he was parachuted fifteen times behind Japanese lines in Burma.

Stafford carried a revolver under each armpit (and would unbutton his jacket 'with apologies' to adjust the holsters so everyone could see them). In charge of twenty Chinese detectives, he lived in Hose Road, Kuala Lumpur, slept with a gun under his pillow in a bedroom lined with mirrors so he could see any part of the room. He dressed himself and his 'killer squad' in black, and was a fervent believer that the only good Communist was a dead Communist. The Chinese called him 'Tin Sau-pah' – The Iron Broom.

Stafford was having a haircut in Kuala Lumpur when the barber, one of his many part-time informers, whispered that an important CT planned to hold a jungle meeting near Kajang south of the capital. He described the venue precisely; a hut in a small valley between two scrub-covered hills. Before dawn the following day, Stafford led his killer squad – with the barber as guide – through a rubber estate to the lip of a valley four hundred feet below, where wraiths of early mist still hung over the coarse lallang* and clung to three wooden huts in the centre. Outside one hut Stafford could see a woman squatting before a charcoal fire.

'That's the place,' whispered the barber – and then, obeying unwritten rules, slid back to a waiting car which sped him to his scissors and shaving soap before opening time.

Bill Stafford edged forward on his stomach, but as he started to slither down the hill the woman looked up, saw him and shrieked. Three men with revolvers rushed out of the hut, shooting wildly. The detectives opened fire as the men wheeled away towards the opposite hill. Two CTs were killed instantly, the third badly wounded. Stafford closed in, leaving the detectives to surround the shacks,

* A wide-bladed grass which grows voraciously in front of bungalows. The Malays successfully stunt its growth by wiping it with oil.

where they handcuffed five more women, one of them Lau Yew's wife. Climbing the hill opposite, Stafford examined the bodies. One man lay in the lalang, a hole the size of a fist in his forehead. A Luger lay beside him. It was Lau Yew.

Inside the hut, detectives found maps, four rifles, three shotguns, three pistols and a jute sack containing two thousand rounds of ammunition. Six detectives were sent back to the road with the booty and to order transport to carry the women and the bodies. Another detective touched the attap roofs of the huts with a match and they went up in a blaze. And Stafford was on the point of moving off when the counter-attack came.

At least forty well-armed CTs opened up with Bren guns from a range of fifty yards – and the police in the hollow were now heavily outnumbered. As the valley exploded with machine-gun fire Stafford managed to withdraw up the hill. Then, deciding to bluff it out, his detectives shouted in Malay and Chinese, 'Here come the Gurkhas!' They all charged, Sten guns blasting, towards the hollow. As suddenly as the CTs had come they vanished, obeying Mao's maxim, 'When attacked, withdraw.' The only police casualty was one detective – cut by barbed wire. On the other hand, the five handcuffed women prisoners left in 'sleepy hollow' had been killed in the crossfire.

'That's bloody promiscuous shooting,' grunted Stafford. 'Now – let's get out of here.'

The loss of Lau Yew was a crippling blow from which Chin Peng never really recovered, for Lau Yew had been the only CT with any real pretensions to military tactics.

'Two-Gun' Stafford, however, had already forgotten the CT military commander, for within a few days he was taking part in the single biggest Communist arms haul of the war. Before the Emergency Stafford had been deeply involved with crime in the underworld, and inevitably, he had built up a network of double agents, part-time informers, one of whom now made a fortune, for it was almost as important in those early days to unearth a cache of arms as to kill a CT – and informers leading the police to dumps were lavishly rewarded at the rate of $50 for a machine-gun, $10 for a rifle and $1 for every bullet.

One informant contacted Bill Stafford through a third man. The next day they met in the back row of the air-conditioned Plaza Cinema in Kuala Lumpur, during a showing of *Tarzan*. Bill Stafford slipped in first, and waited for the informer, who told him of a large arms dump buried halfway up a hill six miles from Kajang, close to the spot where Stafford had killed Lau Yew - and where the Bearded Terror had slit the throats of six tappers.

The tapper offered to lead Stafford to the dump – but only on his own terms: by night. Like everyone else in the Kajang area, he almost shook with fear at the mention of the Bearded Terror. Despite censorship, every tapper for miles around knew how those six throats had been cut on that grisly morning on the Galloway Estate; the trademark of terror, such an integral part of Chin Peng's war, was already being stamped across the country.

The informant was adamant. The Kajang gang, he insisted (doubtless was truth), had spies in every street, every shop-house, every café in the area. No one knew who they were – and for a man to be seen with one of the running dogs was like signing his death warrant. 'If any member of the Kajang gang sees me with you, I'll be killed in a week,' he said, adding, in effect, 'I want the money – but I'll never be seen with you by daylight.'

So there was nothing for it but to operate by night. Whispering in the darkness of the cinema, they arranged a rendezvous at the sixth milestone out of Kajang at eight the following evening.

With four detectives carrying spades and parangs the

party went into the jungle and started climbing – with Bill Stafford worrying about an ambush. Halfway up the hill, the man pointed his flashlight to a clump of young trees and said, 'It's under there.'

'What do you mean – under *there*?' Stafford growled, and looked at the trees.

'The trees were planted after the arms had been buried,' said the contact.

There was nothing to be done but wait for dawn. Stafford made himself as comfortable as possible, spent a restless night bitten by mosquitoes, and at first light they started tearing down the young trees. The eerie greyness somehow reminded Stafford of body-snatching in a graveyard. Nobody spoke and the sound of parangs and spades was magnified as the jungle night noises ceased, so that when one spade clinked against a chunk of rock everyone jumped. The terrified spy urged them to dig more quickly after they had torn away the undergrowth to get at the roots of the young trees. Soon the sun came up, and though it was hidden by the foliage, its heat pressed down until every man was soaked. Finally they uprooted the trees, and as they started digging it was no longer a graveyard, but to Stafford – a great reader of adventure stories – it was Treasure Island all over again, as the spades sliced deeper into the ground until finally they hit the cache.

Even Stafford was astounded. The trees had been planted over a dozen pits, each one lined with timber and containing the circular metal drums in which the arms had been parachuted by the British Force 136. It was the single biggest arms haul of the war, and included dozens of machine-guns, still oiled, Stens, two hundred and thirty-seven rifles, ten-thousand rounds of ammunition.

Stafford wanted to leave a guard and return with sufficient police to carry the booty back to Kuala Lumpur, but the informer flatly refused to travel by daylight and Stafford could not possibly have found his way through the jungle without a guide. Even after he had painted a rosy picture of the reward the informer remained adamant. He would prefer to give up the money rather than risk being seen by the 'Bearded Terror' or one of his men. He would only travel by night. So Stafford had to sit in the jungle until nightfall before being led back, and then wait in Kuala Lumpur until the evening before returning with a large force of police trainees to collect the arms.

Police headquarters was delighted – but also dismayed at the amount of the reward, for at the ruling prices the informer was eligible to collect more than $100,000. Stafford was told to see if the informer would agree to accept a smaller sum, and a price of $60,000 was eventually agreed, though the informer made one proviso: the money had to be paid in dollar bills. Stafford spent a hectic day running from bank to bank, piled the notes into a big rattan basket and took a trishaw to the café where they had arranged to meet.

As he handed over the money, the informer said he would like to offer Stafford a present 'from the basket'. Stafford naturally refused, but did suggest that his detectives might appreciate something for the hours they had put in digging. To Stafford's fury the informer dipped his hand into $60,000 and pulled out a hundred dollars.

'You lousy bum,' shouted Stafford. 'Get out of town today – or by God, I'll bloody well shoot you.'

The impression remains, perhaps, that all this was not really a war, but more a series of sporadic actions; and in those early days this might have been partly true. It was to be many months before the police became really organized. And though the army units were swiftly deployed across the country they could not hope to *prevent* action. Chin Peng's men were in hundreds of camps dotted over the length and breadth of Malaya. No sooner would there be an atrocity in one area than the scene would change and slaughter occur three hundred miles away. The country lacked a powerful leader, and Whitehall did not seem to be in any particular hurry to appoint a successor to Gent.

And also, however worried the planters and miners might have been, the impression gained from reading the files, papers and diaries of the period is that to the ordinary man and woman in Kuala Lumpur the gravity of the situation had not really sunk in. Men like Bob Thompson certainly knew they had a full-scale war on their hands – indeed, a historic war involving a new pattern of conflict – but Thompson remembers a businessman member of the 'Spotted Dog' club flinging down the *Straits Times* and grunting to him, 'Bloody newspapers! Always exaggerating!'

Thompson could not tell the man that in fact the newspapers were, very properly, under censorship, because of the need to keep the CTs guessing, and consequently were printing only a fraction of what was happening.

4 THE HISTORIC DECISIONS

Not until September 1948 did Whitehall appoint a successor to Sir Edward Gent. Luckily for Malaya, he was a man who, even if he did not have the power to win the war, had the foresight to know how it should be won. Sir Henry Gurney – whose tenure of office lasted two years to the day before ending in tragedy – made two profound historic decisions, one military, one social, that were to change not only the conduct of the war but the world's thinking and policies when faced with Communist insurgency.

Gurney had been Chief Secretary in Palestine during the last two years of the British mandate. A slight man of fifty, with receding hair and spectacles and a clipped grey moustache, his panache had become a legend in Palestine during the last frightful months. Unruffled, he insisted on his daily round of golf even on the day before he wound up the administration theatrically by taking the last plane out of the country.

Known to close friends as Jimmy, he had gained a Blue for golf at Oxford and was a keen tennis player (he quickly arranged for a weekly game every Wednesday evening with Bob Thompson). In public he was every inch a Proconsul. In a hot climate where shorts and open-necked shirts were becoming normal wear Gurney insisted on dressing immaculately; he always wore a jacket, tie, felt hat and invariably carried a walking stick.

He was also an old hand at bureaucratic manœuvre who delighted in sly jokes. Soon after his arrival he displayed his slightly malicious sense of humour when a member of the Legislative Council sent the Press an advance copy of a speech which should have been made on a certain day but was delayed. Unfortunately the speech was printed in the newspapers, and when the debate did take place, the embarrassed politician had to plough through his speech while Gurney ostentatiously checked each word against the newspaper version.

He was cast in a very different mould from Gent – perhaps epitomized by the differences in the handwriting on their official reports. Gent had sprawled his gubernatorial red ink over two or three lines at a time. Gurney wrote the neat, precise hand of a reflective, creative mind.

To many he had the reputation of being aloof, distant and 'hard to get to know'. They forgot that there were times when a High Commissioner needed to be aloof. Thompson found him 'warm and human, but he could be cold fish when he had to be.' And though there were some at first who felt the war called for different, tougher qualities of leadership they underrated him. For it was Gurney who quietly devised a classical strategy for eventual victory.

Gurney's first historic decision was, briefly, that on no account must the armed forces have control over the conduct of the war. This, he argued, was a war of political ideologies. He believed that what was needed was armed support for a political war, not political support for an army war. The army thought otherwise. During the long hot summer between the death of Gent and the appointment of Gurney, General Boucher had naturally been running 'the military show' as he called it, with virtually no interference, particularly as at first the police had been ineffectual. Reinforcements, including the Coldstream Guards, had reached Malaya. To a man of Boucher's army mentality, this was 'just a job for an army' and it was unthinkable, as he told a friend, that 'a bunch of coppers should start telling the generals what to do.' Naturally his staff officers backed him up. To the average army mind, force was synonymous with power, with victory. In the discussions at King's House – which never descended to acrimony – Boucher's attitude was plain; in effect, 'Give us the tools and we'll finish the job.'

Gurney's answer – which could never hope to satisfy *any* army chief – was that too many tools would *not* 'finish the job'. If the army were given its head it would, he believed, lead to a pattern of escalation, a need to impress with military might, the inevitable bombing of innocent civilians resulting in a hatred of authority which would have delighted Chin Peng. More guns and troops were needed, of course, but only, Gurney insisted, as an adjunct to the civil power.

Fortunately for the future of Malaya, the country had more than its quota of brilliant, dedicated men whose persuasive powers helped to prevent military domination of the civil power – men like Malcolm MacDonald and Bob Thompson.

MacDonald had seen the danger almost as soon as Gent left, for before Gurney's appointment he had received private word from Whitehall that a general was being considered as the next High Commissioner. MacDonald had immediately telegraphed London and urged that on no account should a soldier be appointed. He felt that, 'This was the first shot in the army versus civilian crisis. I was clear in my mind that it should be a civilian. Whitehall was not hard to persuade – but it might have been a very different story if they had not had someone in a position like mine to persuade them.' Now Malcolm Mac-Donald supported Gurney wholeheartedly.

Thompson also held very strong views on the role of the armed forces. He had just been transferred to the Government Secretariat in Kuala Lumpur, where one of the his major tasks was handling and co-ordinating intelligence reports, a job which brought him very close to Gurney, and he argued, 'It's all very well having bombers, masses of helicopters, tremendous fire power, but none of these will eliminate a Communist cell in a high school which is producing fifty recruits a year for the insurgent movement.'

He knew that Chin Peng's army had been deliberately designed to be immune to large-scale military power and that in fact massive application of such power could contribute to a British defeat, for he felt, 'The very size of an army foments political instability because political power inevitably rests with control of the army.'

This was more than ever true in a war in which, as Thompson pointed out, only a minute fraction of the population were active, positive members. In this kind of war, one stray bomb that killed one innocent child could make a thousand enemies. Successfully, he urged that it was better to police villages than to destroy them. (This was a fundamentally different policy from that adopted later in Vietnam, where vast areas were written off and before long came to be regarded as enemy territory, after which it seemed logical to bomb them.)

It so happened that around this time one highly significant military engagement was fought which proved conclusively that men and machines, however great the number, could never hope to eliminate small determined jungle platoons. This was the 'Battle of Tasek' in which eight hundred crack security forces, with highly sophisticated arms, failed dismally in the war's longest battle to trap fifty CTs in a small self-contained area from which it seemed that not even a rabbit could escape.

The army had received information that several prominent CTs were operating in the Tasek area – a district of limestone ridges and broken country in the Kinta Valley north of Ipoh.

Just after dawn a cordon of nearly eight hundred police and troops was thrown round the area, which consisted of a sloping hill covered with thick secondary jungle, bounded at its foot by an overgrown pineapple estate. Troops based two mortars on the upper edge of the perimeter and began to lob shells into the area. CTs immediately replied with brisk fire – and gave their positions away. Two CTs were killed. During the next four hours not another man was killed, and about ten a.m. it was decided to contract the circle. This, however, had a dubious advantage, for the angle of the mortar shells was now 'straight and down' and several troops had narrow escapes. After several calls to surrender had been ignored, British reinforcements arrived with two flame-throwers, setting alight the jungle. Two more CTs were shot and yet, after nearly five hours, only four had been killed. Now the police formed a line of men and, as the report put it, 'In the manner of a line of beaters moving forward to flush out partridges, started to work through the undergrowth.' Two more CTs were shot.

The battle was called off shortly before dusk, when the scene was obscured by smoke and fire. Six CTs had been killed, including two women. But as to the leaders, there was no sign. With at least forty other CTs, they had proved (as the French and Americans were later to discover) that when large forces attack small groups the jungle is not neutral, but can be very friendly to those who know how to use it.

To men like Gurney and Thompson this was no surprise. Gurney had fought terrorism. Thompson had fought guerrillas. Both knew that arms alone could never win a guerrilla war but that political stability *was* a major key to victory – that normal workaday government had to function, to make the decisions, had to be *seen* to function; otherwise there would be no hope for the millions of bemused, bewildered bystanders caught up in the turmoil of a war of terror. And without hope, without belief in government, the only alternative would be Communism.

At first Whitehall tended to back the army – possibly because of the strong army lobby in Britain; but while Gurney was arguing with Boucher, MacDonald was able to make his views felt in Whitehall, which finally agreed to back Gurney. There was, it should be stated, in no sense a 'battle for power'. The two sides put their views and Gurney's prevailed.

The real significance of this historic decision is that at a moment when the war was going badly Malaya was fortunate to have a man enlightened enough to realize the fundamental principle involved, and strong enough to insist that it should be carried out.

It was useless to have a civil government with power over the armed forces unless it could make some positive move, and it was now that Gurney made his second historic decision. It was breathtakingly simple in concept, and probably Gurney would have been astonished had someone told him that he was about to give the world its first glimpse of how Communist terror tactics could be eroded, that he was launching a plan which marked a social revol-

ution unprecedented in the history of British overseas rule.
For he decided to uproot and resettle the 600,000 Chinese
squatters living on the jungle fringe on land to which they
had no real title. By this enormous removal operation he
hoped to achieve two things: give the squatters grants of
land, so that they would have a permanent stake in the
country; and by resettling them in New Villages under
guard, deprive Chin Peng of hundreds of thousands of
willing or unwilling helpers.

The squatters were not a Malayan phenomenon. There
was hardly a city in all Asia that was not surrounded by
Chinese vegetable gardeners supplying it with pigs, poultry
and vegetables; but in Malaya the number had increased
phenomenally during the Japanese Occupation as starving
Chinese peasants fled from the cities with their families
and settled down on any available patch of land near the
jungle. They built their own ramshackle huts, worked
assiduously, raised families – and had become so much a
part of the Malayan scene that until now nobody had dared
to contemplate the gigantic task of uprooting more than
ten per cent of the country's population from areas in
which they had lived for six years, on the tacit understanding by all parties that possession is nine-tenths of the law.
Some lived by their agricultural efforts; others were
tappers who supplemented their income by the Asian equivalent of an allotment.

Chin Peng had long since realized the value of the
squatters both as food suppliers and as spies, and though
many might have been anti-Communist, he had from the
start launched a ferocious campaign of intimidation among
them. Any waverers were ruthlessly murdered, or even
worse, their wives and children were, often in the most
grisly fashion. On the edge of Amherst, where some of
Peter Lucy's tappers lived with their families in a squatter
area, CTs appeared one night, routed out three men who
refused to pay subscriptions and coldly ordered them to

parade their wives and children. As cold-blooded as executioners, they picked out one child from each family and hacked them to death before their parents' eyes. Their final warning was succinct: 'Pay up or we'll kill another of your children.'

Though CTs did all in their power to foment discontent, to discredit the government and thus increase their control over the squatters. Chin Peng was careful not to murder anyone too popular. For them he developed a guerrilla tactic that was to prove invaluable. The man would be compromised and discredited, as Bob Thompson discovered, 'perhaps by associating him with an unpopular aspect of government policy, or by accusing him of corruption, or better still, rape. There is no shortage of keen female party workers who are prepared to engineer a situation which will justify a charge of this nature'.

No holds were barred in cases of this sort. One highly popular Chinese mine overseer on Ira Phelps's estate suffered just this fate. Tien Chong was happily married and had a good job – until the police, who had been tipped off, raided the top floor of an unsavoury hotel in the town. As they pounded up the stairs, hysterical screams led them to the room. They broke down the door and found Tien bending over a naked girl black with bruises, and with blood streaming from a badly punched nose. 'He raped me,' she screamed. In vain Tien insisted that he had received a message to meet a fellow worker at the hotel, had arrived only two minutes before the police, and had been trying to calm and help the girl, who (he also insisted) had been covered with a sheet which she threw off as the police battered down the door. Tien went to jail – and was only released by chance six months later, when the girl was arrested, found to be a CT, and recognized by one of the policemen who had raided the hotel. She had been such an enthusiastic Communist that she had allowed herself to be beaten by fellow CTs just before the unfortunate Tien arrived.

Somewhat naturally British troops tended to regard most squatters as potential or active spies, but in fact the majority were simply terrified people, caught in the crossfire between the British and the CTs, and keeping as far away from both sides as possible. Many of the British scornfully regarded this as 'sitting on the fence', but this was a grossly unfair accusation. The squatters were being intimidated and murdered all over Malaya - so they followed a realistic policy, one by which victimized peasants throughout the centuries had managed to survive oppression in China. The Chinese in Malaya were only borrowing the tactics of their ancestors.

Many squatters were first-generation Chinese immigrants and Gurney was the first man to see that if they could be removed to land which would be theirs by legal right, if he could protect them in New Villages, they would not only deny food to the CTs, but would also cease to be waverers and become solid land-owning citizens.

As a policy it posed many problems, and Gurney admitted privately that he reckoned it would take eighteen months 'to get it off the ground' because of one stumbling block: most of the agricultural land was reserved for Malaya, and Gurney would have to persuade the Sultans to part with some of it. Every state had to be dealt with separately as each had different laws. Gurney formed a Squatters' Committee and started work, though he never received the real credit for what later became known as the Briggs Plan. Quite apart from Gurney's foresight, it was his patience, tact and understanding which persuaded the Malay rulers that it was to their advantage to give away land titles to form New Villages.

As Gurney was initiating these new measures, the police were beginning to operate more effectively – though not without serious dissension, particularly when Langworthy, the Commissioner, was sacked and replaced by a tough, unpopular, controversial figure.

Colonel Nicol Gray was a strong man in every sense of the word. His DSO as a Commando proved his gallantry. His previous post as Inspector General of Police in Palestine – where he had worked with Gurney – had been highly successful; yet from the moment his appointment was announced Nicol Gray was marked for hatred by almost all the older members of the frustrated, divided police force.

When Gray arrived at Kuala Lumpur to take up duties second only in importance to those of the High Commissioner, he had to hump his own suitcases through Customs and was met outside the airport 'by one reluctant police constable'. At police headquarters he was shown into a room in which two other officers were seated. 'That's your desk,' said his guide, pointing to an empty one in the corner.

Gray, of course, soon took an office for himself, but it is extraordinary that adults in a vital police force should have behaved with such pettiness. It was not because of loyalty to their ex-chief Langworthy; it had a deeper, more fundamental cause. Gray recruited several hundred Palestinian police – out of a job after the British handed back their mandate to the UN – and it was not long before they arrived, conspicuous in their 'Old Palestinian Police' ties of dark blue with Khaki and silver stripes. To the police in Malaya they posed an immediate threat to seniority in a force which the British officers had joined as eager cadets at nineteen, spending all their lives in the country, members of a 'club' in which, under the old easygoing order, the man next on the list automatically gained preferment as an older member dropped out.

The result was that a force already split in two was now divided into three: the ones who had remained in Changi jail after the fall of Singapore, the ones who had 'run away', and now the Palestinians.

And there was another extraordinary factor. Though Gray quickly got more weapons and equipment and created a police radio network throughout the country (with sets borrowed from the army), he seemed to have a phobia against the use of armour on police vehicles. Of course, there were only a few armoured vehicles in the country; but the American tin miners had demonstrated how to improvise by stripping the carcasses of rusted Japanese tanks and many isolated police posts felt they could do the same. Gray would have none of it. No doubt he would have been happy had all vehicles been armed, but since this was impossible he decided on a policy of 'all or none', presumably because he felt it would be unfair to those unable to get armour. It led to the most ridiculous situations in which high-ranking police officers went to extraordinary lengths to deceive their own Commissioner. One officer devised highly ingenious portable armour for his men's trucks. Steel plates from cannibalized Japanese tanks were slotted into position on the sides of each vehicle, hanging from bolts. As soon as word came that Gray was visiting the area, the plates were taken off and hidden.

Gray's policy led to a fundamental dispute over tactics. As Gray called for more action, police losses mounted, for police detachments in non-armoured lorries had to move along roads notorious for CT ambushes. Gray argued that in such attacks the police should jump down from their vehicles and use them as cover when returning enemy fire. It was stratagem which had served him well in Palestine, but it took no account of an important difference in terrain. Palestine had been open country with terrorists lying in ambush a hundred yards from the roadside. In Malaya, the jungle creeping to the very edge of a road gave CTs cover a few yards from their targets, so that time and again they could open with a murderous first burst which gave the police no chance to hit back.

Before long everyone in Malaya – and everyone knew all about Gray's no armour policy – had startling proof of what it meant in terms of human lives. Shortly before Christmas 1949, a police convoy of three unarmed vehicles was attacked by a hundred CTs as it wound up the twisting road across the north-south mountain range on its way to the town of Jelebu.

The ambush had been brilliantly laid. Strips of paper stuck to the roadway indicated the precise ambush position, and as the police swung round a corner, the CTs opened fire. Eleven policemen were killed in the first bursts. Two British sergeants, I. M. Lovie and J. L. Davis, had narrow escapes. As Lovie jumped he was shot through one leg, and while hiding in the jungle he was shot through the other. Davis had the sight blown off his carbine. In all sixteen policemen were killed and nine wounded before the CTs retreated.

Public outcry against Gray was bitter and furious. Mr S. O. K. Ubaidullah, a member of the Legislative Council, put down a resolution demanding immediate armour for the police, while the Malay Prime Minister of the state of Negri Sembilan said bluntly, 'All security force vehicles should be armoured. It should have been done long ago.'

Gurney found himself, not for the first time, in a difficult position. The Commissioner of Police had been his colleague in Palestine, and none disputed the fact that Gray was an acknowledged expert in anti-terrorist operations. So Gurney felt he must support him, but police morale dropped lower than ever.

Despite the problems with the police, Gurney was putting other far-reaching measures into effect. The police could now detain suspects for up to two years without trial. The death sentence became mandatory for any suspects

convicted of carrying arms. Houses could be searched
without warrant, curfews imposed, all movements of traffic
and food could be controlled without warning.

Police and judges were also able to use effectively the
Banishment Act – a long-standing piece of legislature
which had proved highly effective before the war in dealing
with Chinese secret societies, in their way as all-embracing
and evil as the Mafia. The threat of deportation to starving
China from prosperous Malaya had always been one of
the greatest deterrents to crime, though in point of fact
Chinese born in Malaya were rarely banished; the Act was
used to deport undesirable aliens, as in any country.

After a great deal of hesitation, Gurney made two more
far-reaching decisions. The first was to announce a system
of rewards for information leading to the killing or capture
of CTs – with Chin Peng worth $80,000 at the top of the
list. While members of the public frightened of reprisals
could hardly be expected to lead police to violent CTs,
Bob Thompson was a firm believer that, as he put it 'the
natural cupidity of many members of the population soon
involves them in the hunt, particularly if they know that
their identity will not be revealed and that they will be
paid on the nail in cash in accordance with results.'

But the real hope behind the plan was to persuade
surrendered CTs to sell their erstwhile comrades for cash
bounties, and though many deplored the move on moral
grounds, it proved in the end (when bounties were vastly
increased) to be one of the biggest war-winning weapons.
Surrendered CTs were offered a half-rate of the standard
reward, and many a one-time Communist set himself up
in business, for (to quote Thompson again) 'there is
nothing like establishing prospects whereby an individual
can go from terrorist to capitalist in two easy moves.'

The second major decree angered Chin Peng more than
any other. It was an essentially simply manœuvre to beat
guerrilla Communists: the introduction of nation-wide

national registration. Legislation for this had been introduced earlier but until the autumn of 1948 it had been impossible to spare the men to put it into effect. Now every man, woman or child over twelve had to possess an identity card bearing a thumb print and photograph. National registration took many months to complete, for field teams had to be recruited, frightened photographers (mostly Chinese who rightly feared reprisals for their collaboration) had to be cajoled into working for the government, squatters rounded up. It was a masterstroke; for this one decree was also in effect a census; and it would be an invaluable help when the time came to grant citizenship to many aliens. It also meant that security forces were able time after time to separate the sheep from the goats. No CT dared to come forward for a card; yet if a man was questioned and could not produce one, he was immediately suspect.

Soon Registration teams of photographers and young civil servants (armed with fingerprint pads) were scouring the countryside. In the cities it was comparatively simple; nor was it too difficult in the mines and plantations, for when Peter Lucy was told that a team was due to arrive, all he had to do was assemble his labour force to be photographed and finger-printed. It was a different matter with the squatters. A team would arrive only to find that everyone in the area had vanished. And Registration was not made any easier by Chin Peng's violent reaction.

It is highly improbable that, at this stage – the end of 1948 and the spring of 1949 – Chin Peng had any idea of Gurney's first profound decision to resettle the squatters. The resettlement plan needed months of preliminary work before the CT leader ever heard of its existence. Compulsory registration, however, was an instant danger – one that threatened to disrupt the Min Yuen and consequently make life doubly difficult for his terror squads. He decided on immediate and violent reprisals.

5 THE FATAL PAUSE

It is one of the ironies of war that all too often a side poised on the edge of victory has not the faintest idea how near to defeat his opponent may be, and this is what happened in Malaya during the months following the appointment of Gurney.

Despite several spectacular Communist victories, the death of Lau Yew, the CT military commander shot by 'Two-Gun' Stafford, caused such an upheaval in Chin Peng's army that if only the British had been able to make one final effort, the war might have ended in a few months. Without the brilliant leadership of Lau Yew – and certainly there was no one to replace him – several CT leaders began to look doubtfully around them. Their military leader was dead; not a single one of the promised Liberated Areas had been established; the army was already facing a minor crisis in deaths and deserters and Chin Peng was finding it hard to get replacements, for though in theory there were thousands available, he had not yet realized the fallacy of believing that guerrilla warfare leaders can always count on unlimited dedicated volunteers.

One Central Executive document issued at this time (but which did not fall into British hands until much later) soberly announced that the Communist Party was 'disheartened at the way the revolution is going'. Called 'Our Opinion of the Battle', it admitted that 'the campaign has been badly planned and improperly directed.' Had the British known this – and had they been given better trained troops and a united police force – the Communist army might well have been routed by 1949. Unfortunately in these early days Intelligence was not as good as later and the government did not seem to realize how close to total defeat the Communists were. So instead of action there was a fatal government pause – one which added years to the war and gave Chin Peng a golden opportunity to regroup, to re-think his planning – and to prepare for a massive offensive the following spring.

Chin Peng's first priority was to make certain that his CTs were operating from properly equipped jungle camps, and (because he never lost sight of the theory of revolution) to make equally certain that camp commanders never forgot the need for political indoctrination.

No one has ever been able to assess the actual number of jungle camps, though it is known that there were several hundreds, varying in size. We know now – from captured documents together with eye-witness reports from surrendered CTs and from security forces who found some of these camps – that many were as well equipped as that which had been built for Chin Peng's first jungle meeting.

Bob Thompson's company of Ferret Force stumbled on one in the deep jungle near Temerloh in Pahang. It had accommodation for four hundred CTs, a parade ground with the Red Flag flying, kitchens, a bathing pool in the river, with latrines properly sited down river. The officers had separate quarters built of wood. Sentry posts – with the inevitable cord to be tugged in the event of an alarm – formed a loose ring nearly half a mile from the camp. As in every CT camp in Malaya, this one had its 'retreat road', to be used when the cord was pulled.

In those early days, each camp rigorously observed the shibboleths and rules of a Communist state. Each new comrade was welcomed with due ceremony as a 'Reserve' who had to pass through a probationary period before receiving the coveted 'Circular of Approval' which told him, 'You have worked hard, improved your knowledge and achieved progress. The Executive Committee are satisfied with your work and find that you have passed the qualifications for becoming a member of our Party. Today you receive an extremely glorious title: a Communist member, a Bolshevik Warrior. Look upon the Party as your vocation for life. Strive and fight for the Party, fulfilling your duty to the last.

Strict ceremony, starting with the singing of the 'International', was enforced when a new comrade was admitted to the Party. He had to step forward and bow before portraits of the Party leaders, after which, with clenched fist, he recited the six-pledge oath, and the formal meeting ended with the singing of 'The Red Flag'.

A new Communist was also given a list of 'Ten Points to be observed in Camp'. They were: 'Speak quietly; observe custom; return borrowed articles; pay for any damage you do; be honest when buying and selling; treat prisoners well; keep living quarters clean; keep personal belongings in good order; go every day to the lavatory; avoid the fair sex when bathing.'

The shrill blast of a whistle stirred every sleeping camp at 5.45 a.m. The men were given a quarter of an hour to wake up before physical training until 6.30; this was followed by a wash and breakfast, usually of rice and fish or vegetables. At 8.30 the day's first session of political instruction started in the camp 'school', complete with benches and tables. It usually lasted two hours, after which the men rested until lunch at noon. At 1.00 p.m. there was a second period of political instruction lasting for an hour, followed by camp duties or drill and PT on the parade ground until the evening meal at five o'clock, which was followed by a third session of political indoctrination, under a political commissar whose power was often greater than that of the camp commandant. Political textbooks printed in the jungle had been approved by Central Executive, and CTs had to learn books such as the twenty-page *Duties of a Sentry* by heart, apparently on the assumption that if a CT could repeat the instructions verbatim he understood them.

Now and again a curiously inept and unsuitable book would reach the jungle classrooms. Security forces recovered a copy of *Military Weaknesses of the American Imperialists*, which offered a comparison of every Russian and American weapon, plane and ship – none of which could have been of the slightest value in the Malayan jungle – and also a quaint chapter on the imminent collapse of the American capitalist system. This was apparently because (according to the book) US inspectors collected taxes in person from workers but did not hand over all the money to the Treasury, so that Washington was always short of money, this meant that every year the Treasury had to impose new savage taxes to balance the budget.

From time to time each CT received a crisp personal 'Critical Note' showing that the political commissar was keeping a watchful eye on him and pointing out such faults as 'You have a bad temper,' or 'You are showing insufficient enthusiasm when learning.' Punishments were severe.

Harry Miller, the author* who spent the twelve years of the war as a reporter in Malaya, had access to hundreds of captured documents, and discovered that for some crimes 'an offender may be tied to a tree and exposed to the sun for hours without water. He can be beaten with a bamboo pole for as much as thirty-six strokes. Men have been executed by being buried alive. Discipline is in accord with the background. It is jungle discipline.'

There can be no doubt that the iron discipline of the jungle camps produced fine soldiers; and, in those early days, excited and enthusiastic ones, particularly among the social misfits and the more illiterate, many of whom were now taught to read and write. They were mesmerized by Communist lectures which left a deep, inexplicable impression that somehow they had been given a privileged glimpse of a mystic source of power; that for the first time in their lives they had found answers to questions which

* *Menace in Malaya*

had always eluded them; and that they were members of an organized clandestine army with world-wide connections.

It was from these base camps that the war of terror was launched. It was more than a new kind of war, it was history in the making, for this was an army which struck with violent terror and then vanished, which lived off the land by threat, intimidation, or aided by a fifth column that penetrated every cranny of Malayan life to an extent that Quisling could never have envisaged.

Chin Peng's campaign of terror was directed with (for the time being) one objective in mind: wrecking Gurney's National Registration plan. He issued a campaign directive pompously labelled 'Strategic Problems of the Malayan Revolutionary War', obviously borrowing the title from Mao's 'Strategic Problems of the Chinese Revolutionary War', written in 1936. In it Chin Peng envisaged an intensification of guerrilla warfare aimed at the destruction of all identity cards. (Curiously, for such an intelligent man, Chin Peng completely ignored a fundamental precept of Mao's more balanced strategy: that one must wage a struggle on two fronts with equal emphasis – an armed fight in remote areas outside government control, side by side with a peaceful, 'legal' struggle by industrial strife and other means in urban areas under government control. It was to take Chin Peng nearly three years to remedy the error.)

Osman China, the top CT propagandist working in the Pahang jungle, organized a brilliant propaganda offensive, insisting that men were being registered as a prelude to conscription, or to make it easier for the government to levy outrageous taxes. His CT newspaper *Battle News* (printed on an ancient press in the jungle) cried that registration was 'a tyrannous enforcement of Fascist methods devised to consolidate oppression of the people'. He had tens of thousands of paper slips printed in Chinese, Malay and Tamil to be stuck on rubber trees. They threatened death to 'running dogs' who registered, and urged people: 'Use your identity cards as joss-paper.'

Lam Swee, who had been Vice-President of the Pan-Malayan Federation of Trades Unions until he went into the Johore jungle, wrote a cyclostyled 'Letter to workers' which shrieked: 'Sisters and brothers, we are now in the midst of a struggle. This was started by the British Imperialists, who have stripped all liberty from the workers and encroached upon their rights by enforcing registration.'

Side by side with this propaganda, the CTs stepped up their campaign of intimidation. Government registration teams visiting remote kampongs were attacked. Villages were raided, buses halted and every card was collected and ceremoniously burned. Eleven photographers were murdered, for it was for these men, mostly Chinese who had been hastily enrolled into temporary government service, that the CTs reserved their harshest tortures. In Johore one man was pegged on to the ground and left to the sun and the ants – and when he croakingly begged for water, rice was stuffed into his mouth.

When a group of people had been registered, then the CTs attacked, wherever possible through the family – knowing that this above all would induce others to submit. On an estate near Kota Tinggi a hundred tappers and their children were watching the usual free Saturday evening cinema show when CTs attacked, demanding their new registration cards. Four children were shot dead and the fourteen-year-old daughter of Mr H. M. Rice, the planter, only escaped by fleeing into the jungle after seeing her father murdered. In Johore Bahru an eight-year-old girl was burned to death with her family after her father had refused to surrender his card. Another child, six-year-old Georgie Wilson, saw his father shot dead. Mr George Wilson, the 39-year-old assistant manager of the Waterfall Estate, had superintended the registration of his workers and was therefore murdered as an example. He was driving his son to nearby Rawang – less than two miles from their bungalow – when CTs ambushed his car. Wilson opened fire, but was fatally wounded. A CT walked up to the car and told Georgie to run home, where Mrs Wilson was hiding in the rubber as she heard Georgie crying, 'Mummy, Mummy! Daddy's dead.'

The climax to this period of 'registration card collecting' (as the CTs called it) came when an American running a home for a hundred and fifty orphans was murdered. 'Mike' Blake – born A. M. Blake in Boston, Massachusetts – was thirty-one and ran the Serendah Boys' Home, twenty-two miles north of Kuala Lumpur. Two boys saw some men standing outside Blake's house. As they moved forward, a Chinese in uniform pointed a gun at them and said, 'Go back to sleep or you'll get hurt.'

Blake came out of the house. The boys, peeping from the dormitory window, saw him stand on the top step arguing. One Chinese hit him on the head with the butt of a gun. Blake stumbled, managed to crawl through the door. The CTs followed, the boys heard the sound of shots and in a few moments they saw the house burst into flames.

These were the months of the killing. Twenty-five people were badly injured when a grenade was thrown into a packed dance hall in Seramban. After police had beaten off an 'anti-registration squad', CTs killed seven men after an hour-long gun battle on the Ayer Kuning estate in Perak. On the Bidor estate, south of Ipoh, CTs killed eleven men, including a visiting company director, who were inspecting an abandoned corner of the estate. Four people were killed and twenty injured as CTs derailed a train near Tampin to collect cards; five were killed when another was derailed near Tanjong Malim. One man escaped by obeying the polite notice in the carriage: 'In the event of this train being fired on, please lie on the floor.' Buses suffered badly, particularly those plying the lonely routes north-west of Kuala Lumpur. Here thirty-six buses were burned by CTs led by a Chinese woman who held up thousands of travellers and demanded their cards. She was easily remembered for she was fat, well-dressed, and wore make-up and jewellery, which must have made her Sten gun seem slightly incongruous. Bus conductors said she also carried a black book and checked the identity cards of passengers against her list of names.

As the CT attacks mounted, special 'killer squads' concentrated their attacks on British troop reinforcements which had reached Malaya – including a battalion of the Inniskilling Fusiliers from Hong Kong and a Brigade of Guards from London. Many soldiers were national servicemen and often this was their first taste not only of the jungle, but of battle, for most of them had never seen a shot fired in anger. When a train was ambushed in Pahang and an ammunition truck blew up, a black-faced British soldier crawled out from under the wreckage, looked at the flames leaping to the sky, and calmly started to make notes. He had been conscripted, his name was Leslie Thomas, and thousands were to relive that scene when he wrote *The Virgin Soldiers*.

Some youngsters grew up in a matter of seconds. Men of the Fourth Hussars, after only a fortnight in Malaya, drove into an ambush near Sungei Siput, in which their CO was killed by the first grenade. Second Lieutenant John Sutro, aged nineteen, was wounded in the thigh – but he took over and held the bandits while Trooper Jimmy Goodier, also badly hurt, drove the only undamaged Bren-carrier through the ambush to fetch reinforcements. Sutro was wounded again, this time in the back, but he and his troopers killed six CTs before the remnants fled.

The CTs quickly employed devilish new twists in their ambushes against British troops, particularly ambushes laid on one side of a road, for then the troops would

instinctively jump out of their vehicle on the opposite side
– where CTs had planted pointed stakes in the undergrowth on which men would be impaled.

One jungle squad of the Guards ran into the 'Venus
Fly Trap' near Bentong. The sergeant in the lead stepped
on a carefully disguised pit lined with sharpened bamboo
spikes embedded into the sides like teeth. The force of
his fall allowed them to bend, but then they closed in on
him, making the slightest movement excruciatingly painful.
As his comrades tried to rescue him, CTs hiding nearby
moved into the attack, forcing the patrol to make the
agonizing decision to leave their sergeant while they fought
off the ambush.

The CTs had a simpler but equally effective booby-
trap. A sack filled with fifty pounds of sand into which
iron spikes were embedded was tied to the end of a long
rope looped over the branch of a tree, with the other end
of the rope fixed to a trip wire. As the first man in the
patrol touched the wire, the sack swung into the patrol,
decapitating the second man and often seriously injuring
several others. The CTs also quickly discovered simple
home truths – that while Chinese and Malays would automatically walk through big jungle puddles, British soldiers
tended to skirt them, so when possible small land-mines
were laid at the edges of pools.

To the newly arrived troops the psychological effect
must have been frightening, especially when added to the
normal terrors of the jungle – the wet heat, the slime and
ooze of thigh-deep swamp, the fat black leeches, the
sudden frightening cackle of an unknown animal bursting
into the silence, and at night, always and all through each
and every night in the jungle, the hum and the bites of
mosquitoes and the chilling jungle noises. These ceased
only with daybreak, when a tired unshaven patrol would
wake – if they had ever slept – to a half-cold breakfast,
without even a cigarette to sooth jangled nerves before

setting off on patrol, knowing that a swinging sandbag, waiting to pounce like an unseen animal, could burst open your head at any second.

Perhaps the fourteen-man patrol of the 2nd Battalion, the Scots Guards, felt like this on December 11, 1948, as they searched for CTs in the jungle near Tom Menzies's rubber estate at Batang Kali, a village north of Kuala Lumpur. They were led by guides and were examining a hut when sentries fired at two men in jungle green on a hill three hundred yards away.

The patrol was alone – and in a tight corner in CT-riddled territory. The sergeant in charge had no vehicles, no radio, no means of communicating with his platoon officer. He decided to press forward to his 'specific objective' and late that Saturday afternoon reached a working area in the plantation. There were three large buildings, a smokehouse, a rubber store. Men were working, women were cooking. The twenty-five men were separated from the women, the sheds searched, and a handful of ammunition was found in one shed. That was enough to start interrogation of the men. It lasted until dark, when the men were locked up for the night. Three soldiers, including the sergeant in command of the patrol, remained on guard. The rest slept.

The next morning the men were released from the shed to be taken to the nearest town for further questioning. What happened at that moment has remained a mystery ever since. There were three paths leading from Tom Menzies's jungle clearing and first reports said that as the last of the prisoners – all Chinese – left the hut, one shouted, and every man ran towards the three jungle paths. The sentries warned them to stop. The men ran on. Within two minutes every one had been killed.

That was the story the people of Malaya read in the *Straits Times* within a few hours. But soon they were nagged by serious doubts. How was it possible that every single escaping man had been killed and none wounded? How could the troops even be sure the Chinese were CTs? Especially as Mr Justice Laville, a prominent judge in Malaya, pointed out that flight from the police by uneducated people was far from being proof of guilt. Soon there were suggestions- apparently not without foundation – that the Chinese had been murdered in cold blood.*

Within days the outcry forced the Attorney-General in Malay, Sir Stafford Foster-Sutton, to order an enquiry, which published its findings twenty-one days later. It said in effect that 'a bona fide mistake had been made.' This might well have been true, but none of the evidence taken at the enquiry was ever made public, and even more curiously, the report was never sent to the War Office.

The *Straits Times* was so critical that Gurney sent for Allington Kennard, one of its most experienced writers, and asked him bluntly why the *Straits Times* 'was so hostile in its comment on Batang Kali and why the paper would not let the matter rest'.

Kennard replied equally bluntly, 'Because we know more than has been admitted.' Kennard was convinced that suggestions of a 'secret massacre' were 'wildly remote from the truth', but he had heard a story that the sergeant told the prisoners he was going to shoot some of them if they would not talk. He took out three men who were questioned separately, after which came the sound of shots 'to encourage the others'. Actually, according to this version, the three men were locked up in another hut, but, 'This, I am convinced, is why next morning the sergeant's remaining captives assembled in the clearing ran for their lives,' Kennard stated.

* An allegation that was repeated twenty-one years later in a London newspaper which produced affidavits from British soldiers who took part in the incident.

Significantly, Kennard then asked Sir Henry Gurney 'if he could assure me that this melodramatic play-acting never took place. Sir Henry changed the subject.' Perhaps he did so because of one puzzling discrepancy in this version. If three out of the twenty-five suspects were locked in another hut, then only twenty-two could have staged the mass escape the next morning because they believed their three comrades had been shot. How did the other three (presumably still locked up) come to be killed? The question has never been answered.

One thing is certain: the patrol of the Scots Guard had no means of telling whether the tappers were innocent or were CTs. At a time when newly arrived troops were trigger-happy and inexperienced, there seems little doubt that there was considerable truth in the suspicions.

The pity is that the government in Malaya did not remember that the finest weapon against Communism is to let the world see that justice is being done. By refusing to make public the evidence given at the official enquiry, the government encouraged suspicions that some of the Chinese had been deliberately murdered and gave Chin Peng an unrivalled opportunity to make political capital.

Professor Anthony Short, an acknowledged expert on the war in Malaya, placed the event in its true perspective, when he wrote in the *Asia Magazine*:* 'There were, almost inevitably, innocent victims. Some of these victims – like the twenty-five dead in Batang Kali in northern Selangor – were not surprisingly made martyrs by the MCP. But there was nothing like the indiscriminate killing of civilians in Vietnam. And although the figure can never be known, I would put it at less than a hundred from all causes – including misplaced shots and bombs dropped in error.'

---

* December 10, 1967, two years *before* the 'disclosures' in a London newspaper.

Early in 1949 Chin Peng called his second jungle conference, again in Pahang. Despite some signs of dissatisfaction in his ranks, he could look back with some comfort on the results of the first six months of war – 482 police, troops and civilians (including 24 British planters and miners) killed, another 404 wounded. Chin Peng's losses had been 406 CTs killed, 268 captured. And yet – something had misfired, for Chin Peng's grandiose plans to hurl back the British forces had gone awry. There were as yet no Liberated Areas. And the British were getting tougher. A new Emergency Regulation 17D now gave the government powers to uproot entire villages if there was evidence of support for CTs and take them into detention camps.

The jungle conference was attended by several Chinese Red Army officers; some crossed the Thai frontier, others arrived by sea from Hainan Island, apparently to help Chin Peng reorganize his armed striking force. Several major decisions were taken. First the name of the army was changed. The original Malayan Peoples' Anti-Japanese Army had already become the Anti-British Army, but Chin Peng felt that this name might seem odd in view of Malay's impending independence. What was the use of an Anti-British Army if there would be no British to fight? The name was therefore changed to the Malayan Races' Liberation Army – the Malayans being represented by the 10th Regiment, commanded by a notorious killer called Abdullah CD.

Chin Peng was also conscious of criticism that the war appeared (to world opinion as well as in Malaya) wholly destructive. Peasants who had been intimidated into helping were beginning to ask what they were fighting for. Chin Peng now provided an answer by forming the 'Peoples' Democratic Republic', in which he promised that after victory everyone over eighteen would have a vote in a Peoples' State 'controlled by the united revolutions of all races' and in which workers would have equality with the 'armies of state-controlled industries'.

He announced a scheme of national and social insurance, free education, land grants, and free supplies of seed and implements for agriculturalists. (Intriguingly, the British, who were distributing free seeds, farm implements, pedigree pigs and promising independence, were offering much the same inducements to join *their* side – particularly in national insurance, into which all employers and workers paid fixed sums, which the employee could draw out at the age of 55. As Bob Thompson, one of the originators of the scheme, felt: 'Every contributor received an annual statement and when, after a few years, a rubber tapper could see that he was worth several thousand dollars invested in the government and knew that it would be paid when due, it is easy to guess whose side he was on.')

Chin Peng had two more major problems to deal with – CT communications and special recruiting drive in the state of Pahang.

The first problem was serious, for communications were so bad that frequently Min Yuen local branches which needed to co-ordinate efforts did not know what a branch ten miles away was doing. Communications were the nerves of Chin Peng's scattered, mobile army and his vast numbers of Min Yuen supporters, and at the first jungle conference Chin Peng had organized a courier system of 'postmen' who took his directives and letters to major distribution points. But there was a flaw in this plan. Jungle travel – especially when harassed by security forces – was so slow that couriers could no longer be expected to undertake long journeys. It had taken one CT three months to travel the 250 miles from Johore day after day holed up to escape the ambushes in jungle country which, even in normal conditions, was so impenetrable that a man could cover only a few miles a day.

Now Chin Peng had a brainwave. He planned to reopen

the jungle postal routes which had served him and the British so well when Force 136 was fighting behind the Japanese lines. The Chinese had never revealed full details of the jungle courier service to the British, but it had one vital advantage over Chin Peng's first plan. The distances between each 'post office' were short, and the secrecy of their whereabouts was guaranteed by one simple expedient: no courier knew more than two secret hiding-places – the one where he picked up a message and the one where he delivered it. It meant not only a speedier service, but a chain which, even if one link were broken, was still essentially secret.

Now Chinese CTs who had fought with Force 136 would reorganize the courier system with its secret hiding-places. Speed was vital, particularly in north and central Malaya, if only because the Politburo was working in this area, and so Chin Peng made an appointment of some consequence. He needed one person to co-ordinate the system, to be in effect postmaster-general, and he chose a young and pretty Chinese girl called Lee Meng. She had already earned a reputation as a cunning fighter and organizer. Chin Peng told her to go to Ipoh to establish a communications centre. He gave her enough money to find a small room, get a job as a casual labourer in the local tin mines, which would give her freedom of movement when necessary, yet provide her with a cover. She was also told to buy a desk. One with a secret drawer.

The last two men to leave Chin Peng's jungle conference were the Shakespeare-loving Osman China and the Malay Communist Abdullah, both of whom operated in Pahang, and it was here that Chin Peng demanded action. Pahang was essentially a 'Malay state', and in order to present to the world a picture of a *Malayan* uprising – instead of the predominantly Chinese one which in truth it was – Chin Peng ordered Abdullah to start an intensified recruiting drive among the kampong Malays of Pahang, and to step up terror tactics in the state – the terror to be executed whenever possible by Abdullah's all-Malay regiment, with its killer squad.

In Chin Peng's grandiose dreams everything was so simple. As he explained, Abdullah would overrun one village and repeat the process ten or a dozen times until all the villages formed a Liberated District, which could then be enlarged to a region, finally reaching the status of a Liberated Area. And as he told Abdullah and Osman China when leaving, 'It's in Pahang that I want to establish Communism's first Liberated Area.'

6 THE COUSINS

Of all the states in Malaya, Pahang was the most 'Malay' – and to those who lived there, whether Europeans or Asians, it was the most beautiful and gentle. Covering 13,280 square miles, it was nearly twice the size of Johore, the next largest state; yet while nearly a million people lived in Johore, only 278,000 dwelt in Pahang. It was the home of simple devout Muslim paddy-growers who led almost self-sufficient lives in their kampongs or villages on the banks of the Pahang river, or clustered round townships like Temerloh, Jerantut, Kuala Lipis, all of which seemed to take a delight in living in the past.

It was in this area that Abdullah CD had been told by Chin Peng to step up terrorism and recruit Malays to Communism. Abdullah CD* was 29 and had been educated at Ipoh's Anderson School. A bespectacled, chubby, pipe-smoking man, he wore a red star on his velvet songkok, the Malay national hat. He had turned Communist during the Japanese Occupation and, like so many others, had fought with the British Force 136. He was a ruthless

---

* Short for Che Dat bin Abdullah, though he never used his full name.

fighter, and had already planned the single biggest 'Liberation' success of the war, in which his men actually moved into an area and held it for five days – the only time in the war that Chin Peng's dream of a Liberated Area was realized.

With this kind of military operation to his credit Abdullah was already feared in the Malay kampongs and he now set about consolidating his position. Three hundred CTs attacked the railway town of Kuala Krau, burning down the railway station, the houses of the station master and an inspector. Two British railway engineers asleep in a siding were killed. The CTs then attacked the police station, killing four policemen and two women, and derailed an armoured train which puffed into the relief of the besieged town. Within a few days Abdullah and two hundred CTs attacked the Kemayan Estate, also in Pahang, burning the British manager's bungalow, labourers' quarters, the smokehouse and other buildings.

Trouble had become so widespread that troops of the Devonshires were moved in Temerloh, on the Pahang river, and a deputation from local kampongs begged the Sultan of Pahang to appoint a Malay to lead organized resistance. After some hesitation the Sultan 'lent' them Yeop Mahidin, his Malay secretary.

Yeop was an extraordinary man – one of the most colourful fighters thrown up by the war. A stocky, dark-haired, fearless extrovert with a flashing smile, he had escaped from Malaya to India when the Japanese occupied the country, joined Force 136 and was parachuted back to fight with British officers – so gallantly that he was awarded the MBE. Later he shared a cabin with Chin Peng when both travelled to London for the Victory Parade. There was, however, one Communist even closer to him than Chin Peng; one who had occupied the next desk to his when they were both learning English at the Anderson School. That man was none other than

Abdullah CD, and this was no coincidence – for the two men were cousins, now dedicated to killing each other, a point made abundantly clear by cousin Abdullah who wrote to Yeop – in a letter larded with Marxist theories urging him to take to the jungle and join 'the winners'. Yeop felt he should at least try to persuade his cousin to give himself up, and wrote a letter which he nailed to a rubber tree in the area where Abdullah was operating. A week later Yeop received a spine-chilling reply. 'From now on we are not relatives,' wrote Abdullah. 'The enclosed is all you will get from me.' Out of the envelope tumbled a .45 bullet.

Yeop's first task was to form a personal bodyguard, choosing twelve kampong friends who quickly became known as the Vagabonds, and who remained with him for eleven years. So the legendary Pahang Kampong Guards were born. Before the end of the war, Yeop Mahidin was leading a force of 26,000.

Yeop, a devout Muslim, believed passionately that in every bad man there lurked a spark of good and 'my dream was not to kill, but to make bad people into good citizens.' He knew that many Pahang Malays in the jungle were not really Communists; though they were certainly known to be strong-minded nationalists, and as far back as 1892 they had openly rebelled against the British. The rebellion had been quashed, but to many the memory, handed down in the kampongs, still rankled and they dreamed of the day the British would be expelled from their state. Their tragedy was that few Pahang Malays realized that by fighting for Communism they would merely be exchanging one master for another.

A fluent speaker, Yeop toured the kampongs, telling the headmen that Britain had promised independence to Malaya, pointing to countries like India and Burma to prove that she kept her word – and they listened because he could talk on equal terms to families with relatives in the jungle, 'just as I have my cousin Abdullah on the other side'.

When he suspected a family of helping CTs, he crept up to the house alone at night pretending to be a CT, whispered that he had cone for a 'subscription' and more often than not a bag of rice would land with a thud at his feet. The following morning Yeop would return, challenge them and after the usual indignant denials would produce the bag of rice. But instead of arresting men and women who had been intimidated, he promised silence in return for information. Soon a chain of informants was helping Yeop to harry Abdullah CD from one camp to another, and a small trickle of CTs were surrendering to his bungalow, with its enormous flame tree in the garden, on the outskirts of Temerloh.

The most valuable informant of all in those early days came into his hands by chance and almost brought Abdullah CD's reign to an early end. Yeop had spent ten days and nights in the jungle and on the tenth morning he returned to Temerloh. One man went ahead to arrange transport at the jungle fringe, and when they reached the pick-up vehicles Yeop, as usual, remained fifty yards behind in case the noise had attracted any nearby CTs. It had. Through the hissing rain a voice whispered 'Bong!' – Indonesian slang used by Pahang CTs for 'Wait!' The voice added, 'I'm lost.' Slipping back the catch of his Sten, Yeop moved forward in the dark – until a pencil torch lit up his face and he heard a gasp – a girl's gasp. Then she crashed away into the jungle. Dropping his Sten, Yeop ('I was not a wing three-quarter for nothing') brought her down with a flying tackle.

The girl fought like a tiger. She bit, she spat, she scratched. But he held on until a Vagabond came to the rescue and they piled her into a truck. The Malay girl insisted that there was some mistake, but Yeop could always tell. Shining a torch on her face, he saw her unmistakable, unhealthy jungle pallor – the pasty look that showed even on Chinese skins after a month without the sun. Then he looked at her arms. They were covered with small, light-coloured scars, the jungle sores that marked every CT.

Yeop took her home, and while his wife warmed up some curry and found dry clothes, he studied the bundle of rags standing sullenly in front of him. With an emaciated face, cropped hair, flat chest, dirty khaki shirt it was hard to tell whether this was a boy or a girl. Her name, he discovered, was Siti Hadar, and she was twenty. Apart from her torch, Yeop found only one item of interest – a letter she had been trying to post to her father. The gist of it was, 'Don't worry, we are winning, it won't be long now.'

After she had wolfed the curry with the silent intensity of a beggar, Yeop pondered on what to do with her. He had caught her – and that meant a mandatory prison sentence. But soon he learned something about her. She had been a rubber tapper in a nearby kampong whose husband had gone into the jungle in June 1948. He missed her, she missed him, and one day a girl-friend whispered that she was sending food to her husband in the jungle and Siti started to do the same – a little rice hidden in her brassière, a message on rice paper hidden in her mouth. It all seemed rather exciting.

One day she was tapping when, without warning, a platoon commander met her – he 'suddenly appeared in front of me in a uniform with a gun over his shoulder'. He thanked Siti for her help, and said that two uniforms were waiting for her if she would come into the jungle. She went – as a cook. She had never seen any action, had never carried arms.

Yeop decided that if anything were calculated to turn her into a real Communist it would be a spell in prison, so he made a bargain with Siti. She would tell him everything she knew about Abdullah CD and in return he would say she had surrendered, which would mean a rehabilitation camp instead of a prison sentence. But he warned her that she must speak frankly and openly at the interrogation which would be held in the Rest House before Ian Mendel, the District Officer, and a colonel of the Devonshires.

Siti agreed – and then told an astonished Yeop that within twenty-four hours Abdullah CD had a rendezvous at Songsang, a district near Temerloh. With only four hours' sleep, Yeop and the Vagabonds set off, leaving Siti with his wife on parole.

Yeop, who knew every kampong road in the district, decided that because of rain and flood his cousin could take only one of three routes to reach Songsang. He split the Vagabonds into three ambush parties and they settled down to wait. To this day, Yeop does not know what went wrong, but Abdullah CD never kept the rendezvous. He had certainly intended to, for Yeop received an envelope containing yet another bullet from his cousin, with a message, 'We know the traitors among us.' Yeop could only assume that Siti's husband had warned Abdullah.

Siti was duly sent to a rehabilitation camp in Johore for three years,* but only after an unexpected twist during the interrogation. For Siti became terrified when she faced Ian Mendel and the colonel. It had been one thing to talk to a fellow Malay. It was different when faced with two stern white men, and she was tongue-tied. The colonel showed signs of impatience. Finally Yeop asked if he could help. 'Anything to get this farce over with,' growled the colonel. Yeop turned to the girl and said, 'Those are nasty jungle sores on your arms. Would you like some medicine for them?' Siti nodded; Yeop went to the Rest House bar

---

* At the beginning of the war there was only one camp where 'hopeful cases' could be trained to become useful citizens again. Later there were many more. A typical camp is described on pages 144–45.

in the next room, surreptitiously ordered a triple brandy
in a large glass and topped it up with ginger ale. 'Here!
Drink this,' he ordered her. Within twenty minutes Siti
was cheerfully answering every question.

Two days later, Yeop said goodbye to the girl as guards
took her to Johore. Neither could have imagined they
would ever meet again, but they did – in very different
circumstances.

'Yeop's war' – as the admiring Malays called it – was
conducted in a manner different from any other operation
in Malaya. Of course, during the months that he was
trailing Abdullah, troops, planes, police, were heavily
engaged in other areas as the war gathered momentum.
But Pahang was 'different'. True, many troops were operating in the state, but Yeop was a lone wolf who felt that
he and his Vagabonds had a personal vendetta to settle
with his cousin. Inevitably, the methods had to suit this
most Malayan part of Malay – as Yeop recognized when
he made his next move. He trailed Abdullah deep in the
Aborigine jungle north of Jerantut, with the help of one
several Dyak trackers recruited by the British from Sara-
wak and Borneo. This was Sardin – young, laughing, with
his long hair worn in a pigtail down his back and his body
tattooed with intricate designs. (He also had a splendid
set of gold false teeth – bought out of army funds before
he reached Temerloh. Like many Dyaks, Sardin had his
teeth extracted as soon as he had saved up enough money
to buy a gold set – but he had lost them when shinning
up a coconut palm for nuts. His tracking had suffered so
badly, due to depression, that 'in the interest of the country' the army had replaced them.)

Sardin was acknowledged even by his fellow professionals to be in a class by himself. He had been brought
up in Borneo where tribal laws demanded that he should
sleep under a row of shrivelled human heads to remind

youngsters of the deeds of their ancestors. He could speak little English. Armed with his poisoned arrows and blowpipe, Sardin set off with Yeop and the Vagabonds.

For three weeks they tracked Abdullah. Time after time Sardin would scent the trail, which he could follow merely by noticing the way a leaf had been flattened or a twig had been snapped. From time to time they stumbled on an Abo village – the long kongsi hut big enough to hold fifty people next to the banyan tree under which the villagers held their councils. But from none could they glean even a fragment of information. They were not sullen, but they were terrified. They offered meals to the Vagabonds, sold them food, but could not be persuaded to talk – until finally one volunteered the information that Abdullah was in a remote Aborigine kampong living in the headman's kongsi hut, and holding the headman and his family as hostages.

The house was built on stilts on the edge of a fast-flowing river. A balcony surrounded it, with rough steps in front and a primitive ladder at the back, with the shallow water slapping against its lowest rungs. Even if the house had contained only CTs it would have been difficult to launch a frontal assault, but with the headman held as hostage it was unthinkable, for Yeop knew that Abdullah would cut the man's throat without compunction if necessary. Their presence unknown to the enemy, the Vagabonds settled down unseen in the thick surrounding jungle to await an opportunity.

It came after several days, when late one afternoon Yeop and the Dyak tracker crept to the edge of a small jungle clearing which was obviously an old worked-out Abo settlement. Standing on the other side of the clearing was a CT sentry in uniform. To shoot would have given the alarm; nor could they capture the man before he tugged the string which Yeop knew must be there. With the swift, silent movements of a jungle hunter, Sardin plucked a poisoned arrow from his quiver, inserted it, raised the long blowpipe to his mouth, and the next instant the sentry's knees seemed to buckle, and without a sound he crumpled to the ground.

Yeop and the Dyak knew that sentries were always posted in a ring round a camp – and the death of the sentry meant the ring had been penetrated. Now the two men formed a hurried plan. The Dyak would make his way into the heart of the enemy camp and sound out the possibilities of attack. It would be dangerous, but Yeop felt certain that the Aborigines, suffering from the indignity of having their headman held hostage, would not give him away. This is just what happened.

The two men first disposed of the sentry's body, for his absence would eventually be noticed and they could only hope that when CTs came to search for him and found no trace – no blood, no signs of struggle – they would presume he had joined the increasing number of defectors. This done, Sardin crept into the village and Yeop went to fetch reinforcements. Within a few hours Sardin was back – with the welcome news that Abdullah and his guards slept in two cubicles at one end of the kongsi house, leaving the headman and his family under guard at the other end. Abdullah had chosen the end of the house nearest the ladder, and now Yeop knew just what to do. He would launch a feint attack.

At eleven o'clock that night the Vagabonds opened up with intensive Sten gun fire – aiming in the air. At that moment Sardin led Yeop round the outskirts of the village, to the river – and the rickety ladder where, at the last moment, Yeop fished something out of his pocket. It was Abdullah's bullet. Carefully Yeop inserted it into the first chamber of his revolver.

As the mock battle drowned the jungle noises, they could hear the sounds of panic, and barely a few seconds passed before figures came tumbling out of a flimsy back door at the top of the river steps. Two fell headlong into the water. Two more clambered down - and still Yeop waited in the shadows. Then a figure more burly than the others appeared. As he started to climb down awkwardly his hat dropped off, landing almost at Yeop's feet. It was a velvet songkok.

At that moment a CT flashed a torch, and for a split second Yeop Mahidin saw his cousin's face – and his cousin saw and recognized Yeop. Twisting round, Abdullah hurled himself from the ladder on top of Yeop, and the two men rolled and fought in the water. Abdullah was up first and splashed his way to a sampan. As Yeop scrambled to his feet Abdullah jumped in and pushed off. Carefully Yeop took aim as the sampan gathered speed in the current. He pulled the trigger – and nothing happened. His cousin's bullet was a dud. By the time Yeop was firing again the current was taking the sampan away without any help from Abdullah, crouched out of sight.

It was the end of one of the war's most personal battles, for though Yeop failed to kill his cousin, Abdullah was never a fighting power again. Most of his guards surrendered and for two years Abdullah remained in virtual obscurity. He never fought a major engagement, and finally fled the country and took refuge north of the Thai border.

7 THE BRIGGS PLAN

Sir Henry Gurney's scheme to resettle squatters was making slow but sure progress by the end of 1949, but this long-term plan needed a man with special powers to implement it, a man who could call on civilians or army to give it a helping hand. As GOC, Boucher had power only over the armed forces, whereas Gurney, as High Commissioner, could hardly order army units to erect a New Village. Obviously one single man was needed to run the war, to co-ordinate civil and army operations. For some months Gurney had been pressing for a Director of Operations but the Colonial office was perpetually jealous of relinquishing too much power to the armed forces, while the British government, nearing the end of its term, was inclined to rely on the civil services. So nothing seemed to be done.

In the spring of 1950, Gurney again complained bitterly, and one can understand why. As Bob Thompson, who was working with him closely, could see, 'We were running into trouble. No High Commissioner could handle the government, the country, deal with the Malay Sultans – and still have time to co-ordinate the various security forces including the police.'

Despite the problems, Gurney had done a great deal. In September 1949 he had announced surrender terms to Communists, and a million leaflets fluttering into the jungle told CTs that the law had been amended to allow CTs who had not committed serious crimes to surrender under a guarantee that they would not be charged with any offence carrying the death penalty.

At the same time Gray's police force had formed more than two hundred jungle squads ready to dash to the scene of any incident. Police had also been granted powers to offer substantial rewards to informers. Bribery had always been a major weapon against crime in Malaya, but now the rewards were stepped up and in 1949 $763,000 was quietly paid out for information – a fraction of the enormous sums that would be paid later when 'Dead or Alive' rewards of huge fixed sums were offered.

The police had also used the long-standing Banishment Act to deport more than ten thousand Chinese aliens during the year; these were first-generation Chinese, and so in effect were being sent back to China as undesirable aliens.

On the political side, Gurney had been trying hard to

encourage the Chinese to take a more active role and here too he met with some success when Tan Cheng-lok, a Chinese businessman and a staunch anti-Communist patriot, formed the Malayan Chinese Association (MCA) in an effort to convince the government and the Malays that all right-thinking Chinese were anti-Communist. This was important because thousands of Chinese (particularly the squatters) had failed to resist the CTs, making many people doubt their loyalty. Backed by vast funds, Tan Cheng-lok aimed to attract village Chinese away from Communism, and within a few months the MCA had 100,000 members and raised $2.5 million by lotteries to improve conditions in Chinese villages.

Yet despite these measures, none could disguise the fact that 1949 had been a bad year for the government; against 619 CTs killed, 337 captured and 251 surrendered, 344 civilians had been murdered, 160 were missing, and the security forces had lost 229 killed and 247 wounded. Even worse – to those in Malaya – was a feeling that no one outside Malaya (and many in the country for that matter) seemed to take the war seriously. Little news appeared in the British Press. It was almost as though its significance were being deliberately underplayed; not by newspaper reporters but by Whitehall for its own reasons. Even in Malaya itself, the Emergency only rated the status of an appendix in the 1949 Annual Report of the Federation, while in London any reference to the war was usually brushed off with the comfortable question, 'How many bandits have they shot today?' And this, of course, tended to hide the deeper, more serious issues involved.

Donald Wise, the ex-parachutist turned planter, felt 'there was something damned suspicious in the air. You couldn't say the Press were gagged, but time after time when big news broke reporters didn't seem able to get the details. Very convenient – for someone.'

Indeed it was. For as the end of a black 1949 turned

into the first week of January 1950, it became crushingly clear why the British government had hoped to relegate the war in Malaya to just another 'Empire skirmish'. For some months Attlee had been flirting with a new sweetheart in Asia – none other than Red China, and in the first week of January, he gave official recognition to the Mao Tse-tung regime.

Like millions of others, Peter and Tommy Lucy switched on the radio at Amherst on the fateful evening to listen to the six o'clock bulletin on Radio Malaya, and as an impersonal voice announced the news Tommy remembers the tears smarting behind her eyes as she cried to Peter, 'It's like being kicked in the teeth by your best friend.'

Of course there had been rumours – but everyone had hoped that they were just rumours. And though to those outside the country the feeling of black despair that swept Malaya may seem to have been exaggerated, Malaya was not fighting a war of bullets alone, but a war of politics, and with this one decision, Attlee hit Malaya a harder blow than any Chin Peng had ever dealt.

Gurney tried to make the best of it by promising on the radio that, 'Nothing that may happen in China will weaken the determination of the people of this country to eliminate militant Communism here; rather will their efforts be strengthened.' Gurney presumably had to say something; though his suggestion that the recognition of Communist China would *help* the fight in Malaya might have been better left unsaid. The reaction of the average Briton in Malaya was simple: they felt that once again they had been betrayed by Whitehall, as they had been betrayed before the fall of Singapore in 1942.

This was the situation in Malaya when Whitehall appointed the new Director of Operations. They named Lt-Gen. Sir Harold Briggs, who had retired to Cyprus in

1948 after a distinguished military career, including jungle warfare in Burma. Briggs was fifty-five and asked to be excused, but Field Marshall Sir William Slim, an old friend from Burma days, prevailed upon him to accept. Reluctantly Briggs did so – for a year.

It was a happy choice. As Director of Operations 'to plan, to co-ordinate, and direct the anti-bandit operations of the police and fighting forces', Briggs would work directly under Gurney – though as a civilian, and for an ironic reason. Though planters and miners had demanded a strong military leader (and now presumably would get one), General Briggs's civilian appointment was received with sighs of relief by the owners of the rubber and tin companies. Had Briggs appeared in uniform, the insurance rates would have been thrown into the melting-pot, for though civilians were being murdered daily, the government in Malaya had taken great pains to insist that this was an 'Emergency' and not a 'civil war', simply because the insurance rates on stocks and equipment covered losses due to riot and civil commotion, but not due to civil war. The government's consideration no doubt delighted the powerful rubber and tin lobbies, but it was a startling proof of the manner in which it underestimated the gravity of the war.

As soon as the news of the appointment reached Gurney, he sent for Bob Thompson and asked him to make the necessary arrangement for Briggs's arrival, and so Thompson, who was still at the Secretariat (and still playing tennis every Wednesday with Gurney), had to find a car for Briggs, a driver, a house ('All I could get was a Class Three house near the golf course'), servants, an ADC, even arrange how the new Director of Operations would be paid.

The choice of Bob Thompson to engage in these house-hold chores – which anyone in the Secretariat might have performed equally well – was to have fortunate repercussions, because from the moment that Briggs and Thompson met they took an instant liking to each other. Both had been in Burma, but it went deeper than that. The Malayan Civil Servant could see in this quiet general out of uniform a man who might understand his passionate beliefs that this was a war to win people more than a war to kill them, that it was a war of ideologies. And in his turn, Briggs could see in Thompson a man of far-reaching vision who was also a passionate lover of the country.

After Briggs had settled in, he asked Thompson to dine – the first of many working dinners. Briggs – a simple, quiet man – told Thompson over their first meal that he believed 'the whole key to the war lies in getting control of the squatter areas'. But people had to be protected, for, as Briggs added realistically, 'The people matter – they are vital – but you can't expect any support from people you can't protect.'

This philosophy exactly matched Thompson's and over the coffee Briggs expounded his general outline of what he hoped to do and achieve – how he wanted a small supervisory staff to co-ordinate work that the *others* would do. 'The ministries, police, the army have all got to do their own jobs,' said Briggs. 'We're not going to do it for them. We'll co-ordinate – we'll pick up things that go wrong and supervise.'

Thompson's instant feeling was, 'Briggs had got it absolutely right from the start.' But one word used by the General puzzled him.

'We?' he asked.

Briggs nodded. 'I'm going to tell the High Commissioner that I'd like you as my civil staff officer.'

Several dinners later – and after thousands of words of discussion – Briggs turned to Thompson and the army and RAF officers on his staff, and said, 'Well – now I think we all know what I have in mind and what I hope to do. Will you please draft out a directive.'

Thompson was delighted for he felt he knew exactly what Briggs had in mind. The matter, however, was urgent.

'How long have we got?' he asked the General.

'A few days – will that be enough?' asked Briggs.

It had to be. A few days and a few nights burning the midnight oil, for this would be perhaps the single most important policy document of the war. Happily Thompson was a past master at putting his thoughts on paper simply and coherently. He and his service colleagues virtually lived together for nearly a week before Thompson was able to go to Briggs and offer him the rough draft of a directive which Harry Miller felt 'will endure in the history of the Emergency as the "Briggs Plan".'

Briggs hardly altered a word, particularly in the statement of four vital suggestions for conducting the war:

(a) to dominate the populated areas and to build up a feeling of complete security therein which will in time result in a steady and increasing flow of information coming in from all sources.

(b) to break up the Communist organization within the populated areas.

(c) to isolate the bandits from their food and information supply organizations which are in the populated area.

(d) to destroy the bandits by forcing them to attack us on our own ground.

A master-stroke of power and simplicity, the Briggs Plan meant briefly that from now on security forces would protect the unpopulated areas, cut the enemy lines of communication between CTs and villagers, and force the CTs out to battle. Briggs planned to give the populated areas the confidence which only protection could bring, to implement Gurney's squatter plans, and by resettling half a million people, isolate the CTs from their food supplies, knowing that, in the words of Edgar O'Ballance,* 'without them the guerrilla fighter, like a fish out of water, gasps helplessly until he dies.'

It was a gigantic task, and it might well have failed had not Briggs and Thompson singled out the one factor which would prevent military escalation; the Briggs Plan confirmed that the authority for running the war must rest squarely on the shoulders of the civil government and the police. The troops were there to help. With one stroke Briggs allayed the fears of both the police and the civilian administrators that a new general might not realize that this was a war of intelligence, of CT defectors leading the police to others; a war demanding patience, in which a military patrol blundering into the jungle could in a day ruin months of painstaking work. But with the civil government in control, Special Branch could firmly restrain troops (who by the very nature of their calling wanted to produce results) from entering any areas they chose to freeze.

To thousands of Asians, a civil government in control was also a great morale factor, for to them the consequences of rule by military juntas in Asia were only too painfully visible. With the military in command, a country could be transformed into a wasteland of war in which civilians counted for nothing and were not even left with the one last human emotion of hope.

Briggs immediately formed a small War Council consisting of himself, the Administration heads, police, army and RAF. They would plan policy. Each state had a similar council, headed by the State Prime Minister, and each District also had War Executive Committees – always under the chairmanship of the local civilian British District Officer. Thus at these daily meetings – irreverently

* Author of *Malaya: The Communist Insurgent War.*

referred to as morning prayers – the civilians were in control.

More than any other decree, the Briggs Plan and 'morning prayers' awoke the people of Malaya to the fact that they were in effect helping to direct the war, that everyone had a part to play because they knew it was their war, a civilians' war; for, as Miller put it, 'Through these little war cabinets, Briggs took the strings that were tugging in all directions and wove them into a rope of co-ordination. He brought what might be described as 'joint thinking' into planning the end of the Emergency. Ideas were pooled. The good ones went all the way up to the Federal War Council to be examined, approved, and disseminated all over the country.'

8 THE SOCIAL REVOLUTION

Gurney and Briggs were now poised to implement at speed the largest social revolution ever known in Asia – the resettlement of 600,000 squatters into New Villages; a revolution which ironically might never have been initiated but for the threat of Communism, and one which was to prove a brilliant, unorthodox tactic in the war against guerrilla Communism – one which military leaders would study in every future Asian war.

After eighteen months of plodding work, Gurney had finally persuaded the Sultans to give the squatters titledeeds to agricultural land where they could be resettled and protected from intimidation.

In fact Gurney had met with little serious opposition, but it had needed a man of Gurney's stature (and time) to make the Sultans realize that this was not only a question of military survival, but a vital step in promoting racial harmony and equality, without which the date of independence might well be delayed. The main problem faced by Gurney was not opposition to giving the Chinese land-leases, but leases to the *kind* of land Gurney wanted. Obviously many Chinese in Malaya held land-leases (there was no freehold land). Rich Chinese owned cinemas, hotels, office blocks. In the countryside about fifty per cent of all the rubber grown in Malaya consisted of estates of less than a hundred acres, mostly Chinese owned. And there was still 'rubber land' to spare, but Gurney did not want this – he could hardly afford to resettle squatters on land which would not bear its first crop for five years. Gurney wanted agricultural land – and this was really the only land the Malays wanted.

However, Gurney had gained agreement from the Sultans to all he asked, and now that he had broken the barrier and now that Briggs had arrived – with powers over the army which Gurney did not have – the time had come to put Gurney's dream into effect. In essence, the problem that faced Briggs was simple: but to carry it through demanded the complex co-ordination of a military operation. After the site had been agreed, the plans of each new village were drawn up by surveyors. Each plan had provisions for a police post, school, a clinic, together with luxuries few squatters had ever dreamed of – electricity (needed for perimeter lighting), water stand pipes, space earmarked for roads and shops. The plans made, field teams pegged out village plots, allowing eight hundred square yards for each family, with two acres each outside the perimeter for cultivation. This done, the army was called in to haul vast quantities of building materials to the site – everything from barbed wire, roofing, timber, to hammers, saws and nails.

Planters had to be included in the planning, for some squatters were primarily tappers who employed their spare time (or family) in growing vegetables or raising pigs. They had to be regrouped into 'dormitory' New Villages – and this was not always popular with the rubber companies, for if the New Village were five miles from the plantation, production might suffer. Briggs and Gurney were soon receiving protests from the London offices of some major companies – and ignoring them.

No one could disguise the massive preliminary work that was being carried out all over the country – but the strictest secrecy was essential when it came to the squatters involved. None of those about to be moved could be told where or when they were going until the actual moment of departure, for Chin Peng was trying to form Communist cells among squatters *before* they were resettled so that they could continue to work from behind the security of wired-in settlements.

Meanwhile European 'camp officers' were being appointed, together with schoolmasters and nurses (if available) to run the village clinics. Fortunately there was no real shortage of welfare officers, for Gurney's plans for dealing with the squatter problem had received wide publicity in Australia and New Zealand – both intimately concerned with the dangers of encroaching Communism; and from those two countries a steady stream of young men and women volunteered for service. In their twenties, brought up with a sense of adventure and a love of the open air, they came as a sort of 'Peace Corps', willing to do anything any official asked of them. Soon the broad Australian twang and the more 'English' New Zealand accent could be heard in every state of Malaya; all the volunteers were ready and waiting – very touchingly – to offer a genuine and practical welcome to men, women and children uprooted by war from their homes.

All this was happening in many parts of the country, often against a background of dangerous escalation in CT violence as Chin Peng instructed his platoons to fight resettlement plans in every possible way. Squatters were told they were going to be sent to concentration camps, that they must refuse to budge from plots of land on which they had lived for years. Despite this, thousands of unnamed British conscript soldiers cheerfully became members of the world's largest furniture-removing organization, as Peter Lucy discovered when tappers near his estate at Amherst were resettled in a New Village called Padang Gedok, six miles away; he remembers that 'the Briggs Plan could not have succeeded without the good humour of the British troops.'

On the actual day of removal Lucy rose at 4.00 a.m. to join troops and police who threw a cordon round the entire area on the edge of his estate from which squatters – including some of Lucy's tappers – were to be taken to the New Village. He had to be on hand to calm any of the more bewildered men and women when the troops moved in.

In the eerie half-light, with the first blue wisps of smoke from kampong fires trailing upwards, the troops quietly moved into position and watched as four hundred people – ranging from parchment-faced old women to babies still at the breast – woke up to what they blithely supposed would be just another normal day. The women blew at small fires on which to heat the morning rice. The men, mostly in shorts, made for the river to wash. Sleepy-eyed boys and girls emerged from the hovels they called homes and piddled where the fancy took them; and then, like kids the world over, started throwing stones at the fluttering chickens, scampering, squealing pigs, slinking camp dogs.

The squatters were scattered over a fairly wide area, but they tended to group their houses together, and at five o'clock Peter Lucy – known to all of them as the Tuan of Amherst – walked into the largest 'village' with a Chinese affairs officer. Briefly he told them what was going to happen. And that it was going to happen *now*. His breakfast audience, grouped round pots and pans over crackling twigs, knew of course that the squatters were being resettled in various parts of the country, but it seemed to

Peter that – as with so many events in life – they had never thought it could happen to them.

Blank dismay filled their faces. An old woman started to rock and wail – and immediately started dozens of children crying. Dogs barked. Men started talking at the tops of their voices. They did not seem angry, only stupefied by shock. And as each one insisted over and over again, none of them had *ever* helped the Communists, so why should *they* be removed.

Patiently the Chinese affairs officer extolled the virtues of their New Village – water, electricity, medical facilities, education for children who did not even know what a school looked like. It made no difference. Like people the world over, they preferred the humble home they knew to any promised but unseen palace.

Lucy felt, 'We'd never sort the mess out,' but slowly some sort of order prevailed and the families were grouped together, helped by Malay policemen and British troops. One or two tried to run for it but were caught. Others defiantly announced that they would *never* go. But when the Chinese affairs officer announced that plots in the New Village would be allotted on a 'first come first served' basis, a surprising number of Chinese fathers held up their hands. There was some alarm, even among those who willingly agreed to go, when army photographers moved in, for as part of the protection plans, it was essential for every member of the New Village to carry a special identity card to stop CTs slipping past the guards at the village gates.

Suddenly Lucy heard a low rumble. The leading lorries in a convoy of 150 army trucks were grinding their way from the main road along the rough path to the settlement. There would be one lorry for each family and everything it possessed.

The willing squatters – including those who realized the value of having first choice from a variety of plots –

posed no problem. Nor were there any really defiant families. The difficulties came with those who were just terrified; and it was here that the British troops behaved so magnificently. It would have been easy for them to regard all squatters as possible CTs and bundle them by force into the waiting lorries, but they never did. Patiently, and with an abundance of good humour, they sweltered in the tropical heat, helping the people to sort out their problems and their belongings.

Lucy watched them deal with one family. The Chinese father seemed to understand, but he was burdened with an ancient mother, a wife who seemed stupid, and four children including a baby in arms. Father and troops loaded the lorry with his pitiful furniture – a table, two rickety chairs, sleeping mats, pots and pans, water buckets, and – of all things – an ornate mahogany wall clock hanging on the flimsy side of his homemade hut. Then came a chase – which the children at least seemed to enjoy – after four squealing pigs, an assortment of chickens, a recalcitrant cockerel who tried to peck at everyone who approached it. All this time the two women of the family sat by the embers of their breakfast fire, moaning and wailing. The animals were finally put on the truck. The older children scrambled inside. Then Lucy watched one young, fresh-faced soldier gently take the baby from the crying mother, crook it in his arms, and hand it up to the father before returning to the mother and politely giving her his arm to lean upon. The mother went – but the toothless grandmother refused point-blank to budge, even after an irate sergeant yelled, 'For God's sake get her in – we'll be here all day.'

The cockney soldier flashed back, 'Blimey, Sarge! Have you ever tried to tackle *your* mother-in-law?'

Finally two soldiers approached the woman from behind and grabbed her, protesting, and carried her into the truck, already alive with the noise of squealing animals.

'Okay – let's go,' cried the sergeant – at which moment the eldest son, who might have been twelve and who had behaved perfectly, suddenly let out a yell that drowned even the noise of the pigs. Almost immediately he started sobbing bitterly. And none of the soldiers knew what the trouble was until Lucy, standing nearby, was able to translate that the boy's dog had been left behind.

A soldier jumped down, held his arms up to lift the boy out of the truck as the sergeant yelled, 'To hell with the dog, we'll buy him a new one!'

'Come on, Sarge,' said the conscript. 'Didn't you ever have a dog when you were young?' Adding to Lucy in an aside, 'If the son-of-a-bitch ever *was* young.'

Not until they had found the puppy did the lorry join the convoy.

(As Harry Miller, who saw much of the resettlement programme, wrote: 'All through the country the friendly attitude of the British troops was praised. In Perak a group of resettled people were so grateful for the way they had been treated by the husky Coldstream Guards that they asked for and received permission to name their village Kampong Coldstream.')

Peter Lucy got into his car and drove ahead, passing the convoy once he reached the main road – a seemingly endless line of assorted military trucks, all overloaded, with furniture that towered above the sides as though it would fall off at any moment – and every truck alive with animal noises. Hemmed in by the jungle that swept down to the roadside, it reminded Lucy of an ancient Biblical caravan winding its way to some promised land.

Once in Padang Gedok, Peter Lucy watched the first lorries arrive at their new home, a fenced-in blank space on the map with each plot – roughly the size of two tennis courts – pegged out waiting to be claimed. Each family was given free material and help to build a new house, generally much better than the one they had left, but even this material advantage could not console families torn from homes in which they had lived for so long, and as the troops lifted off the old women or the wide-eyed children clutching pathetic bundles, they behaved with great compassion.

Lucy knew that, quite apart from the fact that he was witnessing a remarkable new method of beating Communism, this would be the start of a new life for hundreds of thousands of illiterate children. As the families settled in and the ring of hammers and grinding of saws showed that the first houses were being knocked together, troops were building the school and doctors were giving every villager a medical examination, treating – for the first time in their lives – any who were ill. In another hut a clerk was handing out money, for each family received a government subsidy for up to six months until it could reap the first harvest of its short-term crops.

Of course the CTs made great play with the fact that the lives of the New Villagers were totally controlled. So they were. Padang Gedok was hemmed in by a double barbed wire fence seven feet high,* lit by perimeter lights. The gates were manned day and night. Every man, woman and child in the village was registered with the resettlement officer, but there was one factor to which Chin Peng would never be able to find an answer: the people in Padang Gedok might be homesick for a few days, but the land on which they were knocking up their houses was *theirs*, on long leases for peppercorn rents. For hundreds of thousands of peasants all over the country who believed in the old Chinese proverb, 'A land title is the hoop that holds the barrel together,' this was the fulfilment of a dream: to own a plot of land which a man could pass on to his sons when he died.

* Later the barbed wire was replaced by a chain link fence as an answer to CT propaganda that New Villages were 'concentration camps'.

Among early visitors to the New Villages was James Griffiths, Colonial Secretary in the Labour government, who had so far been unable to visit any of the fifty-three colonies for which Britain was still responsible because of (in his words), 'the tiny majority of the government', whose survival was threatened with every division bell. Finally, Griffiths managed to visit Malaya, though only after receiving an extraordinary warning: 'Before I left for Malaya,' he remembers, 'I had been advised not to refer to the operations as a "war" but as an "emergency".'

Griffiths made an extensive tour of Malaya, and saw many of the New Villages, as well as meeting the planters, some of whom gave him a fairly rough time, particularly at the Semantan estate near Mentakab, where a tall, weary planter looked the Colonial Secretary in the eyes and said, 'There must be something wrong with a campaign that's costing a million dollars for every bandit killed.' As the Colonial Secretary looked up, startled, the planter added, 'Give *me* a million dollars and I'll get Stalin for you.' Without another word the planter picked up his Sten and headed homewards.

The New Villages were springing up so quickly that Gurney sent an SOS to the Red Cross for help and by 1951 two young pretty faces appeared unarmed and unescorted on the lonely jungle roads of Malaya. Two English Red Cross girls, Teresa Spens and Janet Grant, both in their twenties, started the first jungle service in the New Villages. They were based on the Nurses' Home at Batu Gajah, a township in the tin-mining country fourteen miles from Ipoh, an area of bluish mountains, a scattering of sandstone hills with steep cliffs, and worked-out mines.

Every morning the girls set off in their van, easily recognizable with its scarlet wheels, a silver roof and several Red Crosses. 'The inside,' according to Teresa's diary, 'is a delicate shade of pale green with spaces for bottles and jars plus all the paraphernalia.' The girls never took drugs in bulk in case CTs should be encouraged to ambush them, and they had two rules: they never employed a driver, but travelled alone; and whenever they were approached by police officers and asked to report the presence of any wounded CT, they replied firmly, 'Certainly not.'

Travelling from village to village, they no doubt treated CTs one moment, loyal citizens the next. They visited at least three villages a day, sometimes setting up their clinic under a tree, at other times in the headman's house, and at one New Village in a stable next to a large buffalo. They had to fight ignorance and superstition. (Their first woman patient insisted that her headache had been caused by a slap in the face by evil spirits.) Yet they slowly won the confidence of villages often afraid of any contact with 'officials' because they had relations in the jungle.

They also had to fight competition from rapacious Chinese doctors skilled in hocus-pocus. One wounded CT refused to have his broken leg set because a Chinese had covered it with a plaster of mud and leaves – and charged him $150. Another time the girls had to treat a baby with severe burns caused after a so-called doctor had applied a ginger dressing on an infection.

Teresa and Janet were the forerunners of hundreds of Red Cross and St John Ambulance girls who volunteered for service in Malaya and worked in areas of considerable danger, sometimes alone, sometimes with the doctors on their rounds of lonely planters' bungalows.

The doctors faced an even more nerve-racking life, for whereas the girls could plan their journeys ahead, a doctor had to dash out into the night the moment the police reported an ambush. It would have been easy for the CTs to kill them; on the other hand, the CTs doubtless knew

that most doctors treated thousands of poor Malays, Indians and Chinese and never charged a fee.

One such doctor who never refused a midnight call was
Dr Reid Tweedie, who had lived for twenty years outside
Sungei Siput and had in fact been the first doctor to reach
the scene after the first murders in 1948. Tweedie was
company doctor to several estates and was a 'character',
one of those eccentrics who always seem to be thrown up
among Britons in the tropics. Short, with an alert face, he
dressed in a shirt of towelling, 'Oxford bags' held up with
a piece of string, and a topee worn back to front (surely
the last European to wear one). Planters arriving for a jab
at 'Harley Street', as he called his ramshackle clinic in the
main street, would see Tweedie's spare shirt drying on
the bonnet of his Buick, and around lunch-time the doctor
would be removing his sandwiches from the depths of his
medical refrigerator. He had one phobia, strange for a
doctor: he was terrified of catching colds, and hated air
conditioning, so that on his weekly visit to the cinema in
Ipoh he dressed in an overcoat, carried a rug and hot-
water bottle, and wore a skull cap or beret. As an added
medicinal precaution, whisky stengahs arrived in the front
row of the circle every fifteen minutes.

By the middle of 1951, with 400,000 squatters already
resettled, Briggs decided that in order to make them better
citizens they should be given more responsibility, and he
sent for Bob Thompson, who during this period had married a dark-haired Malayan-born English girl. Thompson
had also asked Briggs to be transferred for a time to more
active work; he found too much office work irksome. He
liked to move around, to grasp a situation on his own, to
solve it on his own. So after a brief honeymoon in England,
he was posted as Chinese affairs officer in Johore Bahru,
the capital of the State, where he lived next door to Malcolm MacDonald. He had often discussed the possibility

of creating New Village Councils with MacDonald, who had mentioned the idea to Briggs. Now Briggs told Thompson to go ahead and see how this lesson in 'instant democracy' worked out.

It worked magnificently, but only because Thompson realized one fundamental truth: 'It was no good electing village councillors without some sort of real power. Otherwise, the whole experiment would sooner or later slide into oblivion.'

Thompson started by sending for government information teams to prepare the way with lectures and film shows. In order to encourage big audiences, some bait had to be offered – and there was one sure-fire winner: the film *Tarzan*. Bob drove across the causeway to Singapore, where he persuaded the leading distributors to let him borrow without payment sixty copies of *Tarzan* to go the rounds of New Villages.

After the movie and a documentary had been shown, Bob or the Resettlement Officer would explain what they planned to do – that after everyone had voted democratically for their councillors, those elected would run the village affairs on their own, raise local small taxes – the equivalent of rates – look after clinics, health, cleanliness.

There was only one snag at first – getting enough people to stand for election. Most villagers were terrified that CTs would see their election as an anti-Communist stand and would kill them the moment they left the village. Slowly Thompson won them over, and finally, after months of preparation, the tin voting boxes were brought into the village school and each villager slid his secret ballot through the slot. Even then there was trouble. After one election, all the men who were voted on to the council were so frightened that they bolted for Singapore and safety.

The CT reaction to village councils was violent, particularly in Johore, which was one of the black spots of Malaya.

Outside Yong Peng – a particularly notorious Communist-infested town – CTs lay in wait for two councillors from a nearby village. They were ordinary Chinese ex-squatters – as terrified as the next man of CTs – who, like so many others, had stood for election, realizing that at last they had a literal stake in the country. As they reached their allotments outside the perimeter, four CTs appeared out of the jungle and abducted the councillors. Three days later their wives each received a grisly parcel containing one of their husband's arms, with a note demanding food; and with a warning that if it did not arrive within the week the other arm would be amputated. Thompson never found out what happened to the men for they were never seen again; but after many similar attacks, the government realized that a great deal of food was being smuggled out of the New Villages, either because of coercion or sympathy, for not all New Villagers were paragons of virtue. So Briggs introduced all-embracing regulations to prevent food, medicines, and fighting materials reaching the jungle CTs. It was the most sweeping measure of its kind since 1948. A list of restricted goods, ranging from rice and dried fish to paper and printing materials, was drawn up. None could be sold without a written record of the sale, including the name and address of the purchaser. In restricted areas no food could be taken out of the home. Tappers could not take a midday meal with them when they set off before dawn for the rubber estate. They had to wait until they returned home. In towns like Yong Peng, Briggs also restricted the number of shops in a given area; he closed countless restaurants and cafés; he prohibited the movement at night of all foods except perishable articles and these consignments had to be covered with roped-down tarpaulins, and could only move on main roads.

Many Chinese squatters themselves had demanded these stringent regulations, telling Briggs in effect, 'If the Communists come with a gun and demand food, we are killed if we refuse to help. Do something by law which the Communists will know makes it impossible for us to help them.'

So 'Operation Starvation' came into being – and provided yet another new task for British troops. Each soldier memorized the long list of restricted articles before becoming an amateur customs officer. They coped cheerfully. Boards at check gates apologized to the long, impatient queues, many of them girls carrying babies almost as big as themselves, riding on their elder sister's left hip. All were searched. Those in cars also proceeded to searching sheds – 'Women to the left, men to the right'. There belts were undone, ballpoint pens scrutinized, shoes checked (were they new?) and fingers dipped into water bottles to see if the liquid tasted of sugar. Other teams were examining the cars – everything from the engine compartments to the upholstery, the boot, the underneath, even the inside of a hub cap. Before long troops could examine a car in three minutes.

Rice was the main objective of every search, for rice was both the strength and the weakness of the CTs – a strength because it was abundant, easy to smuggle and, being virtually tasteless, could be eaten for years without any revulsion; a weakness because CTs who were denied rice for a long period suffered physically and morally.

Every CT sympathizer who lived through those days invented extraordinary tricks to smuggle rice, often to relations in the jungle. Peter Lucy saw one worker limping, yet remembered that he had seen the man half an hour previously walking normally. Suspicious, he had him stripped. Strapped by sticking plaster to the inside of the man's thigh was a bulky packet of rice. One searcher found rice in a girl's brassière, another a few grains in a bicycle pump.

Bicycles, indeed, were often used for smuggling. Colonel Richard Miers of the South Wales Borderers arrived at a village near Kluang one day just as two soldiers were completely dismantling a bicycle in front of a tearful, protesting Chinese boy of nine. An officer told him, 'This kid's been learning to ride his bicycle, or pretending to, for the past week. He's always in and out of the gate but today I thought we'd go over him properly, and here's the result.' The officer led Miers to a mound of rice and several dozen large antibiotic pills – the main CT jungle medicine. All had been poured out of the frame of the bicycle.

At another camp one old woman passed the control point daily carrying two heavy tubs of pig swill dangling from a bamboo bent across her frail shoulders. Suspicious police put their hands daily into the filthy mess – with no result. Not until a month later did one realize that she was not hiding tins of rice in the swill, but grains in the hollow bamboo.

Rice became such a vital product that in some areas the uncooked rice station was abolished and all the rice had to be communally cooked before the rations were distributed – because cooked rice is perishable and bulky.

As food from the squatters dried up, CTs started growing vegetables in deep jungle clearings, some on an enormous scale. Security forces found one garden of several acres, planted with rice, maize, tapioca, sugar, tomatoes, cucumbers, tobacco. The nearby camp even had its own rice mill. The moist climate, the rich soil, offered quick results, though at first CTs, with typical Chinese neatness, planted vegetables in straight rows, making it easy for the RAF to spot them and spray the gardens with hormone plant killers. After that CTs, copying the Aborigines, planted their gardens haphazardly, making them more difficult to detect from the air.

To follow up the CTs in the deep jungle, Briggs brought in Major 'Mike' Calvert, who, like Bob Thompson, had fought in Burma with the Chindits, and asked him to form a Special Service Regiment – known as the SAS – to penetrate and live off the deep jungle as Spencer Chapman had done.*

Inevitably, the CTs stepped up terror-tactics, and if they could not penetrate all New Villages, then they launched ferocious attacks on lonely police posts, plantations and mines – not only for food, but to increase their image of terror. Chin Peng knew that the New Villages and the election of councillors were giving thousands of simple people a genuine voice in democracy at work – and this was something he could not allow to happen. At the same time his jungle squads were being robbed of food supplies by Operation Starvation. This was the basic reason behind the fact that in 1951 there were 6,100 CT incidents.

Naturally, to most people the increasing tempo of CT attacks appeared to be a sign of defiance, but as Harry Miller wrote: 'Looking back, it seems to me that their vicious attacks and their atrocities [in 1951] were also born of desperation.'

9 THE DEFECTOR

As Briggs was squeezing the CTs, the first deep rifts in the higher echelons of the Malayan Communist Party occurred in Johore, the most southerly state in the Federation. Johore was the vegetable garden of Singapore, supplying the city with most of its pigs, ducks and vegetables; yet the state had a record for violence among the worst in Malaya, with townships like Yong Peng and Kluang completely dominated by CTs. Now the CTs started quarrelling among themselves on a scale so serious that it

---

* The highly unorthodox Calvert trained his force by sending two men into the jungle armed with miniature airguns. Though their faces were shielded, their bodies were not – and the first one to be seen by the other was peppered with stinging pellets.

caused the defection of a political commissar to the security forces, and the formal execution of a high-ranking officer. Referred to by Communists bitterly as 'The South Johore Incident', it revolved round a meek, short, unsmiling but intelligent man called Lam Swee, who had been an active Communist since 1940, finally rising to the post of acting-Secretary General of the Pan-Malayan Federation of Trades Unions, and then its Vice-President. With the Emergency he had gone into the jungle to become political commissar of the 4th Johore Regiment. Lam Swee had refused to meet Chin Peng at the first jungle conference in 1948 because he suspected trade union funds were being illicitly used; but this had not prevented him from making bitter attacks on the British in leaflets produced in the jungle.

He was a thoughtful man, one of many idealistic Chinese who had seen in Communism an attempt to produce a better life for the working classes of which he was a member. 'I was influenced by the surging waves of young men all over Malaya,' he remembers. 'I longed for the realization of a new, free and equitable order, in which each would be given full opportunity.'

Once in the jungle, Lam Swee quickly became disillusioned, and 'though I had no confidence in the success of the revolution, I did not have the slightest idea of surrendering.' But as time passed, he found it more and more difficult to refrain from criticizing the inefficiency of CT platoon leaders, or, worse still, to stifle his nagging doubts that the rank and file were being duped – and killed in the process – by Politburo members living in comparative comfort. As a member of the South Johore Regional Committee (as well as being a political commissar) he saw men wantonly sacrificed, starving, some of them 'really heroic, indomitable figures in the Communist Party'. He also had to meet members of the Politburo (if only to receive orders and directives), and found that, 'while our troops were struggling, members of the Central, including Chin Peng, were living near Mentakab, eating three meals a day. Such was the manifestation of the Central's "Equality in Livelihood".'

Lam Swee was not the only disgruntled Communist in the South Johore regiment, but fear of spies prevented matters from coming to a head until he received proof that his troops had been duped. Lam Swee's men had been ordered to undertake a particularly gruelling forced march to help set up a new jungle camp a hundred miles north of their base. It had taken them six nightmare weeks in the jungle, fighting sickness, insects, rain, the damp heat that could never evaporate in the soaking air; for days at a time they had been holed up, hiding from British jungle patrols, and when they reached their destination the little band of forty men was in rags and tatters. Fortunately Lam Swee had an official note from the Central Committee ordering the local political commissar to provide food and money. To Lam Swee's astonishment the man insisted that he had neither. Quite by chance one of Lam Swee's platoon commanders discovered that the political commissar had in fact more than enough food to spare and $2,000 in notes.

'That night,' Lam Swee recorded, 'a full meeting of all platoon commanders was called as the direct result of their demands.' Lam Swee presided, and a certain Beng Kwang, 'who had once said he felt good only when members of the Central Committee were shot', took down the minutes.

Inevitably, the Politburo heard of this meeting, and Chin Peng acted swiftly. One platoon commander was shot, and Lam Swee was relieved of his pistol and grenades – a move which made it patently obvious that 'they were getting ready to murder me secretly.' On June 27, 1950, Lam Swee gave his guards the slip and walked into the police station at Bentong in Pahang. He had $1.75 in his pocket.

This was by far the most significant surrender of the war, and the news was kept secret for nearly four months, as Lam Swee started writing 'My Accusation', a powerful tract of which tens of thousands of copies were dropped in the jungle. He was then presented to the Press on November 8, and had lost none of his quiet, unassuming diffidence. Leslie Hoffman of the *Straits Times* described him as 'inconspicuous. He wore a white shirt, white trousers, brown leather shoes and a poker face.' Hoffman asked him bluntly if he were still a Communist, to which Lam Swee replied, 'I believe there should be equality for every man and he should have food and a job to do.'

Other CTs were also beginning to criticize the Communist leaders openly. In nearby Malacca, the political commissar, Shao Liu, questioned the 'correctness' of Chin Peng in starting an armed struggle at a time when most people had barely recovered from the Japanese Occupation. He attacked the Central Committee for its policy of wanton terrorism, which he said, was losing the support of the masses – a valid criticism which Chin Peng did not realize was true until a year later. Shao Liu was no mere verbal critic. A former schoolmaster, a theoretician to his fingertips, he wrote several theses analysing what he considered to be the errors made by Chin Peng – an open case of that particularly Communist disease known as 'deviationism'.

Chin Peng was particularly incensed by one called 'Keynote of the Malayan Revolution' in which Shao Liu drew several highly critical conclusions: the weight of British armour had, he said, forced the Communist Party to adopt a 'passive' policy, and resulted in 'an inability to establish a firm supply base'. He also criticized the 'inadequate arms and the loss of operational grounds' – a reference to the very real truth that Communists had, since the start of the armed struggle, been unable to use their trade unions to foment unrest. Under these conditions, wrote Shao Liu, any prolongation of the armed struggle was suicidal, and he could see no hope of success until the Party created 'a strong racial front and a large army founded on the mutual economic interests of the three main races, the Chinese, Malays and Indians.'

Shao Liu was by no means *against* an armed rebellion; indeed he believed that 'armed revolution is indispensable in dislodging British Imperialists.' But equally he was convinced that the Malayan Communist Party was going about things the wrong way.

Chin Peng lost no time in counter-attacking. In a long directive, sent by jungle couriers to all regional headquarters, Chin Peng announced, 'Shao Liu and his supporters are unwilling to accept the basic principles of democratic centralized policy of the Party – the minority should submit itself to the majority – the whole party should submit itself to the Central Executive. His booklets are a tissue of lies.'

In true Communist fashion, Shao Liu was now given a chance to recant. He refused and, as Professor Anthony Short comments: 'There was something unmistakably mediaeval and theological in the way in which he was called upon to recant, refused to do so, and continued to publish his views.'

This Chin Peng could not allow. He issued fresh instructions for dealing with the deviationist* making it clear that he was to be demoted, and 'at the slightest suspicion of defection he is to be destroyed without hesitation. It is essential to isolate and destroy his influence.' With the cold impassivity of an executioner, Chin Peng added: 'If watching his movements and actions becomes tedious, then it will be better to destroy him without further waiting.'

Still Shao Liu continued to write, including letters to

* Later recovered by security forces from the body of a shot CT.

friends urging them to side with him against what
he contemptuously called 'Ngau Kung' – 'Buffalo
Communists'.

In the spring of 1950 Chin Peng ordered his execution.
In early summer Shao Liu, his wife and three of his closest
supporters were arrested by CTs near Kluang. There were
no beatings, no tortures, no bitter recriminations by one-
time Party comrades. The captives were taken through the
jungle to a major CT camp where they were kept for three
days in captivity, during which time they were subjected
to no indignities.

On the fourth day, they were led to the parade ground.
Each man and woman was tied to a stake near the camp
flagpole from which the Red Flag was fluttering. Every
man in the camp was called to parade. With their fists
clenched they sang the 'International'. Only then did the
firing party carry out the execution.

The deviation of Shao Liu was a bitter shock to Chin
Peng, perhaps because in his heart the Communist leader
realized that there was a great deal of truth in what the
'traitor' had preached. Possibly Chin Peng felt that now
there was no turning back; the struggle had been launched,
and though it had failed in its objective to create Liberated
Areas, it could hardly be said to have failed in creating
disorder; for five thousand men were keeping a nation of
five million in terror. The one thing, however, that Chin
Peng could not allow was criticism.

Shao Liu's deviation was bad enough, but the defection
of Lam Swee caused a major upset in the Politburo. It
was one thing for a comrade to question authority and be
shot for his temerity; it was very different for a highly
placed man like Lam Swee to go over to the enemy – for
that was in effect what he had done; and Lam Swee's
defection was an even more serious setback to the Communists than they realized, because by chance the British
acquired, almost at that very moment, a brilliant Chinese

psychological warfare expert who was able to make the fullest use of Lam Swee.

10 THE WAR OF WORDS

C.C. Too was a short, balding bespectacled Malayan Chinese of thirty, with quick, decisive gestures, a perfect command of English (including its spicier words) and a round face perpetually creased in smiles or chuckles. He had first joined the government's Psychological Warfare Department in Kuala Lumpur as an assistant with little authority, but his knowledge of the Communist mind – and how to deal with it – was so remarkable that before long he was in virtual control of all propaganda aimed at CTs. His flair for understanding Communist words and activities was no mere chance. Before the Emergency he had for months attended Communist meetings in Kuala Lumpur, for the Party had been looking for intellectuals and was so impressed by Too's string of degrees that it tried to enrol him. Too's answer was, 'I'm not one of you but I'm open to conviction,' and indeed he admired many aspects of their beliefs, particularly their resolution and sincerity. But even when the Party offered him a tempting six-months' scholarship in the US as an inducement to join, he preferred to remain on the outside, looking in.

Bob Thompson was still responsible for channelling intelligence through to Gurney, and he soon came to admire the beaming cheerful Chinese. They thought alike, they met regularly, and soon Thompson had arranged for Too to be given a free hand within the general guide lines laid down by policy. The psychological warfare philosophy that resulted was such a remarkable factor in helping to erode Communism that it would become a standard pattern in many parts of South-East Asia.

'It's no good hating the CTs in your propaganda,' said Too. 'You may hate some of the things they do, but you have to remember that when you are sending leaflets or messages to CTs in the jungle, you can never be sure what kind of a Communist you're going to address. He might be genuinely sincere – he might be a waverer who realizes he's made a mistake and wants to escape but daren't – or he could be a criminal who doesn't really know what Communism is about. You've got to find a formula that fits every kind of CT.'

Too's major rules were: Don't preach. Don't theorize. Never say 'I told you so'. No propaganda based on hatred. One of Too's favourite lines was, 'You are a human being and we all make mistakes.'

He believed that every item of propaganda must be factual and true and he scored a big success among CTs by admitting in a leaflet that a CT whose death he had previously announced was alive due to an error in identification.

Too knew that many CTs who had spent months in the jungle were so starved of news that they would be unable to resist picking up a leaflet which dealt only with hard facts, so he produced a monthly news sheet with photos of CT casualties, names of surrendered CTs, and particularly pictures of the mistresses of high-ranking officers, for the rank-and-file greatly resented this privilege. To this he added the ever-recurring message: 'We know that what you have done was in the name of the Revolution. But you are still human. Surrender and all will be forgiven.'

Too was after the CT so dispirited that he was on the verge of giving in, the man who realized he had made a terrible error, but needed one extra push of persuasion. But that act of persuasion needed the greatest tact for Too knew that the more abject a man, the more he hangs on to the last shreds of his self-respect.

Very soon Too became something of a legend in Malaya.

Richard Clutterbuck,* who served on the Director of
Operations' staff in Kuala Lumpur, felt that 'the forceful
and imaginative Too . . . was adept at forecasting CT
policies and his psychological warfare approach was based
on the understanding gained from constant contact with
current Communist thinking. It took us some time to
learn the obvious lesson that psychological warfare *must* be
directed by a local man. It is amazing how many Europeans
think they understand the Asian mind.'

This belief, widely-held by many Europeans, might have
retarded Too's progress, despite his brilliance, had he not
found such a powerful ally in Thompson, who had already
made his views on the importance of psychological warfare
known to Gurney. They were: 'The main basis of a successful psychological warfare campaign will depend on a
clear and precise government surrender policy towards the
insurgents. Such a policy has three main aims: (1) to
encourage insurgent surrender; (2) to sow dissension
between insurgent rank-and-file and their leaders; and (3)
to create an image of government both to the insurgent
and to the population which is both firm and efficient but
at the same time just and generous.'

Thompson was one hundred per cent behind Too's 'no
hate' policy. Indeed, he would never have given Too moral
help and government backing had not Too's beliefs
coincided with his own.

Too had many ways of reaching CTs – Malaya Radio
which broadcast daily in twelve languages or dialects,
jungle leaflets, 'voice aircraft' in which planes with recorded messages flew low over the jungle; whatever the
method employed, the preliminary work had to be of a
calibre high enough to tempt CTs to read or listen, and

* Author of *The Long, Long War.*

it was now that Too's staff of two writers was augmented by Lam Swee, the defector.

Between them, Too and Lam Swee could 'place' any surrendering CT exactly. They could tell his rank or status merely from the way he talked or behaved – because they knew that Party indoctrination varied on different levels. Often Too could tell from a captured letter something of its author's status.

When it came to writing pamphlets, he and Lam Swee had an enormous advantage. They both knew 'CT shorthand' – for due to lack of paper in the jungle, CTs had started abbreviating some of the cumbersome Chinese word pictures. Too had made a study of it, wrote it automatically. (The Chinese word for Imperialism is such a complicated picture that CTs abbreviated it to a square with the letter 'T' inside – 'T' being the pronunciation of the Chinese word for Emperor, and a square being part of a picture word for nation or boundary.)

Their specialized knowledge enabled Too and Lam Swee to make far better use of captured material than the British had done. Every time the British had captured what appeared to be wordy routine duplicated CT pamphlets they had given them to students to translate 'on the assumption that if they were cyclostyled they were so much bumf'. Too went through every captured document, letter or booklet – a wearisome task for, in Too's words: 'When two CTs met it became a meeting. They never trusted each other, so both wrote their accounts of what transpired.' Time after time student translators had missed significant points which Too was now able to pick out.

Too's 'no hate' campaign did not prevent him from attacking weak elements in the CT organization. He would shower leaflets over the jungle showing a photograph of a CT, starved and emaciated at the moment of surrender, together with a later picture of the same man, plump, smiling, perhaps with his wife or girl-friend. Any propaganda that made use of women always struck home, and Too never lost an opportunity of telling the truth about women in the jungle, who inevitably became mistresses of the higher ranking officers – an aspect of jungle life that infuriated thousands of CTs, who had to watch their officers taking mistresses while the rank and file could not. It was not long before Too scored a major success when a platoon commander surrendered following a quarrel over a woman in his CT camp.

Too told Lam Swee, with his knowledge of the vernacular, to 'ghost' a letter under the name of the surrendered CT, who was called Chin Kuen and fought with the 5th Regiment in Perak. Lam Swee had spent years in the jungle, he *knew* what CTs wanted to read, and the letter, signed of course by Chin Kuen, had a message hard for a lonely jungle fighter to ignore. 'Comrades,' it ran, 'I surrendered after my commanding officer had stolen my girl-friend. The officer was not only well fed but he had girl-friends whenever he wanted. Have you a girl-friend? The upper ranks can make love in their huts, but if you want to find a lady friend then you will have to wait until there is one left over from the upper ranks.'

Half a million copies of this letter were dropped. Its strength lay in its truth, and soon several CTs were defecting because of women. In Kedah, a CT and his wife shot their guard and surrendered because one of them was about to be transferred to another theatre. In the rubber-growing area of Layang Layang in Johore, the branch secretary, Ho Cheong, an ex school-teacher, surrendered to Gurkha troops because he pined to see his wife. Two of his colleagues surrendered with him because they wanted to get married.

Captured documents showed an increasing bitterness among CTs in the deep jungle, as when one highly-placed CT 'deliberately set out to buy the affection of a girl belonging to an inferior'. This captured document noted that among other favours bestowed by the CT officer, 'he even awakened her from her sleep and offered her Ovaltine.'

Soon the Politburo was forced to issue stern warnings, and a captured document, issued by the Central Executive, told CTs: 'The frequency of our comrades' misdemeanours in sexual and love-affairs is great. Many of our comrades, not abiding by our organization discipline about love-making, are doing it without the knowledge of the Party. Such improper occurrences are frequent and must be corrected.'*

Not all attempts to capitalize on the human errors of CTs were so successful, for as Bob Thompson remembers: 'The predilection of some insurgent leaders for either brandy or girls can provide plenty of scope for psychological warfare experts and artists. One political commissar in Malaya made, and meant, the unfortunate remark: "The only way to liberate women is to loosen their trouser belts!" Subsequent attempts to exploit and illustrate this in leaflet form were considered unsuitable for publication.'

The increasing number of surrenders, though still only a trickle, posed one problem: what to do with them. Already one rehabilitation camp had been started in Johore. Now, as C.C. Too produced more and more Surrendered Enemy Personnel (SEPs as they were known), a new and more ambitious rehabilitation camp was built on Taiping racecourse. Called the Academy of Peace and Tranquillity, it had room for six hundred men and its establishment was inspired by experiments made at Macronisson in Greece, where ex-Communists were prepared for entry to the Greek army. The model for half-a-dozen later rehabili-

* Police found this document, which was headed 'Appearances of personal licentiousness', in the pack of a CT shot in Mentakab in 1953.

This graphic photo shows how a bus travelling down a tree-flanked road in the steamy Malayan state of Perak was ambushed by Communists. Without warning a shot was fired and the bus braked to a standstill. Passengers scrambled out as a grenade fired the bus. By the time the armoured car had reversed and returned, the stricken vehicle was ablaze, a total wreck.

The still-smouldering embers of the fire which devastated the village of Simpang Tiga. This picture shows only part of the terrible and senseless destruction. February 15th, 1950.

The scene in the cabinet room in the Parliament building in Kuala Lumpur, as the Prime Minister signed a proclamation repealing the Emergency which was declared in 1948. *Left to right:* Dato Abdul Aziz (*standing*), the Minister's Secretary; Mr Tan Siew Sin, Minister of Finance; Tun Abdul Razak Bin Hussein, Deputy Premier; Tunku Abdul Rahman, Prime Minister; Dato Dr Ismail, Foreign Minister; and Dato Sulaiman Bin Dato Abdul Rahman, Minister of the Interior.

Left Sir Henry Gurney, British High Commissioner in Malaya, was killed by terrorists when his car was ambushed on the road from Kuala Lumpur. September, 1948.
Right Police officers count the bullet holes in Sir Henry Gurney's Rolls-Royce. Police counted thirty-seven in all, some of which are ringed in this picture. October 7th, 1951.

Above Tapping rubber on the McKenzie estate, *whilst* a guard stands by, alert. March 29th, 1952. *Below* Malaya's unhappy neutrals. Communists swoop at night on villages of Chinese squatters to extort money. The police suspect them of hiding secrets, and search by day. March 29th, 1952.

Left Members of the Scots Guards are seen here clearing an area that is suspected to be the hiding place of Communist bandits. The area is mortared and then searched carefully either by the military or Malay Special Police. April, 1949. *Right* British fighters landing by helicopter.

Left Evacuation of casualties from the Malayan jungle. February, 1953. *Right* In the Ulu Keneboi area of Malaya, a member of an Army patrol of the Special Air Service has been wounded by a Communist terrorist. His comrades blow up trees to form a clearing where a helicopter may land. February 21st, 1953.

Troops searching the
Malayan jungle for
Chinese squatters. July
27th, 1950.

Troops of the Assault
Pioneers, 1st Battalion,
Royal Hampshire
Regiment, ford a jungle
stream near Kuala
Lumpur, February 8th, a
few hours after the five-
month amnesty offer to
the Communists had
expired. There was an
estimated 3,500 terrorists
still at large, and the battle
against them was resumed
at once.

A member of the Malay Special Police is seen here checking the identity card of a suspect. April, 1949.

Harry Hopkins touring Malaya meets the fighting planters and sees how they assist the authorities in their anti-bandit campaign. November 7th, 1951.

Left General Sir Gerald Templer, British High Commissioner in guerrilla-harried Malaya, congratulates a platoon of the 2/10th Gurkhas in the Tangkak area of Johore during his tour of the state. *Right* Dyaks (head-hunting trackers from Borneo) in action against the Communists in the Malayan jungle. They have been attached to military units to help track the evasive gangs of Reds who strike quickly from the jungle and have vanished before help can arrive.

Left A Gurkha stands guard on a Malayan rubber estate. March, 1951. *Right* Suspected Communists are brought out of the dense jungle by men of the various regiments working on 'Operation Rugger'. The insurgents' hands are tied behind their backs before they are led away.

Above Chin Peng, Chen Tien, Abdul Maidin and John Davis who served with the Communists during Japanese occupation. *Opposite* The Chief Minister of the Federation of Malaya, Tunku Abdul Rahman, photographed at the Federation of Malaya Constitutional Conference. January 18th, 1956.

A full dress rehearsal for the installation of His Majesty Tuanku Abdul Rahman as the Yang Di-Pertuan Agong of the Federation of Malaya. August 31st, 1957.

tation camps built in Malaya, Taiping was run by a brilliant Chinese-speaking Malayan civil servant, George Rotheray, who felt that his camp 'conditions men so that they can take their place in society without danger to that society, and educates or re-educates them mentally, morally and physically, into the type of free citizens who will be a credit to their land of adoption.'

It did not set out to convert Communists into Democrats, but Rotheray hoped that the life in the camp – a practical demonstration of the 'democratic way' – would be sufficient training to enable the inmates to take their place in the community as law-abiding citizens. The single barbed wire fence around the camp was certainly no bar to escape and it would be hard to imagine more agreeable conditions for detention than in Taiping. Between the long attap-roofed kongsi houses were flower gardens and vegetable allotments, side by side with pitches for basketball and badminton, and a summer house, built by the inmates for their coffee club. The old racecourse grandstand housed offices, classrooms and workshops for carpentry, tinsmithing, motor mechanics, bicycle repairs, tailoring and cobbling. Under the shadow of the hills, and adjoining George Rotheray's house, were poultry, duck and rabbit farms.

Each day in camp started at 6.00 a.m., with roll-call a quarter of an hour later, followed by breakfast at 7.00, and physical training. 'School' started at 9.00 a.m., and basic educational subjects included Chinese, Malay, English, arithmetic and book-keeping.

Rotheray was a great believer in vocational training simply as a way of keeping a man's mind off Communism, and if necessary he gave SEPs parole to follow specialized training, so that before long the camp had even turned out its own women's hairdresser. The SEP who wanted to learn this art was permitted to work in town on parole.

Taiping was a remarkable experiment in eroding Communism, for as Richard Clutterbuck noted: 'Few [SEPs] had any desire to return to Communism; their mental break had been too violent for that. The police keep their eye on them – and so, perhaps, do the Communists (if they have run them to earth under their new names). For their part the SEPs seem happy and secure.'

11 THE MONTHS OF KILLING

One of the problems of a war of counter-insurgency is that the measures necessary to combat guerrilla warfare show results only slowly, during which time the guerrillas can increase the tempo of terrorism.

This is what happened in Malaya during the months of the killing in the summer and autumn of 1951 – perhaps the blackest period of the twelve-year war. In 1950, 646 civilians were murdered and 106 missing, and the figures for 1951 showed no signs of dropping. On the credit side, more troops, nurses, volunteers had arrived, the police force had been increased, Home Guards established; national registration had been completed, the Briggs Plan had resettled most of the squatters, while the food squeeze was choking the supply lines to the CTs. But none of these far-reaching measures – all essential to ultimate victory – seemed so far to be showing results. It reminded Peter Lucy of a business which everyone said was booming, but which still had no money in the bank.

The troops were everywhere – but many were still training for jungle warfare and others were occupied with resettlement. Many ex-members of the Palestine police force had settled down magnificently, but despite the increased numbers there rarely seemed to be a soldier or policeman at the lonely spot where an outrage occurred. Nor could there ever be, for the moment there was evidence of serious protection, the CTs switched their attacks elsewhere.

These CT attacks were being stepped up for two reasons. First, because Chin Peng had increased the size of his army, for while the hard core of 5,000 trained guerrillas remained fairly constant and acted as a spearhead force of killer squads, the government estimated that 5,500 members of the Min Yuen were also carrying arms. Secondly, because of the success of resettlement and of Brigg's food control measures, CTs now had to fight harder to get food and increased killing followed automatically.

This the average planter and miner could hardly be expected to realize. To them, now in the third year of a war, it seemed that Chin Peng's guerrilla army could, despite a few defectors, flaunt the security forces and strike at will.

And there was something else: a disturbing feeling that nobody in Whitehall was taking the war seriously enough; that it was not being prosecuted with enough vigour by the government leaders in London from whom the people of Malaya were taking their cue. The government, said the critics, had got its priorities wrong. The fact that the government recognized Red China did not mean they had to avert their eyes from the possibility of a Red Malaya. This indifference in London was reflected among the British and Chinese businessmen in the major cities of Malaya. In the wet, enervating heat that sapped a man's energies, it was only too easy to live the sort of life London had led during the 'phoney war' of 1939; to carry on manfully with one night a week of Home Guard duties, while the mems met at tea-parties to roll bandages. Any visitor sipping his stengah on the veranda of the 'Spotted Dog' club in Kuala Lumpur would have been hard put to realize that only a few miles out of the city men, women and children were living in conditions of extreme danger.

Only seven miles out of Kuala Lumpur Peter Lucy was under constant attack, despite the fact that he had by now been given two ex-Palestine police sergeants to guard the plantation. During one two-week period in the summer of 1951, there were twenty-five attacks on the Lucy bungalow. On one night alone there were three. The first opened with a fusillade about eleven in the evening. Peter and Tommy scrambled out of bed, Peter picking up his gun as Tommy ran to bring in the twins from their nursery. Peter could hear the bullets pinging like hail on the galvanized iron roof. He and Tommy had long since adopted a routine drill to meet the nightly attacks. Tommy naturally wanted to be with the boys, so the Bren gun had been moved near to them; as Tommy opened fire she could keep an eye on the amah waiting by the bedside to soothe the boys if they woke up. Peter dashed outside to lead his special constables – not that there was anything positive they could do, for the spurts of flame came from the blackness of the trees and it was quite unthinkable to counter-attack. Yet Peter had to return the fire – for if he did not the CTs would certainly creep up to the bungalow.

This attack lasted twenty minutes, after which they thankfully returned to bed. An hour later it started all over again, lasting for another twenty minutes. And they seemed to have barely dozed off into a troubled sleep before gunfire woke them again at 4.00 a.m. After that, Peter had an hour and a half's sleep before he got up to go on his pre-breakfast rounds.

Yet the Lucys remained unperturbed. 'Our defences have been improved,' Tommy wrote in her circular letter. 'We now have two lines of barbed wire round the bungalow area, with two barbed wire gates that are kept locked. We have floodlights at night, eighteen Special Constables on shifts. They are armed with rifles; but we have other weapons about the place; it wouldn't be "security-minded" to tell you how many. We won't starve, for the vegetable garden supplies us with spinach for the boys and the dogs, sweet corn, brinjals, radishes, mint and watercress.'

'The Twinnery', as Tommy described the nursery, was 'a model nursery and the boys are a lovely bronze colour as they have the sun in the morning and the pool which we have built in the garden each evening. Once seen, never forgotten.' Even Nicol Gray, the Police Commissioner, who visited the Lucys regularly, was so captivated by them that he gave them two miniature uniforms and made them 'Honorary Police Officers'.

Life in fact had to go on – and it did, sometimes calmly, sometimes with overtones of grim humour, as on the night when the bungalow was attacked and Tommy called up the police station, to find a new recruit manning the switchboard.

'We're being attacked,' she said.

'Attacked, madam?' answered the voice. 'By whom?'

'Bandits, you fool,' snorted Tommy.

That same week Tommy, whose calm beauty was matched by an equally beautiful figure, did a three-day stint as a model showing off the latest fashions in Kuala Lumpur at a charity bazaar. The Lucys were determined that 'life had to go on'. For, as Tommy wrote: 'If you were sitting with me at the moment, you wouldn't believe I was surrounded by terrorists, that the house was full of guns, that the bar in the living-room is stacked with hand-grenades, and that we might be attacked at any moment. The early mornings in Malaya are astonishingly beautiful; the blue hills are in front of me, bright flowering shrubs and plants in the foreground. The lawn-mower sounds very English and the boys are gurgling on the veranda. We try to carry on as if nothing was happening. It's the only answer to our present situation.'

Even so, Peter Lucy was too old a hand to fall into the one trap for which all CTs prayed – a set routine. He had long since changed his pattern of living. When he left the bungalow before breakfast on his rounds, he always took a different route, never told his clerk when he would return; breakfast became a moveable feast. Times of lunch and dinner were varied to avoid the possibility of a hand-grenade being lobbed through the dining-room window. And on the rare occasions when he had to drive into Kuala Lumpur in the Monster he would never tell anyone the hour of his expected return.

The miners were having a tough time too, but it was not CTs who caused them trouble. Ira Phelps, manager of Pacific Tin's mine at Kampar, woke up one morning to find that 'someone had just laid a barrage of mortar shells across the mine and hit the number six dredge.' He immediately phoned Norman Cleaveland in Ampang, whose first thought was that CTs never used mortar fire. Ira had already telephoned the army, who knew nothing of the attack, so Cleaveland cabled head office in New York: 'Number six dredge mortared stop No casualties damage superficial stop Army denies knowledge.' New York cabled Singapore – and then the fat was in the fire, for the news leaked to the *Singapore Standard*, which ran a page one headline: 'Communists attack American dredge with mortars.'

Army headquarters in Kuala Lumpur was furious: what had happened to the rigid censorship? An irate British major arrived at Ampang and told Cleaveland, 'You've been talking too much to the Press, and I've been told to ask you to make an official denial of the story.' This was the sort of situation which appealed immensely to Cleaveland's sense of humour, for obviously the army had fired the mortars in error.

'Listen, Major,' Cleaveland retorted, 'the first item on the agenda is: Who fired the mortars? Can you answer that?'

The Major didn't say a word. 'Right,' continued Cleaveland. 'Sort that one out and then we'll sort out how the story got into the Press. Okay?' Cleaveland never heard another word from the army.

With increasing attacks on Pacific Tin's mine at Ampang – at one stage there was heavy firing on twenty-one consecutive nights – Norman Cleaveland insisted on a regular show of armament and force. 'Doing the High Noon stuff,' as he describes it. He kept the mine on a fully armed basis twenty-four hours a day, with eight fortified posts straddling the mining area in commanding positions. Every shift was escorted by armoured cars between the mine camp and the dredges. And twice when bandits attacked the village of Ampang, Cleaveland and his armoured cars tore down the hill 'with guns blazing' to save the township's police station.

Cleaveland even formed a pack of hounds. 'We might as well get a laugh out of the war,' he said. Importing Australian dogs and Rhodesian ridgebacks, he and his friends hunted in the secondary jungle nearly every Sunday. They usually killed a wild boar (a perfect centre-piece for Cleaveland's regular Sunday barbecue) and also found constant evidence of hurriedly-evacuated CT camps. Once they found a CT peaked cap complete with red star which had obviously been dropped by a fleeing Communist. They put it on a dead boar and paraded it through the village, driving solemnly past the lines of wooden shanties, the Chinese school with its wide eaves, Ampang's green duck pond, before leaving by the south gate for the rutted, sandy track leading through the lallang and tin tailings to Cleaveland's bungalow – and kitchen.

Though sixteen European and American dredgemen were murdered during the war, Pacific Tin did not lose a single European in any of their mines, but costly equipment was smashed up month after month. The manager of Rahman Hydraulic Mine near Kroh in the north looked out of his bungalow one dawn to see with stupefied half-awake eyes more than twenty CTs tipping his valuable machinery over a precipice.

Peter Lucy had two particularly narrow escapes. The first came when, accompanied by a Malay special constable, he was making a routine inspection in a part of the estate which was terraced. Peter carried a twelve-bore shotgun. He looked up, and to his astonishment, 'I saw a bandit in full uniform lying on the ground about twenty yards away. He was facing me and he had a Sten gun pointing straight at me.'

Before the CT could squeeze the trigger, Lucy – using the same technique he had perfected when pheasant shooting in England – twisted round and fired in one swift movement. He shot the man through the head. Almost at the same time the constable saw another uniformed CT ready to fire. He too was shot through the head after which 'two other CTs began firing at us and we decided to retreat.' Lucy's bandit was identified as a local leader called Sin Seng. Peter was awarded the Colonial Police medal and a reward of $2,000 which he promptly decided to bank. Tommy had other ideas.

'Oh, no!' she said. 'I hope you'll never have to shoot another CT – so let's have a memento of the occasion.'

As Tommy noted in her diary: 'Finally (!) Peter agreed, and we bought a sapphire and diamond eternity ring (it never leaves my finger) and Peter had a gold cigarette case and studs and cufflinks.'

Within a few weeks, Peter Lucy was again in the thick of the fighting – but this time it was Tommy who received the shock. She was sitting on the bungalow veranda when a police car tore up and a white-faced policeman told her that Peter was missing after an ambush on a nearby estate. Peter had been accompanying Mr J. H. Clarkson, a fifty-year-old director of several firms, when ten CTs attacked them as they walked down a path along a small ravine.

The first rifle shots were followed swiftly by Sten gun fire. Clarkson emptied all the chambers of his revolver before he received the full blast of the Sten in his stomach. Peter was two feet away, and as one policeman fell dying, another saw Peter stand up and fire. Then, said the police, 'he just vanished'.

In the mêlée following Clarkson's death, Peter had been knocked out, but he had managed to crawl into the bottom of the ravine. The CTs melted away, but though police reinforcements found the bodies of Clarkson and the dead policeman, there was no trace of Peter. They raced to the bungalow to break the news to Tommy.

Four hours later a dishevelled Peter with a bump the size of an egg on his head reached Amherst. He had fallen into undergrowth, fainted, and then had managed to crawl to the estate bungalow, only to find that the wires had been cut, so he had been unable to telephone Amherst.

Within a few days, Peter Lucy received an official visit from a high government officer. Police had uncovered evidence that Lucy was on a CT death list, and the repeated attacks forced the government to warn him that he should leave the country, as they could no longer guarantee his safety.

Lucy's first reaction was to snort, 'Give in to them? Never!' But there were other considerations – particularly the twins. For the Lucys it was an agonizing decision to make. Amherst was their home, Malaya was the country they loved above any other in the world, and they spent many wretched evenings arguing whether or not they should leave.

Both wanted to stay – and both decided firmly that they would not in any circumstances leave immediately; they wanted some weeks, even months, to think it over.

Of course there was another alternative – but neither dared to bring it up at first: that Tommy should take the twins and Peter stay.

Carefully they shunned the question when talking to each other – though not when talking to friends. All Peter's colleagues wanted him to stay; all Tommy's friends urged her to go. But as Tommy wrote: 'One of the main reasons why I feel we should take the government's advice is that the twins can no longer stand the constant shooting and their nerves (and mine because of them) are at breaking-point. But I don't want us to go without Peter – for that will mean a broken family.'

As the long, hot summer of 1951 burned itself out, the ferocity of CT attacks seemed suddenly to be directed more against women and children. On a nearby estate two-year-old Susan Thompson, daughter of a planter, was murdered while her father and mother were in Kuala Lumpur. Susan was riding in the estate Land-Rover with the cook when CTs ambushed the vehicle and shot her through the head.

Then the first British woman was murdered. An ambush – on the classical pattern – was laid on the main Taiping-Selama Road north of Ipoh. Two logs straddled the road, and a dozen or so CTs in jungle green with Sten guns waited.

The first car arrived. In it were George Burne, a tin miner, and his wife Mary. One CT signalled the car to stop. Burne pulled up, stepped out. Without warning, the CTs opened up, not at Burne, but at the car, killing Mary who was in the front seat.

It was after this that Tommy turned to Peter and said, 'I think it's time we *all* went'. Peter hated the idea, but he knew that Tommy would never leave unless he did; and he knew also that she had to go. Sadly he agreed, but suggested that at least they might stay until the following year. Peter wanted another six months at Amherst.

Tommy found this reasonable, but that night she wrote in her diary, 'The trouble is that all the fun and beauty seems to have gone out of this country which we love so much.'

They had talked a long time, and it was nearly midnight when she switched off the light. Only a few minutes were left before the start of a new day – the blackest day in the history of the war.

Shortly before noon on Saturday, October 6, a platoon of thirty-eight guerrillas, led by Siu Mah, commander of the Eleventh Regiment in Pahang and a friend of Chin Peng's, were at ambush stations. They had chosen a two-hundred-yard S-bend on the narrow twisting road leading to Fraser's Hill, a hill resort in Malaya. They had been in position for two days and two nights, waiting patiently to ambush a military convoy which they had been told would pass that way. They were not after men, but badly needed arms.

It was perfect ambush terrain. The narrow road wound round a hill, its sheer slopes covered by jungle with here and there prominent clumps of tall bamboo. Siu Mah had laid his plans carefully, placing his men in positions extending for the two hundred yards of the bend. Palm leaves and attap screened their gun positions from the road twenty feet below. Each ambush position had a flag, including one made from a pair of red underpants which hung from a bamboo pole at the main firing point, a twenty-foot boulder masked by bamboo. Tracks connected the three Bren-gun firing positions. Another track had been beaten into the jungle behind; this was the prepared withdrawal route without which no CT ambush was ever laid.

But then the stakes were high – arms. And Siu Mah's plan was to kill and wound as many troops as possible in the first minutes of ferocious fire, then send his men down the bank to collect all the arms possible.

Only one thing had marred the plan: faulty information,

for the military convoy had not arrived. Trucks and motor-cars had passed regularly up and down the hill, which was a few miles north of Tras, a township with a particularly evil reputation. Two senior officers in cars flying pennants and with escorts had passed, but Siu Mah had held his fire. He wanted bullets, not bodies.

Around midday, he decided to withdraw, but the more aggressive CTs grew restive and suggested that they might as well attack the next convoy that came along. Siu Mah agreed.

A few minutes before one o'clock a three-car convoy came round the bend. Forty yards in front was an open Land-Rover carrying six Malay policemen. Behind was a black chauffeur-driven Rolls Royce flying the Union Jack. The third vehicle was out of view round the bend. Its engine had stalled.

Siu Mah waved the red flag. The attack opened with a burst of machine-gun fire. Not one of the CTs could have had the faintest idea that inside the Rolls was Sir Henry Gurney, the High Commissioner, his wife and secretary, Mr D. J. Staples, on their way to Fraser's Hill for the week-end. The two vehicles drove straight into the first furious burst. Only one sergeant in the Land-Rover escaped injury, and he coolly started to return the CT fire. In the Rolls the chauffeur was wounded instantly and the car slewed to a stop as bullets ripped its tyres.

Suddenly a door of the Rolls opened and out stepped Gurney. Almost leisurely he banged the door shut, and started to walk towards the high bank – and the shooting. As he reached the deep gutter by the roadside, the High Commissioner seemed to hesitate for a moment. There was another murderous hail of fire. Gurney, the man who initiated the greatest social revolution in Asia, the man who realized the fundamental truth that to win a political war the civil government must remain in control, crumpled on the grass verge, killed instantly. Inside the Rolls Lady

Gurney and Mr Staples crouched on the floor. Suddenly a bugle sounded. It was Siu Mah's signal for his CTs to withdraw. Gurney was dead, but his wife and secretary were unharmed, though thirty-five bullet holes were counted in the Rolls.

So the second High Commissioner of Malaya's war died, though not by deliberate planning, as documents captured later proved conclusively. Certainly there had never been an ambush on this stretch of road since the start of the Emergency three years previously.*

One puzzle remained. Why had Sir Henry Gurney got out of the car? Harry Miller, who visited the scene and spoke to survivors, believes that he deliberately walked into the road to draw the fire from his wife. 'He had secured his intention with the loss of his life,' Miller wrote. 'The terrorists did not concentrate on the Rolls-Royce any more.'

To the shocked people of Malaya, this was a disaster of the first magnitude. If the British High Commissioner with an armed escort could be assassinated in broad daylight, what would happen next, where would it all end? In the hierarchy of British Imperial rule the person of the High Commissioner was as inviolable as that of the Queen. It was hard for them to believe that such a disaster *could* take place. Numbed by shock, it was not possible for Malaya to see what had happened in its true perspective – 'that', in the words of Professor Anthony Short, 'the importance in Malaya is that the event came after three years of consistent and public underestimation of the strength of the insurrection. The irony that Sir Henry was killed by chance was not apparent. This, the end of 1951, was the low-water mark of Emergency Operations in Malaya.'

* Siu Mah lived in the jungle until March 9, 1959, when he was betrayed by two of his men and shot hiding in a cave near Ipoh.

12 THE OCTOBER DIRECTIVE

No novelist would dare to deploy his characters, tax the imagination or stretch coincidence to the point it reached in the fateful month of October 1951, the turning-point of the war. Here were two protagonists locked in an implacable conflict of ideologies, played out against the dank, sunless background of the jungle; with the Lucys and Puckridges fighting to protect a country in which victory could mean independence followed by a passage home by P & O and a cheque to tide them over till they found new jobs, with the Chin Pengs living like hunted animals in order to 'protect' a country against the hated Imperialists who had already laid their plans to leave.

And yet, as the pitiless October rains heralded the autumn monsoon, with British fortunes apparently plummeting lower than ever before, this was the moment when Chin Peng had to admit that he was on the verge of failure.

One of the ironies of war is that the power and brilliance of the enemy becomes magnified out of all proportion. In three years, Chin Peng's elusive CTs, able to pick the time and place of any battle before sliding into the obscurity of the jungle, had, to the Security Forces, taken on almost superhuman qualities. It would have stupefied the people of Malaya to learn that almost at the same time as the chance assassination of Gurney, Chin Peng had called yet another jungle meeting at which he admitted that his first plans had failed and offered entirely new tactics in their place.

So both sides were at their lowest ebb since June 1948. Neither looked like winning – though each thought the other was. And, after three years in which each side had refused to acknowledge truths, they now took stock.

For the British, the murder of Gurney would pave the way to victory. It had needed his death to galvanize the British government in Whitehall into serious action, to make them realize that without a supremo to run a real war, there could be no victory. By chance, Gurney's death coincided with the last breaths of the Socialist government in Britain, so that within a few weeks one dynamic man would at last see the threat in Malaya for what it really was.

Meanwhile, despite the apparent successes of CT terrorism, Chin Peng faced a deeper problem and at a full meeting of the Politburo, again attended by several Red Chinese officers,* he produced the historic 'October 1951 Directive'. In it the Malayan Communist Party admitted that the initial campaign from 1948 to the middle of 1949 had misfired. The deliberate campaign of terrorism, with which the Communists had hoped to win the support of the population and force the British out, had been a dismal failure. Terrorism, said Chin Peng, had alienated Communism's most valuable asset – the very people they were trying to 'liberate'. The Party had acted on a totally false premise – that terror tactics which had worked during the Japanese Occupation would produce equally dramatic results against the 'British Colonialists'. In fact the opposite had occurred. After three and a half years of Japanese Occupation, all the people wanted was to be left alone, to be given a chance to work freely again. They were weary of living in constant fear.

Similar reactions had followed Chin Peng's policy of damaging machinery and slashing rubber trees. Ordinary people who had to earn their daily rice disliked intensely having their livelihood taken away from them. It might be

---

* In his excellent book, *Malaya: The Communist Insurgent War*, 1948–1960, Edgar O'Ballance mentions that changes of view were 'perhaps pointed out by the Chinese Red Army Officers', and again that the conclusions were 'probably implanted by a few visiting Chinese Red Army Officers'. Osman China also remembers seeing these Chinese officers.

heroic to fight for a cause, but it was a different matter if one's children starved for it.

Therefore, said the October 1951 Directive, in an astonishing *volte face*, all unnecessary 'inconvenience' was to be avoided in an attempt to win the support of the masses. No identity or ration cards would be seized. There would be no more burning of New Villages and coolie lines, no more attacks on post offices, reservoirs, power stations or any public services. Civilian trains were no longer to be derailed with high explosives; great care had to be taken when throwing grenades or when 'shooting running dogs found mixing with the masses to avoid stray shots hurting the masses.'

There was no suggestion that attacks on troops or police should be curtailed, though the directive enumerated several subtle distinctions: while British officers and troops, together with managers of production centres, could be killed with impunity, British health officers should not be touched. (Nor would it be permitted, according to a footnote, for gold teeth to be extracted from corpses.) Possibly influenced by Red China, one obscure paragraph insisted that the prevalent Malayan view that the Chinese peasant was worse off than his Malayan brother 'must be corrected'.

In place of bloodshed the Min Yuen would now control the masses 'legally', involving them in 'revolution' by exploiting lawful disputes, demanding concessions from capitalists, penetrating the trade unions. In other words, the government's progressive measures, which the Communists now found embarrassingly like their own promises, had to be exploited rather than attacked.

With a curious irony, the main points of the directive embodied many of the heresies advanced by the unfortunate Shao Liu, the Political Commissar of Malacca who had been executed with his wife for his temerity in suggesting them. And there was another interesting point – one that would seem to indicate Chinese pressure. Under the new directive, Chin Peng at last committed himself to wage war on two fronts – terrorism against police and troops on the one hand, legal infiltration on the other. It meant that for the first time Chin Peng had accepted Mao Tse-tung's classic principle of a struggle on two equal fronts with equal emphasis.

Most of the top Communists attended the conference, and Osman China remembers that though all realized the gravity of Chin Peng's admissions, none entertained any thought of eventual defeat. It might no longer be feasible, as Chin Peng had hoped, for CTs to seize regions, towns or even villages, and set up Liberated Areas; but they were still a fighting force. The general feeling was that Communism was dealing with a shrinking colonial empire discredited in many areas of the world, and the morale of the meeting was inflated by the dramatic victories of Communism in China, and now by Chinese intervention in the Korean war.

The Communist October 1951 Directive was a momentous admission of partial defeat, a document that was to change the whole course of the war. One wonders what would have happened had it not taken nearly twelve months for the first copy to fall into the hands of British Intelligence.

Phase Two
COUNTER-ATTACK
1952–54

13 THE OLD WARRIOR

On October 21. 1951, Attlee's Labour government was defeated in a general election in Britain and Winston Churchill became Prime Minister. True, his Conservative government had only a majority of seventeen seats, but to the average Malayan this provided the one tonic that was required, for Churchill was above all a man of vision, capable of translating what he saw into direct action.

He needed all his energy and resources now, for in his first survey to Parliament, he found Britain so near the verge of bankruptcy that he cut all cabinet ministers' salaries by £1,000 a year and his own by £3,000. It seems incredible, looking back only as far as 1951, to realize that food stocks in Britain were lower than in 1941, at the height of World War Two, and that Britain's food was still strictly rationed. Solemnly Churchill warned the country that there was no immediate prospect of easing the rationing. Abroad, he faced a crisis in the Middle East where a new threat faced the world. In the second week of October Egypt took the first steps towards nationalizing the Suez Canal. Churchill's answer was to order an airlift of six thousand troops. In the Far East a new place name had sprung into the news – Panmunjon, where peace talks to end the Korean war were taking place. Yet, however grave these events might have been, Churchill's immediate interest lay in Malaya. 'If Malaya goes,' he growled to a friend the day after he took office, 'all the Far East goes.' Churchill was the first man – after three tragic, wasted years – to place the picture of Malaya in the frame of Asia.

The war in Malaya, where 3,000 men and women had been killed, was costing $500,000 a day, and rubber and tin production was in danger of falling. To Churchill it was part of a pattern in which democracy's manpower was being drained all over Asia – 800,000 men fighting Communism in Korea, 100,000 French in Indo-China; and in Malaya 40,000 British and Colonial troops, 25,000 fully-trained Malay police and 50,000 special constables. One of Churchill's achievements was his immediate awareness of the global gravity of Malaya's guerrilla warfare, and his unshakeable belief that a means could be found to beat it.

He knew this was a battle which, if lost, could change the course of history between warring ideologies; for this was a conflict not only at the crossroads of history, but at the crossroads of Asia. What happened in Malaya would have a profound influence on the rest of the world – and not just in a corner of 'the Empire'. Churchill therefore demanded immediate action.

His first move was to call for a complete report on the situation in Malaya. He found it depressing beyond belief. The country was in a state of frustration; there was divided control at the top; the civil administration might have quickened its tempo by Malayan standards, but it still seemed to move at the leisurely pace of a country at peace. The police force was still bitterly divided. As the *Daily Telegraph* commented: 'The trouble [has been] not only murder but mugwumpery.'

Within days, Churchill decided that his new Colonial Secretary must go immediately to Malaya. 'The rot has got to be stopped,' was how he put it.

Oliver Lyttelton had been appointed to the Colonial Office. A burly, good-natured, typically Conservative product of Eton, Cambridge and the Brigade of Guards, Lyttelton was fifty-eight and could claim some affinity with Malaya, for in 1937 he had been chairman of the London

Tin Corporation, which with its subsidiaries owned or managed fourty-four dredges in Malaya – probably the largest dredging enterprise in the world.

Lyttelton took over from James Griffiths, who on his visit to Malaya in 1950 had announced that 'the difficulties' – great though they are – can be assessed squarely and confidently.' But that had been more than a year ago and now, as he handed over his papers and his desk to Lyttelton, Griffiths had to confess sadly: 'At this stage Malaya has become a military problem to which we have not been able to find the answer.'

Lyttelton had been told to fly out immediately, but he delayed his trip for a week or two for a very good reason. Churchill had been in correspondence with General Briggs, whose term of office in Malaya had almost expired. Briggs had lodged some harsh criticism about the police force and its leader, Nicol Gray, and Briggs had also complained about his own lack of authority over the police despite his grandiose title of 'Director of Operations'. Churchill and Lyttelton had taken heed of Briggs and had quickly decided that something must be done, so it seemed more politic for Lyttelton and Briggs not to meet. Lyttelton therefore decided to fly to Malaya two days after Briggs had left, which the General did on November 27, after twenty months in Malaya.

The quiet capable soldier whose 'Briggs Plan' was already a household word in Malaya left the country a sick and bitterly disillusioned man. He had been not a commander, but a 'co-ordinator under civilian control' – a half-and-half man in a country where for too long half-hearted half-measures dictated by Whitehall had so restricted his powers that even as Director of Operations he did not have the control he wanted (and needed) over the police force. On his last day before leaving, Briggs admitted, 'I have not been completely satisfied with my powers.' He was, however, able to promise that his successor would have fresh powers for putting the entire Defence Branch and 'the complete policy of the police' under the Director of Operations. So, as well as implementing a social revolution which was to have a lasting effect on South-East Asia, Briggs gained a bloodless victory over the police. By dealing quietly with Downing Street, he had set in train events which were to transform the police into a force so brilliant that its Special Branch would be second to none in the world.

Two days later, Oliver Lyttelton flew to Malaya to see for himself what needed to be done – and to discuss the question of Gurney's successor. Two thousand police ringed the airport when he landed in Singapore, to be met by Malcolm MacDonald. Lyttelton had hardly stumbled off the plane (he almost fell) before the Press asked him, 'What have you come for?' Perhaps without thinking, Lyttelton made what in normal circumstances would have been an innocuous reply.

'To restore law and order is the first thing,' he answered. 'When I know more we will have a Press conference.'

As the two men drove off with an American-style motorcade escort, MacDonald seemed glum. 'I wish you hadn't said that about law and order,' he told Lyttelton. 'The effect will be bad. You see, it's political advancement that will solve these problems, not bullets.'

MacDonald was right. As Lyttelton remembers, 'the general tone of the Press was "Secretary of State denies Constitutional changes" and "Continuance of police state forecast." ' Thereafter he treated the Press with its strong Asian influence a little more warily.

Before going to Kuala Lumpur, Lyttelton stayed a night or two with MacDonald at Bukit Serene (where the Sultan had restored the water supply to the pool), and where 'the comfort of the East began to lap us round.' Dirty shirts were whisked away to be washed immediately. Lyttelton

was able to take time off to be measured for a sharkskin
dinner-jacket and a couple of tropical suits before settling
down to the serious business of finding out why such a
rich and powerful country was being kept in thrall by less
than ten thousand armed Communist fighters.

'The situation,' he noted at the time, 'was far worse
than I had imagined: it was appalling. From a long life in
administration, I could draw no parallel.' By the end of
his tour, Lyttelton had become determined on one point
above all others: Malaya should be led by one man in
control of both military and civil affairs. He would have
to be a general. He would have to be supported by a
post hitherto unknown in Malaya – that of Deputy High
Commissioner responsible for shouldering the day-to-day
chores.

After leaving MacDonald, Lyttelton moved into King's
House at Kuala Lumpur, and set about persuading the
Sultans that a change in the constitution was necessary to
allow for this Deputy High Commissioner. The Sultans
agreed, though they all expected that the post would be
filled by a Malay, who would serve under the Supremo.
Lyttelton, however, had firm views on this: 'I did not think
that a Malay of the necessary calibre was available.'

Lyttelton then decided to dismiss Nicol Gray, the
Commissioner of Police ('a gallant officer but not a professional policeman'), and Sir William Jenkin, the Head of
Special Branch, after realizing that 'the police were divided
by a great schism ... Intelligence was scanty and unco-
ordinated. I secured their resignation.' These moves were,
however, kept so secret that no one in Malaya had an
inkling of what was happening.

Then Lyttelton set out to meet the planters and miners,
including one informal gathering with fifty of them at the
planters' favourite meeting place – the Coliseum Bar in
Kuala Lumpur (where he accidentally fired one of the
many revolvers heaped on the mahogany bar counter).

The planters told him bluntly that if things did not improve within the next six months they would resign in a body. They particularly wanted heavier sentences on the many Chinese known to be paying protection money to the CTs. To his credit Lyttelton flatly refused, insisting that until the government could guarantee safety for civilians, it was cynical to prosecute men and women protecting themselves in the only way possible.

'At the point of a gun, you would pay rather than be murdered,' he retorted to one obstreperous planter, 'and so would I and you know it.'

Lyttelton did, however, promise to ask Churchill to unblock dollars so that American carbines could be bought for planters, and also promised more armour for police and special constables on the estates, adding, with an obvious reference to Gray's 'no armour' policy, 'I cannot subscribe to the theory that protecting a man from rifle fire reduces his fighting spirit.'

All this time Churchill was watching from afar. Daily cables from No. 10 reached King's House, some of them not without a flash of typically Churchillian humour, as when the London Press reported one particularly wordy encounter between Lyttelton and the planters. 'Lyttelton must live,' cabled Churchill jokingly.

Before leaving, Lyttelton broadcast some details of the plan he would place before Churchill on his return to London. It contained six main points: Direction of civil and military forces by one man; reorganization of the police; compulsory education programme 'as a means of winning the war of ideas'; more protection for squatter areas; a Home Guard to include 'large numbers of Chinese'; and finally, a review of the civil service with a view to recruiting the best men available in Britain and Malaya.

On his last night at King's House – where the security might be expected to be of the best – Lyttelton was astonished to find the imposing great hall filled with anxious police officers. They had good reason to be there, for the butler who had gravely handed the Colonial Secretary his coffee after dinner each evening had turned out to be a Communist agent. 'As a result of this somewhat overdue discovery', as Lyttelton tartly noted, every servant had been dismissed on the spot, and until new ones could be screened, police officers were there to heat the bath water and prepare breakfast.

The next morning Lyttelton flew back to London to report to Churchill. They met within a few hours of Lyttelton's arrival, and Churchill immediately started looking around (via his Colonial Secretary, of course) for 'our general'. He did not prove quite so easy to find as Churchill imagined, and with Christmas approaching in Malaya, and CT incidents mounting, the *Straits Times* in a leading article headed 'Indecision in London' warned that 'the long delay has begun to be harmful.' The higher echelons of the Malaya Civil Service were also having some doubts about the wisdom of the 'Supremo theory' – a doubt shared by Malcolm MacDonald, who had told Lyttelton in Malaya that another civilian was wanted, to which the Colonial Secretary had replied, 'No, it must be a soldier.' These doubts were now expressed in the *Straits Times*, which after discussing rumours that a high-ranking general would be chosen to replace Gurney, added that: 'It should be increasingly clear in London by now that the essential qualities which are required are those of an administrator and that there is no short cut through the jungle which the magic of a big name can open.'

Christmas came to Malaya – marking the virtual end of a bad year in which 532 civilians were murdered and 505 members of the Security Forces were killed. Still there was no news of Gurney's successor – and all that Malayans could do was to celebrate and hope for the best.

Bob Thompson and his wife Merryn spent their first

Christmas together in Malaya in their house overlooking the Straits of Johore next to Malcolm MacDonald's – very convenient as Merryn loved horses, had acquired an Australian ex-racehorse called 'Kashmiri Song' which she kept in the garage, and could now ride over the vast grounds of MacDonald's Bukit Serene.

Peter Lucy's Christmas was inevitably tinged with sadness, for within a few months they would be leaving to start a new life planting sisal in Kenya. All the arrangements had been made. None the less, as Tommy wrote: 'We celebrated in the good old tradition; we spent all Christmas Eve decorating the bungalow. The Christmas Tree had of course to be a casuarina. On Christmas morning there were stockings for all, old and young. Father Christmas distributed the presents from the tree, but was not able to keep his warm headdress on too long in this climate! It was our first Christmas with the twins, so a very special celebration. Christmas dinner that night, with many special guests who braved the dangerous trip out to the estate, was gay and cheerful, with turkey and plum pudding, champagne, and the toast to "Absent Loved Ones" was particularly moving, as people living on estates are never sure whether they will ever see their loved ones again – and we could not help wondering when, if ever, we would see all our tried and trusted friends.'

Christmas and New Year had barely passed before a new bombshell hit Malaya. Nicol Gray, the controversial Federation Police Commissioner, left secretly. He had, of course, been relieved of his appointment, but this was not generally known, and what shocked Malaya now was the manner of his going. Without a word to any colleague, he packed his bags, asked for an RAF plane to fly him to Singapore – a perfectly routine flight – and was on the way back to Britain before even the Police Secretary in Kuala Lumpur knew he had gone.

It was an extraordinary way for Gray to leave. He did write to Peter Lucy apologizing for not saying goodbye, and the note gave a clue to his behaviour. 'If I were to say goodbye,' he wrote, 'my presence might well aggravate a difficult period for the police.' To a friend he merely said, 'I thought it best to get out of the way.' The *Malay Mail* was bitterly outspoken on 'why Mr Gray's resignation was announced only after he had left the country'. 'A veil of secrecy' had been drawn over the affairs of the police, said the *Mail*, adding: 'It does not seem to be realized in official circles how much harm has been done to morale and public confidence by the steadfast refusal to reveal even an outline of the facts. For more than two years the Federation has been buzzing with rumours about dissension in the police.'

The *Straits Times* felt that the way in which he had left the country before any announcement 'emphasizes once again the lofty disregard of public opinion which is one of the major faults of the Malayan administration . . . The public are entitled to a more full explanation than has so far been offered.'

This 'lofty disregard' annoyed thinking people in Malaya far more than the fact that Gray had left in such curious circumstances, for as the *Straits Times* added, after paying a tribute to Gray: 'Equally the fact cannot be disguised that his achievements did not embrace a genuine consolidation of the force and its cohesive working as a unit.'

This might have been true, and Gray had certainly been a controversial figure, but it is also indisputable that the early animosity which had greeted him in the police force had changed to a grudging respect,* for he had after all expanded a force of 11,120 men, including only 154 gazetted officers, into one of 25,154, including 481

---

* This changed feeling was most noticeable among all senior police officers with whom the author talked.

gazetted officers, 617 inspectors and four hundred British lieutenants.

Now the country had neither a High Commissioner nor a chief of police, and in Whitehall Lyttelton was trying to find successors to Gurney and Gray. In an effort to find the right man, Churchill even asked the advice of Montgomery, inviting him to luncheon with Lyttelton. Montgomery's presence had a curious repercussion. The Press learned he had been there, and someone jumped to the conclusion that he was being offered the post of High Commissioner. The matter did not arouse much interest in London, but in Malaya the *Straits Times* was horrified. 'Mr Churchill could make no bigger blunder than by sending Field Marshal Montgomery to Malaya,' it said. 'Montgomery's appointment would be regarded as disastrous. We believe without any qualifications whatever that Field Marshal Montgomery could lose Malaya as surely and as quickly as he won North Africa.'

It is doubtful if Montgomery was in fact ever approached, for both Churchill and Lyttelton felt the best man would be Sir Brian Robertson, who was at the time in the Canal Zone. Churchill cabled Robertson to visit London for consultations.

One thought, however, had never crossed Churchill's mind: that Robertson might refuse the post. But Robertson did refuse. He spent a quarter of an hour alone with Churchill, who then summoned Lyttelton. As soon as the Colonial Secretary entered the Cabinet Room Churchill in his best rhetorical manner told him: 'Sir Brian Robertson feels obliged to decline. He would dislike leaving the Canal Zone at the moment, and when he does, he urges that he should not be asked to undertake another long period of foreign service.' Robertson had, in fact, spent twenty-eight of the last thirty-one years abroad, and as

Churchill put it, 'feels entitled to be excused and to enjoy, at long last, some settled family life.'

Lyttelton now had to cable Malcolm MacDonald that he was looking for another general 'with the right qualifications, but a few days must pass before an appointment can be announced.' To this MacDonald rightly replied that he could not be responsible for the safety of Malaya if there were further delay 'and above all if a general was appointed, with all the implications of military dictatorship which it implied.'

Lyttelton had to admit that 'I was somewhat at a loss to find the right man.' He approached General Slim of Burma fame, but this doughty warrior felt himself 'a little too old to go flipping around in an Auster aircraft in the trying climate of Malaya.'

Lyttelton was also looking for a new police commissioner, and here he had better luck. Colonel Arthur Young, the forthright Commissioner of the City of London Police – a professional to his fingertips – was summoned to the Colonial Office, where Lyttelton told him bluntly, 'I want you to go to Malaya.'

In the shock of this sudden declaration, for which the 44-year-old Arthur Young was totally unprepared, he nearly blurted out, 'Where is it?' Fortunately Lyttelton gave him no chance to talk, explaining that the Home Office had given him a short list and 'I've chosen you because your age is right.'

Lyttelton assumed that Young would automatically be prepared to take up a permanent appointment in Malaya – until Young made it clear that he would only go on secondment for a year. Lyttelton replied tersely, 'That's no good to me!'

'If I can't do the job in a year,' retorted Young, 'I doubt if I can do it at all.' With that Lyttelton had to be satisfied.

Young had one more question to put to the Colonial Secretary. Who was going to be his High Commissioner?

Lyttelton replied, 'I wish I could tell you, but I'm afraid we're back to square one. We've asked several generals, but they've all found reasons not to go.'

It was Churchill who 'discovered' the man who would lead Malaya to victory. And he did it in, of all places, the Rideau Hall in Ottawa. Towards the end of January 1952, Churchill was presiding in Canada at a 'council of war' on Commonwealth problems. Lord Ismay, Lord Cherwell and Field Marshal Alexander – all old wartime comrades – were present. And the first priority on the list was Malaya. There was, however, one question to which no one present could find an answer. Who should lead the fight?

In a moment of exasperation Churchill sent for the Army List, and as his finger reached the fifth name on the list, he paused. That night a cable was sent to Cobham, Surrey. The next day, 54-year-old General Sir Gerald Templer was flying to Ottawa.

Templer was every inch a soldier – and looked it. Stiff-backed on parade, with steely eyes and a choice range of language to any who displeased him, his military background was impressive. Educated at Wellington and Sandhurst, he had, as a good Ulsterman, first seen active service with the Royal Irish Fusiliers in World War One at eighteen. A keen sportsman, he was a member of the British Olympic hurdles team in 1924 and was also bayonet-fighting champion of the army. In 1936 he won a DSO and bar in Palestine, and in World War Two became, at forty-four, the youngest lieutenant-general in the British army.

That night forty guests assembled in the pale green banqueting hall in Ottawa. Amid the cigar smoke, with Churchill, the old warrior, obviously enjoying the role of premier, few noticed the slim British general who had just arrived. Not until the brandy was served did Churchill talk to Templer. And when he growled bluntly, 'Malaya!'

Templer never hesitated. 'I regarded it as an order,' he remembers.

Three weeks later Templer was in Malaya, armed with military and political powers greater than any British soldier had enjoyed since Cromwell.

14 THE SUPREMO

Almost from the moment General Templer arrived at Kuala Lumpur in February 1952, the people of Malaya were left in no doubt that a dynamic, unconventional figure with immense energy had landed among them. On his way to King's House, an aide told him that forty servants would be lined up to receive him. Templer asked, 'What do I do? Shake hands?' The shocked aide replied, 'But the High Commissioner *never* shakes hands with them.' 'This one does,' said Templer crisply, and on arrival proceeded to shake hands with every one of the servants and gardeners. This done, he demanded to see the servants' quarters, and, after an inspection, discovered there was a credit of £4,000 in Whitehall's annual budget for repairs and renovations to King's House.

'Spend the lot on improving the servants' quarters,' said Templer (adding later to a friend, 'After what happened to poor Gurney I thought that at least I'd better get the staff on my side.')

After taking one look round the extensive ornamental gardens of King's House, he ordered it to be fenced in with barbed wire. Three days later he telephoned the Public Works Department and asked, 'Is that PWD?'

'Yes sir.'

'This is General Templer. Can you hear me? Clearly? Are you sure you can?'

'Yes sir, quite clearly,' replied the startled head of PWD.

'Well then,' said Templer, 'where the hell is that bloody barbed wire?'

Within a few days Templer's withering language – and his insistence that every order be obeyed at the double – was the talk of every club and bar in Malaya. He was merciless to anyone who smacked of old-time colonialism. When he heard that the all-white Lake Club in Kuala Lumpur had refused entry to a distinguished Malay, he called the committee together and told them in a fury: 'For the security forces there is no such thing as a colour bar. British boys, Rhodesians, Gurkhas, Africans and Fijians are risking their lives side by side with Malays, Chinese and Indians. These men see the real enemy in Communism. They also see their real friends.' The club committee resigned – and a new committee agreed to multi-racial membership.

When he found that Chinese and Malay Muslims refused to co-operate in a pig farm project because non-pork-eating Malays did not like to work with the Chinese at breeding pigs, he said, 'I want a pig farm here in a week.' Despite religious objections, he got it – and won the admiration of the local people. Two days later he indented to London for half a dozen prize British boars to improve the stock.

Working with an astonishingly small staff of nine, which included a policeman and a civil servant, he spent as little time as possible in Kuala Lumpur. He wanted things done – and done quickly. He had no time for woolly thinking, and this made him totally unpredictable and at times unfair. There is some truth in the observation of Victor Purcell, the author: 'With him "theoretical" was a term of high opprobrium, while "academic" was his nearest approach to obscene.' He was a new phenomenon in British Colonial administration, and could be venomous against someone who displeased him, so that the *Straits Times* soon found itself apologizing to readers for giving 'only a milk-and-water version of his unprintable remarks.'

He greeted one British newspaper reporter with the sneer: 'I know all about *you*. Everyone says you're a—.'

Though he recognized that most planters were brave and resolute, he despised those on small estates who refused to look after the labour force. These were the few planters who could not, or would not, realize that poor labour conditions fomented militant Communism. When visiting one rubber plantation he told the planter to whitewash the worker's houses. And when the planter asked who was going to pay, Templer roared, '*You!*' and stalked off without another word.

He could be equally unpleasant with some unfortunate subordinates in King's House, but he was also forgiving. One who received a tongue-lashing was disconcerted to be invited for drinks a few days later, when the General greeted him cheerfully, 'Well, how are you, old cock?'

He was ruthless with inefficiency. As soon as he settled down, he realized that the War Committees on State and District level which Briggs had started were often valueless because the civilians, soldiers and policemen could never agree.

Templer let it be known that he was interested in their troubles. 'My advice is for you to thrash out your problems over a bottle of whisky in the evenings,' he said. 'If you can't agree I don't want to know why. I'll sack the lot of you and bring in three new chaps.' When necessary, he did just this.

A man who liked to know precisely where he stood, Templer decided the first time he met Malcolm MacDonald that their relationship should be clearly established. Of course, Templer knew he had 'supremo' powers, but he wanted to make certain MacDonald with his rather ill-defined job, realized this too, so he asked MacDonald bluntly, 'Well – which of us has the final responsibility?' MacDonald made it clear that Templer had, 'Right,' said the General. 'Give me all the advice you like, but keep out of my territory.'

Templer also started a system of 'Red minutes', subconsciously copying Churchill. Each evening after a tiring trip visiting sites, listening to complaints, he would be greeted in his air-conditioned office at King's House with a large whisky and soda, and start writing brief notes demanding instant action in the area just visited. It might be the need for a new water pipe or a demand for more arms. Many Red minutes were libellous. One read: 'When I visited the camp near Yong Peng the European who was to meet me was late. He also smelt of hair oil. Anything the matter with him?' The recipient of the minute *had* to report back within a specified time. And if there were no action, the man was dismissed.* A few heads were bound to roll, though Templer hated dismissing long-term government servants, some of them now out of tune with a grim war. One high-ranking but obstructive police officer called Masterson did have to go and was persuaded to resign. Thereupon Templer sent for Masterson, and as he entered the room, the General got up from his chair, shook him by the hand and grunted, 'Masterson, you've been a difficult and awkward bugger, but you've been a man. Goodbye.'

All this did in fact give the people of Malaya an erroneous first picture of Templer – perhaps deliberately on his part, for his brusque army manner hid the brain of a shrewd politician sensitive to every nuance of political thought, whose policy was outlined in the thirty-four words of his first circular to Malayan government officers; 'Any idea that the business of normal civil government and the business of the Emergency are two separate entities must

* In all Templer wrote 1,500 or so Red minutes. He never kept personal copies, and most of the office copies have disappeared, possibly because of their outspoken nature.

be killed for good and all. The two activities are completely and utterly interrelated.'

Extremely handsome, slim, pale, highly-strung and intense, with a deceptive look of frailty, he brought to Malaya two significant aspects of character, formed in two of his different post-war appointments. In 1945 he had become Director of Military Government in the British Zone of Germany with wide powers over a country naked, on its back, starving, and the easiest of preys to the Communists waiting to take it over. To this threat Templer had offered a simple philosophy: 'You've got to offer people in trouble a big carrot,' and to the Germans he promised aid, dollars from the US to put them on their feet – if they would help him to get rid of Communism. They did, and now in Malaya, the carrot was: 'You can and should have independence if you help me to get rid of these Communists.'

After Germany. Templer had been appointed Director of Military Intelligence and this in its way had an equally fundamental bearing on his attitude to the war in Malaya, for he *thought* in terms of Intelligence and Special Branch. 'Malaya is an Intelligence war,' he said more than once. 'You can never beat Communism with troops alone.' He realized from the moment he arrived that the country needed a first-class Intelligence service with the widest possible powers. And this he could promise, for Templer now had overall responsibility for military operations, the police and civil administration – a post, in fact, analogous to that which the French government had given in vain to Marshal de Lattre de Tassigny as High Commissioner in Indo-China.

Above all, Templer realized that he was helping to shape a tremendous new era in Asia, that the old Empire concept was dead. Churchill's orders to him had been clear and enlightened: 'The policy of the British government is that Malaya should in due course become a self-governing nation.' Templer was thus able to proclaim to the world that the Communists and the hated 'Imperialists' were now fighting for exactly the same common goal: Independence for Malaya.

Templer never forgot that his basic role was to prepare the country for Independence, that the home front was as important as the jungle. Within two days of his arrival in Kuala Lumpur he sent for Guy Madoc, a brilliant, tall, blue-eyed member of the Intelligence hierarchy, one of the anonymous plotting brains. Madoc also happened to be an ornithologist, and the author of a standard work on Malayan birds.

Madoc, sure he would be dealing with 'the army complex', arrived warily with a dossier of carefully prepared notes. Almost as soon as he had been waved to a chair Templer leaned back, kicked open the bottom drawer of his desk and stuck his feet in it, a sure sign that the General was 'at ease'. Madoc waited for his instructions. There was only one at the first meeting.'I understand you're a bird watcher,' said Templer. 'I want you to get some unusual birds for the aviary at King's House. Send me the bill.'

The following day Templer convened a meeting of the local museum directors and told them to brighten up their museums. Better museums had, he felt, a bearing on the slogan he was to make famous: 'The battle for the hearts and minds of the people.'

The curious thing is that though Templer quickly achieved the image of a fearsome, short-tempered general who got things done by riding roughshod over opposition (which he did), he realized with much more subtlety than people gave him credit for that success would depend more on what he did *not* do than on making any startling changes. A great admirer of Gurney, whom he had never met, he made it clear from the outset that his job was not only to provide the effective tough command which he had been lacking, but to implement the plans he had inherited from Gurney and Briggs. Thus there were no major changes of policy that might have been expected from a dynamic general. As John Gullick put it: 'Templer himself likened his position to that of Montgomery before Alamein. His predecessors had learnt by their mistakes, it was up to him to apply those lessons.' Added to this was the lesson of West Germany, and his deep conviction that Malaya's independence would only succeed if the Malayan nation were united, if he could create a way of life for Malaya, 'not necessarily the British way, nor the American way; it must be the Malayan way of life.'

A start towards this life was made within a month of Templer's arrival, when the municipal elections were held in Kuala Lumpur. Their significance was not that any real power had passed to the Asians who were elected to the city council, for in truth they had very limited power, but that the elections created a racial alliance that was to have far-reaching effects and brought to the forefront a Malay who would one day be the leader of his independent country.

This was Tunku Abdul Rahman,* a handsome, soft-spoken man with a delightful sense of humour, a passion for the racecourse, who had taken twelve years in England to pass his bar finals, admitting cheerfully, 'I spent too much time at the races.' But he was, as Malcolm MacDonald, who had known him in London, observed, 'a man with a heart and a belief in his country – and a man who knew instinctively what was right and what was wrong.'·

No one had expected the Tunku ever to become a major political figure, but chance had placed him at the head of the United Malay National Organization (UMNO) after his predecessor had resigned. And then, with a shrewd political sense that few realized he possessed, the Tunku

---

* Tunku, which can be spelt in several ways, means prince.

quietly formed an Alliance with Tan Cheng-lok, the leader of the Malayan Chinese Association (MCA). By agreeing not to field candidates against each other, they won nine out of eleven seats on the Municipal council and formed the Alliance Party with the Tunku at the head. This was the moment when, as independence approached, Templer recognized him as the man with whom he, or his successor, would have to negotiate.

Templer now set about 'winning the hearts and minds of the people' in many different ways. He visited schools, hospitals, received delegations, while his wife worked eighteen hours a day starting woman's institutions, new Red Cross branches, community centres, so that for the first time Asian women could become involved in communal affairs; for until 1952, most had lived secluded lives – not from male pressures so much as from habit. All that was needed was a jolt from another woman – and Lady Templer provided it.

One of Templer's first thoughts was that the more the Chinese (some of whom tended to sit on the fence) were given responsibility, the more they would integrate into the community. What better way than to arm Chinese Home Guards in the struggle against Communism? Yet this had its dangers, so Templer sought the advice of one man who he knew would honestly answer whether his plan was feasible. It was a man of whom he once said, 'He has one of the clearest, most lucid brains I know.' That evening Templer sent a signal to Johore – and the next morning Bob Thompson flew to King's House.

Templer and Thompson got on famously. Templer liked the younger man's keen intelligence, his knowledge of the Chinese and the enthusiastic way in which he expounded on his theories for beating Communist guerrillas without escalating armed forces; and Thompson admired the older man who, however crotchety his public image, seemed determined to exert his whole energies to the winning of the peace as much as the winning of the war.

On that first meeting the two men walked alone in the gardens of King's House for nearly two hours. Thompson had quickly allayed Templer's doubts on arming the Chinese by agreeing that it was an excellent idea, but suggesting that it might be wise for Templer to let the MCA choose the first recruits.

After that, their talk roamed over many areas. One of Templer's pet schemes was for more schools to be built, but he was adamant that they must be staffed by properly trained local teachers. There were plenty of willing would-be teachers begging to be trained, and with the rubber booming because of the Korean war, there was money enough. But with a war on, there were no buildings available, and every skilled carpenter (now charging $40 a day) was occupied on war work. Then Thompson had an idea – just the kind of idea to appeal to Templer. He asked for permission to buy two big country mansions in England, and soon he was chartering aircraft and transporting six hundred Asians to England for a year's course.

Bob Thompson had another brainwave. He suggested to Templer that they should let the people – the ordinary, simple people – see just how the war was being conducted, for Thompson had noticed in Johore how the average tapper or clerk regarded the war as an indefinable phenomenon with which he had to live, but which was no real concern of his. He added one suggestion: that any conducted tour should include a brief appearance by either General or Lady Templer. The scheme was a magnificent success. Tappers, coolies, miners, secretaries, trishaw men were arranged in groups from time to time and taken on a three-day tour which included every possible aspect of the war machine, from the inside of an aircraft to a visit to an Operations HQ. Dressed in their Sunday best, the men and women – fetched and fed – ended the tour with tea on the lawn of King's House, with Lady Templer in attendance. The more sophisticated Malayans had their conducted tour too – and theirs invariably ended with a pep talk by the General.

Nothing seemed too big a problem for Templer to solve. Now he turned his attention to the police force, which was led by Arthur Young, a man for whom Templer had a high respect.

Young had responsibility for a command of over a quarter of a million men if the Home Guard and auxiliaries were included. But apart from numbers, everything else seemed to be lacking – organization, training and equipment. He quickly discovered the lack of necessary units and cohesion and the 'three separate camps with deep-seated animosities' among the gazetted officers. He was particularly worried by the animosity displayed by the old regulars towards the newly-arrived Palestinians, whose 'gendarmerie outlook and less refined behaviour was not tolerable by the "old Malayans" and set them apart.' The fact that many fine Palestinians had rightly been promoted to senior commands over the heads of local officers 'did nothing to add to their popularity'.

Templer immediately backed Young's request for 120 armoured cars, 250 scout cars, 600 armed personnel carriers. Young estimated that he would need two thousand vehicles, plus large numbers of tommy-guns and twelve-bore pump guns for jungle work. But what he also needed desperately were experienced officers to train his men.

Templer seconded a number of technically expert army majors. Some majors might have been dismayed at suddenly becoming 'policemen', but Templer introduced them to Young at King's House with the words: 'This is Colonel Young, your new commander. Serve him well - otherwise I'll send you all back to the War House.'

This was the start of Young's year – in which £30 million was spent on the Malayan police.*

It was also the start of a new phase in the war, one in which Templer and Young banished (in effect, anyway) one of the most popular words in the Malayan vocabulary, one which had been used by the British as often as by the Malays. That word was *Tidapah*. It means 'Never mind'.

By now more than 40,000 regular troops were engaged in Malaya – 25,000 from Britain (including navy and RAF personnel), 10,000 Gurkhas, five battalions of the Malay Regiment, two battalions of the King's African Rifles and one battalion of the Fiji Infantry Regiment; in addition there were some 60,000 full-time police and nearly 200,000 Home Guards. Yet nothing could prevent the hit-and-run tactics of a mobile guerrilla force, and in March an incident occurred which was to have a profound effect not only on the conduct of the war, but on General Templer himself and on his reputation. For some weeks CTs had stepped up their activities in the area of Tanjong Malim, a rubber-tapping town of 20,000 people straddling the main highway fifty-one miles north of Kuala Lumpur. Seven men of the Gordon Highlanders had been killed in an ambush and since the start of 1952 seven civilians and eight policemen had been murdered. As an added insult, CTs had cut the water pipeline between the town and its reservoir, in the jungle five times. On the night of March 24, CTs cut the line again, and for the sixth time a repair party went out to mend the pipe. It was 7.00 a.m. on Tuesday, March 25. The repair party was accompanied by a police jungle squad of fifteen, Mr W. H. Fourniss, the Executive Engineer of Public Works in the area, and Michael Codnor, the 32-year-old local Assistant District

* Twice the amount expended annually on London's Metropolitan police force.

Officer. Codnor had been born in Malaya and was recognized even by CTs as a devoted administrator. He also
happened to have achieved fame in World War Two by
escaping dramatically from a German prisoner of war
camp; his exploits had later been recounted in *The Wooden
Horse*, by Eric Williams.

The party followed the pipeline from the town into the
jungle hills behind. After two miles they walked into a
planned ambush by about forty CTs. As the first burst
killed Fourniss, Codnor was wounded and tried to crawl
into the jungle. He too was shot dead, together with ten
others, seven of them policemen. Eight other policemen
were grievously wounded. One man only escaped injury.
Then the CTs crept up to the dead and wounded and
made off with a Bren gun, several Stens, rifles and pistols.

Three days later Templer, burning with a cold fury,
descended on the township. He ordered 350 community
leaders to assemble in the hall of the local Sultans Idris
Training College. Leslie Hoffman of the *Straits Times*,*
who came to know Templer well, remembers 'the shivers
that went down my spine as I watched Templer speak with
a savage anger I wouldn't have believed possible.'

'It doesn't amuse me to punish innocent people,' Templer said through Malay, Chinese and Tamil translators,
'but many of you are not innocent. You have information
which you are too cowardly to give. You are all aware of
the savage outrage that took place hear here forty-eight
hours ago. It could only have taken place with the knowledge of certain of the local inhabitants. Of that I· am
certain.'

For an hour he lectured them, and when he announced
that a new administration, backed by more troops, would

---

* Hoffman later became Editor-in-Chief of the *Straits Times*. He is one
of the central characters in *Sinister Twilight*, the story of the Fall of
Singapore in 1942.

be installed, some of the stunned listeners near him nodded as though in agreement.

'Don't nod your heads,' shouted Templer. 'I haven't started yet.' He then announced his collective punishment for 'the crime of silence'. There would be a 22-hour-a-day curfew on the town; people would only be allowed to leave their homes between noon and 2.00 p.m. No one could leave the town; schools would be closed, buses would cease to run, the rice ration would be halved.

Templer, though angry, did realize that it was not easy for men threatened with brutal reprisals to give evidence, so now he arranged for a letter and question form to be delivered to the head of every household in Tanjong Malim. It was timed to arrive after a week of the curfew when the town was running down. Trishaw men, coolies, tappers were workless; the streets were deserted; even the local pawnbroker had run out of cash and could no longer help those trying to raise a few dollars on their paltry belongings.

Every form had to be returned whether it contained information or not, and in spectacular fashion Templer now proceeded to prove that no one but he would see the contents. British troops collected the first batch in sealed boxes which were taken to King's House by six local community leaders who watched Templer open every box personally and destroy the forms after making notes. Only then were the timid community leaders allowed to return to Tanjong Malim. 'Go back and tell them how their letters were brought straight to me,' said Templer.

Inevitably Templer's collective punishment produced a storm in Britain. *The Manchester Guardian* described it as 'odious' while *The Observer* thought it 'lamentable'. In the House of Lords Lord Listowel felt that 'collective punishment will turn many people into Communist sympathizers,' and Lord Stansgate, after likening it to the Black and Tan activities, remarked sarcastically, 'It's not a bad idea to

introduce an element of morality when you are trying to
govern a country.'

But Templer had no time to be concerned with bicker-
ing in Whitehall, for he had sent a second batch of question forms to Tanjong Malim under the same guarantee
of secrecy, and some of these were being returned with
important information – so much so that at 7.30 a.m. on
April 9, detectives knocked on a door in Tanjong Malim
and made the first of thirty-eight arrests. That day the
curfew was lifted, and this was followed by a new surge
of spirit which must have astonished even Templer – and
which certainly encouraged his belief that fear alone had
prevented many townspeople from giving information to
the police, and justified a form of punishment which he
admitted was unfair. within days, the guerrilla platoon
which had infested the area realized that its members had
been named, and split up. Before long 3,500 men in a
district with one of the worst records in the war volunteered for the Home Guard, though even they could not
have believed that for the remaining eight years of the war
Tanjong Malim would be one of the most peaceful areas
in the country.

With the success of Tanjong Malim behind him, Templer
was now firmly in control, and by one of those lucky
flukes which even great generals need to help them along,
Templer's first few months in office were marked by a
sharp drop in incidents. The luck lay in the fact that
though the public attributed this to the stern punishment
meted out at Tanjong Malim, it had little to do with this.
It was the direct result of the October 1951 Directive in
which Chin Peng had ordered CTs to switch from terror
tactics to 'legal' unrest. Of this directive Templer was as
yet unaware. He thus reaped the benefits of an improved
public image.

Since the drop in incidents *was* an established fact,

Templer's political antennae warned him that this was the moment to encourage all waverers to give information as they had done at Tanjong Malim. He did this by offering rewards for information so staggering that the eyes of tappers goggled at the tremendous sums involved. Knowing that the amounts must stun public imagination, Templer announced that from May 1, 1952, Chin Peng would be worth $250,000 alive, half of that amount dead. (All rewards were halved if the CTs were dead, for it was obviously important to question men.) Any member of the Politburo was worth $200,000 alive, with the amounts decreasing to $120,000 for regional committee secretaries, and so on, down to $4,000 for CTs with branch committee rank and $2,500 for those of inferior status.

Templer had acted on the advice of the Chinese. C.C. Too of Psychological Warfare and Lam Swee had for long insisted that big money was the simplest way to tempt informers to talk.

Bob Thompson, who had by now been transferred to Templer's Planning Staff, also had a hand in this, for it was Thompson who realized that the reward announcement must be phrased in such a fashion that they would appeal particularly to the thousands of innocent relatives of prominent CTs; people who might despise Communism (particularly from the safety of their New Villages) but who had some tenuous links with husbands or brothers in arms. For them there was a significant phrase in the announcement. Bringing CTs in alive included 'the positive arranging with the authorities of the surrender of a known terrorist now in the jungle'.

The results were immediate. In Perak thirteen CTs surrendered after a deputy-commander of the 5th Regiment and his wife had walked into the small police station at Sungei Rotan, in the Sitiawan area. They handed over their arms and surrendered. The man, whose wife was expecting a baby, confessed, 'We've wanted to surrender for a long time, but we hesitated because we'd been told we would be put to death.' He was so astonished at his treatment that he returned to the jungle and brought out eleven more CTs – for which he and his wife shared a reward of $12,875.

There were some ready to criticize a scheme that could hardly be said to rest on sound moral principles, but Templer brushed these aside, for he knew that he had the backing of the British government.

Templer was not, of course, always successful, and he faced one serious problem that took some time to resolve: this was the running sore of Malaya's northern frontier with Thailand. The Thai police might have been friendly on the surface, but no one could deny that hungry, tired CTs could find a safe haven whenever they wished, simply by crossing the frontier into Thailand. The border was ill-defined, sometimes following the Golok river, more often a valley or mountain range. In the wildest part of this uninhabited terrain there were no markings, no boundary fences, no police, no customs areas. At one moment a CT was a hunted man in Malaya. The next step he was a free man in a country which did not outlaw Communism.

By the spring of 1952 the CT leaders had established a number of base camps in the Thai jungle just north of Perlis. Here they trained recruits, refitted seasoned men, openly ran a rest camp within a few miles of impotent British troops. Equally important, CT leaders were able to organize food supplies, largely from the four million Chinese living in Thailand, some of whom must have been sympathetically inclined armchair warriors.

The British vice-consul at Singora in Southern Thailand, Mr R. W. Harper, admitted frankly* that Malayan CTs were smuggling arms across the frontier. He was also in no doubt that CTs were 'refitting and retraining'.

* In a broadcast on Radio Malaya on April 20, 1952.

The Commander of the Thai police at that time was a colourful character named General Phao, noted for his resplendent uniforms, and Templer arranged for him and Arthur Young to exchange visits and find a formula for joint patrol of the border. Phao seemed polite enough and not obstructive, but Young had the feeling that the Thai general could not spare the time to interest himself in the problem. No doubt it was a minor item on the Thai police agenda. But it is also possible that General Phao was far more interested in Bangkok's night life than in such trifles as border disputes; for the scintillating after-dark life of Bangkok at this time revolved round a magnificent, exclusive, expensive nightclub called 'Chez Eve'. It was coining a fortune for its owner – who happened to be General Phao.

Templer might have been powerless to influence the policies of the Thai police, but he now turned his mind to one potential war-winning machine which had so far been neglected. This was the mysterious cloak-and-dagger organization, peopled by unnamed shadows, known as Special Branch.

15 THE FEMALES OF THE SPECIES

No one can really single out one particular branch of the Security Forces or Government and say, 'These were the people who showed the world how Communist guerrilla warfare can be beaten.' Should that accolade be reserved for men in the hierarchy like Templer and Bob Thompson, without whose liberal thinking the war could never have been won? Or for the jungle-bashing troops, the courageous planters, the police? Without any of these the war might have been lost, but these were people who could be seen and known. Behind them, in conditions of the most stringent secrecy, a dedicated band of anonymous men and women played perhaps the single most effective role in eventual victory. This was Special Branch.

No one knew their names or faces. In its simplest form the all-powerful Special Branch can be defined as the internal security department dealing with internal subversion, internal revolution and counter-espionage. It is a little like the British MI5, and bears some similarity to the CIA, though without its wide powers, and never setting up external spy networks. Until 1952 the Special Branch in Malaya was part of the CID. Templer and Thompson decided that it could do better work if it were left to its own devices – devices being a carefully-chosen word – and split it from the CID, though for the purposes of administration it remained part of the Police Department. In truth it was answerable to nobody, and nobody knew what it was doing.

Thompson had spent much of the war in cloak and dagger operations, and he felt strongly that 'in an insurgency the army is one of the main consumers of intelligence, but it should not be a collector except in so far as its units obtain tactical intelligence through their operations. If a Special Branch intelligence organization is established throughout the country the army can hook into it at any point where its units are stationed.'

The head of Special Branch, with his unlimited powers, and his anonymity, was in many ways the single most powerful man in Malaya after Templer – not in policy-making, but in initiating action, particularly secret action. Special Branch salaries and expenses were quietly paid by the Malayan government. Small groups of British milⁱ...y officers attached to it for the Emergency received their salaries from the British army. To this day it is not possible to reveal the total strength of its personnel, but Templer – who had served in Intelligence – regarded its activities as so vital to victory that he asked Desmond Palmer, one of its chiefs, to come and see him privately and report in confidence at least once a month.

'No, sir. if you'll excuse me,' said Palmer modestly but firmly. 'I don't think it would be a good idea for me to be seen around King's House.'

'Right!' snapped Templer. 'I'll come to see you.' And he did regularly – alone and at a secret rendezvous near Special Branch headquarters, a 'Special Centre' hidden behind a rubber plantation on the outskirts of Kuala Lumpur. Here, covering ten acres and surrounded by a ten-foot barbed wire fence were bugged cells, two-way mirrors, a laboratory for processing documents, a machine shop for work on secret devices, and a nation-wide dossier of CTs which was being completed patiently over the years.

In one section Special Branch radio experts were quietly working on scores of ancient battery sets which had been quietly bought up. Each one was taken to pieces, re-made (using only old wire connections and dirtying the solder as anything new would have aroused suspicion), after which each set was quietly 'leaked' to shops known to sympathize with CTs. Special Branch could be sure that sooner or later such a set would reach the jungle – and when it did, when the CT tuned into Peking or Radio Malaya, the set emitted a bleep-bleep homing signal that could not be heard in a jungle camp, but gave precise directions to the nearest monitoring team.

Intercepted messages at this time played a particularly important role in Special Branch activities, for it was along the CT courier network set up by the Chinese girl Lee Meng that all messages to and from Chin Peng, or between local units and regimental commanders, had to pass. The courier system was so secret that no jungle postman knew more than two 'post offices', so that as soon as one link was discovered, work had to start all over again to find the next. It was a long, painstaking job, but fortunately Special

Branch had several surrendered CT couriers on its secret payroll who, as double agents, would carry on normally in the jungle, but on the way from A to B would lend the documents to Special Branch, who would photograph them before the CT returned to his normal duties.

This procedure was not as simple as it sounds, for all messages were in code and were concealed – sometimes in fruit, a tube of toothpaste, sometimes in an innocuous-looking cigarette – and every message had to be returned looking as though it had not been tampered with – a particularly difficult task when some CTs started using invisible ink. Special Branch were able to make this visible, but this served no purpose for the CTs would know they were discovered; fortunately Special Branch scientists discovered a way of making it invisible again.

Messages had to be opened (and closed) with meticulous care, for the Special Branch knew that when they were returned to the jungle, every fold, every marking, even the gum, could have a special meaning to those eventually receiving them. A special set of tools was devised that would leave no marks when messages were opened – bamboo knives, probes, rollers of different sizes, so that documents could be opened while the gum was put on one side and used to reseal them.

Urgency was the keynote with every message, and rarely could the experts be allowed more than an hour before returning a document. Sometimes Special Branch had to exercise its all-embracing powers - as when one trusted double agent went into a humble Chinese hotel near the Coliseum Bar in Kuala Lumpur to pick up a message. Special Branch waited at a nearby rendezvous, but the CT did not come out of the hotel. The officer felt he had probably been detained by nothing more sinister than a 'comrade' eager for a chat, yet time was pressing and someone had to get the man out of the hotel. It was done – by a simple expedient. One officer nipped round to the

Coliseum and phoned headquarters, who sent down a large packet of opium which was planted in the hotel lobby – after which the regular police conveniently raided the hotel, discovered the drug, questioned several guests and arrested the double agent and spirited him away.

This was run-of-the mill cloak and dagger stuff, but so far Special Branch had been unable to discover who was the head of the courier system or where he was operating. Obviously someone was masterminding the courier traffic between the northern and southern areas; someone who must have known the locations of many jungle posts; someone running a kind of sorting office. If this head office could be cracked, then Chin Peng's entire courier network would crumble, and he would have to start a new one.

Special Branch could not possibly have known that this was Chin Peng's choice, Lee Meng, nor could they have the faintest inkling that she was working in Ipoh, that she was the virtual boss of the Communist courier network. Not until early in 1952 did they receive the first clue – a clue to a long, long trail lasting many months and involving Lee Meng and an equally beautiful Chinese woman detective.

A bleep signal from a planted radio gave Special Branch the first clue; it led to a jungle camp, where, as so often happened, the birds had flown. But one CT had left a haversack behind, and in it were several light spools of thin paper, not unlike toilet paper. They had been folded carefully, and a line had been drawn up the side and over the top – looking 'rather like the lines on the end of a Swiss Roll', according to one detective. Each roll had been sealed with a curious jungle gum. In one of them was the name of a woman courier operating in Singapore – not, of course, Lee Meng. The head of Special Branch decided that this was a job for a woman and in February 1952 sent for Detective-Inspector Irene Lee.

It would be hard to imagine anyone less like a policewoman. Irene Lee was a delightful Chinese girl in her early twenties, full of life, and in fact had only joined the force early in the war after her policeman husband had been murdered by CTs. She also happened to have the reputation of being the 'fastest draw in the East'. Because her breasts were small, she could not wear a holster under her arm, so Special Branch had devised a special holster for a flat Beretta automatic which lay over her left breast. (The right breast was padded.) Just below her left shoulder, her black Chinese samfoo contained a slit pocket with press studs. She could whip the pocket open and draw faster than any man using a holster.

Irene was also a brilliant lock-picker, an expert with a mini-camera, an accomplished thief (in the course of duty) with an unerring instinct for discovering hidden documents. She also had a delicious sense of humour. On one occasion when an officious army major boasted that no CTs could enter his well-guarded camp, Irene smuggled arms into the camp, hid them, then told the red-faced major where he could find them.

Irene immediately went to Singapore with Special Branch officers. For three weeks they kept watch – particularly when the woman went shopping at Robinson's, the big store in Raffles Place. Several times Irene saw her meet another woman there and skilfully switch identical shopping-bags.

Irene shadowed her into the air-conditioned Robinson's around five o'clock one evening, watched her as she met the other woman. The two carried identical flowered plastic bags, stood close to each other at the beauty counter, and when one dropped her bag the other smilingly helped her – and switched bags. Not a word was spoken as the woman with the message calmly walked out into Raffles Place. Outside, Irene's male colleagues were waiting in a Plymouth car, the engine ticking over. Irene followed the woman on foot, then by trishaw. In Stamford Road, by the YMCA tennis courts, the woman got out and started walking. So did Irene. Suddenly the Plymouth drew abreast. Irene stuck her gun in the woman's back and before the startled passers-by could scream, the woman was bundled into the Plymouth which roared off to a house on the outskirts of Singapore. Late that night they found the message, hidden in a sealed tin of Johnson's Baby Powder. The bottom had been removed, then put back (which meant that a detective had to persuade an irate shopkeeper to open up and sell him another tin so the message could be replaced).

The woman CT was finally persuaded to return to the jungle with the message. Money was promised (and was in fact banked for her), and when the woman asked, 'But how can you trust me?' she was photographed with two smiling policemen and told, 'If you don't behave, 50,000 leaflets with this photo will be scattered in your jungle area.'

The information took Irene only one stage further along the courier line, to Yong Peng in Johore, where another woman courier was living. Posing as a CT courier, Irene went to see her. She reached the house, made herself known to the woman CT inside and was accepted. Finally she persuaded the woman to come out for a meal 'to celebrate'.

'Celebrate what?' asked the CT. Irene Lee always believed that the more exciting the 'cover', the more readily it was believed. A policeman had been killed in an ambush not far from Yong Peng three days previously, and Irene modestly answered, 'I led the ambush and I fired the shot.'

An ancient taxi happened to be cruising by (conveniently manned by a Special Branch officer) and Irene's newfound friend talked gaily. Irene particularly remembered her comment, 'I've been told not to talk to anyone, but taxi-drivers are usually with us.'

Four hours later a very frightened woman CT had

'surrendered', but before being interrogated she had an unnerving experience. Knowing that women were usually more difficult to crack than men – they were often emotionally involved whereas men were intellectually attracted – Irene decided that a little 'softening up' would do no harm. After dinner inside the Special Centre at Kuala Lumpur, the CT was taken to a small room at the end of a long corridor. As the door was opened, bright naked bulbs, mirrors, strange-looking chairs made her blink and hesitate. Two women in white overalls heightened her dread (as she later admitted to Irene) that she had entered some strange torture chamber.

'Don't worry.' Irene guided her to a chair – where to the girl's astonishment one woman started waving her hair while the other rubbed pumice stone on her calloused, cracked fingers and then gave her a manicure ending with pink polish.

She became a valuable double agent, though it took some time, for like many CTs she had undergone a psychological trauma in surrendering more difficult in many ways than when she had joined the Party. She had to justify her reasons for abandoning the God who had failed her. As she put it to Irene, 'I've made great sacrifices, but they've let me down.' Then she added, with unintended irony, a sentence used by women the world over, if in a different context: 'I've wasted the best years of my life.'

Soon she was begging to be allowed to work with Irene, whatever the risks, doubtless because the lingering effects of Communist indoctrination impelled her to join an equally powerful organization in order to retrieve the comfortable sense of 'belonging'. What more suitable organization could there be than the police? Before long, she had led Irene one more step towards Ipoh. It was the name of a tapper on a rubber estate near Jerantut, and for several weeks Irene worked as a humble tapper.

The estate was called Jenderak. Though of course she never met 'Puck' Puckridge the planter, she often saw him. He seemed perfectly happy even though no roads led to the estate, and no visitors ever arrived. Irene probably found the 'tuan' a little eccentric when he blew his home-made bugle every night as the Union Jack was hauled down, but Irene was used to eccentrics.

Penderak was a 'comfortable' estate, with several hundred tappers, a small co-operative shop, football teams to play on the padang behind the factory where the latex was processed. Every morning Irene was in the rubber by six o'clock, making her swift, downward curves in the mottled bark, and the last tree was usually dry by 11.30. Then she started her real day's work – shadowing the spare-time activities of a fellow tapper called Chen Lee, known to be a Min Yuen member. Irene felt that to begin with she should watch him, but take no action until she had solid proof of his activities. Everything depended on this man – on his co-operation, not his death – for Special Branch chiefs were by now convinced that they were only separated from the head of the courier service by one or two contacts. But patience was vital – for without this man at Jenderak they could not find the next address along the line.

So Irene tapped – and waited; and became for several weeks part of the large 'family' of the Puckridges – for the Puckridges treated their isolated labour force as a family, and Mollie was a daily visitor at the crèche, while the tuan regularly inspected the 'lines' – rows of two-roomed shacks where the food was cooked and eaten in one room and the entire family slept in the next. Puckridge was always ready to order a leaking roof to be repaired. He inspected the milky liquid at the co-operative toddy shop; he watched the football games.

Irene soon found evidence that Chen Lee was a courier and was smuggling food out to dumps on the jungle fringe.

When the opportunity came, they met 'by chance' and after that often tapped together in the same area. As soon as Irene was sure the man was deeply implicated she threw up her job, made her way to Temerloh, and late one night tapped on the window of Yeop Mahidin's house, Special Branch having warned him to expect a 'visitor'. Under the shadow of his big flame tree Yeop saw a girl and asked the 'tapper' in. She refused, said she had been too afraid to use a local telephone, but gave Yeop a phone number in Kuala Lumpur, and asked if he would relay a message for her. She would take the bus to Mentakab (a few miles west of Temerloh) and she wanted a taxi to pick her up there the following afternoon. She would, she said, recognize the cab.

After that it was easy. An old taxi arrived, the driver took her up as near to Jenderak as possible, and when Chen Lee made one of his regular visits to the jungle fringe, he was picked up on a lonely road where the chances of observation were slight. In the back was Irene, a past-master in the art of 'soft' interrogation.

Sitting in the inky blackness, she gently spelled out every detail of Chen Lee's recent Min Yuen activities. 'Last week you filled your bicycle pump with rice,' she said. 'Three days before that you bought ten dollars' worth of drugs and hid them in the jungle.'

Chen Lee, who must have been sweating with fear, hotly denied everything as the damning evidence piled up. He had never smuggled food, he had never bought any drugs.

'Oh yes you have,' said Irene, opening her bag. 'Here they are. We dug them up after you'd buried them.'

These were the master tactics in breaking down resistance on the part of Chen Lee. For now he was trapped. If the CTs had the faintest idea that he was suspect, they would cut his throat. If he denied everything and carried on he would be caught red-handed and arrested. In a panic he asked to be taken into protective custody.

'Not a chance,' said Irene. 'We know that on one occasion you bought three bullets – and that means the death sentence if you're arrested.'

Now there was only one way out, and Chen Lee had to take it – as Irene knew he would. He admitted everything (though insisting that he had been coerced), and promised to help Irene. That was all she wanted – for him to carry on as if nothing had happened and report all information he could to her; and above all, tell her the name of the next link along the courier chain. It was a bookshop in Batu Road, one of the busiest shopping streets in the Federal capital of Kuala Lumpur.

The trail was now getting very 'hot', and indeed Special Branch believed (wrongly, as it turned out) that this might be the *end* of the trail. Breaking into the shop posed one of the trickiest operations of the war and it involved detailed planning. The bookstore in Batu Road was not a shophouse, so it was locked up and empty on holidays and Sundays. Somehow it had to be entered, searched and vacated without the owner's suspicions being aroused. It had no rear entrance and because it was in such a busy street Special Branch had to make their plans look so legitimate that no prying CT could find fault with them. For above all else, it was vital that no suspicions should be aroused *after* the raid had taken place, or contacts along the line would be warned – and would vanish.

With these thoughts in mind Special Branch, using a respectable alias, formed an import-export company which bought a small pineapple estate and cannery in Johore. The sale was reported in the local Press. The directors – all bonafide on the surface – then bought a large second-hand six-wheeler lorry which was transferred legally to the company with the correct papers. One Saturday the lorry set off from Johore for Penang, with a full load of cases of tinned pineapple for shipment to Britain.

A driver and a clerk – both fully-trained detectives – occupied the front of the lorry which would take a day to reach Kuala Lumpur on its way north. Thus it would pass through the Federal capital on a Sunday. Even if the Min Yuen were watching the empty shop, this could not possibly arouse suspicion, for not only had the groundwork been thoroughly prepared, but the pineapples were destined to be loaded on a ship sailing from Penang on the Monday, so the lorry's time-table fitted in perfectly.

By arrangement the lorry had a back wheel puncture in Batu Road – almost opposite the bookshop, which was closed, though Special Branch had noticed several men in relays lolling around the shop on holidays, and were sure they were Min Yuen spies. Now these men came in useful in a way that must have allayed any latent suspicion. Owing to the weight of the pineapple cases, the lorry's rear wheel could not be jacked up, and so, stressing the urgency as the ship was leaving the following day – and waving his papers to prove it – the driver offered handsome payment to the loiterers if they would help to unload the cases. They had to help, for they must have known that otherwise they could have been suspect. A couple of Malay policemen joined in. The cases could not be dumped in the road because of the traffic so they were piled high on the pavement, many up against the bookshop windows.

Everybody buckled down to the job. The driver sent a boy for some bottles of Tiger beer after he and his assistant had unloaded one particularly heavy case – and placed it carefully, for crouched inside in the stifling heat was Irene Lee, one of the finest lock-pickers in the force. While the wheel was being changed, she worked through a trapdoor in her packing case, picked the front door lock, entered the shop, searched it, made photocopies – and was back again in her packing case before the perspiring men had started reloading the lorry.

It was in the shophouse that Irene found the two final clues to the courier network for which Special Branch had been searching for so long. Now they knew two vital points: the centre of the CT network was not in Kuala Lumpur as they had supposed, but in Ipoh. And it was run by a girl.*

The FMS Bar in Ipoh, which had been run by the same family for three generations, was unlike any other in Malaya. Not far from the station, a firm favourite with the planters and miners, it had the swing doors of a Western movie, an L-shaped bar with a big fridge behind it, a Victorian pendulum clock on the wall, and an abacus rattling at one end of the bar. At the far end of the room three curtained cubicles awaited those who wanted dinner.

Every night it was crowded – but on this particular night in the last week of July 1952 it was more crowded than usual, for six plain clothes Special Branch officers, including Irene Lee, were waiting for zero hour – at 8.00 p.m. They had an 'appointment' in a small Chinese house two blocks away. Now they were waiting for the local police superintendent, and when he arrived the Special Branch chief explained that they were going to interview a girl and if, as they expected, it would be necessary to arrest her, the Ipoh police would take over. It was not part of Special Branch's philosophy to be in any picture.

At last the trail had reached Lee Meng, the ex-schoolteacher, now twenty-four, and Chin Peng's personal choice as a top Communist courier. It was the result of

* The thoroughness of this plan was justified; when the pineapples (which were later sold in Britain) were loaded at Penang the following day, the lorry driver was approached in Penang harbour by a 'dock labourer' who was obviously a CT and knew about the previous day's breakdown. He was checking the story right to the end.

months of work, but none who were there that night could have imagined that Lee Meng would shortly become a pawn in a Cold War barter offer between Russia and Britain, and that for a reason totally unconnected with the fighting, Malaya would become front page news the world over.

When Irene knocked on the door it was opened by a young and pretty girl. She was alone. She worked, she said, on a tin mine, and she was certainly dressed for the part. Two detectives sidled into the room, closed the door and explained who they were. The questioning was gentle and it took a long time, for Special Branch believed in making a suspect feel the police didn't really have enough evidence to make an arrest as this encouraged a relaxation of control. So for two hours the questioning continued – questions, apparently innocuous, about the girl's parents, where she had been educated, where she bought her clothes, her boy-friends and so on.

Confidently Lee Meng produced her identity card, which, of course, bore another name, and, without apparently reading it, Irene saw that it had been issued in Ipoh in early 1949. Casually she asked the girl how long she had been in Ipoh. Just over two years, said Lee Meng. Before that she had been in Singapore.

The chief of Special Branch saw Irene Lee stiffen slightly. 'Something doesn't add up in her answers,' she whispered. 'She can't have been in two places at once.'

The police started to turn on the pressure. The questions became tougher as perfunctory queries gave way to a kind of third degree. Lee Meng was given no time to think up answers. How long had she lived in Singapore. Who had she lived with? Had she worked? For whom? As the girl started to falter in her answers, Irene shot out the question, 'You say you lived at the same address in Singapore for at least two years – what was the name of the shop where you bought your food?' Lee Meng couldn't remember. 'All right then – what was your nearest coffee shop called?' As Lee Meng began to lose control, to fumble for an answer, Special Branch, still not absolutely certain this was Lee Meng, started 'to take the room apart'. Finally, in an old Chinese desk against the back wall of the blue-painted room – the desk Chin Peng had told her to buy – Irene found a false drawer. It was stuffed with Communist documents awaiting dispatch by jungle post. And there was ample proof that the girl was indeed Lee Meng, who Special Branch were convinced, 'had done murder herself and had plotted and schemed other murders'.

Special Branch quickly vanished and the Ipoh police made a formal arrest. Lee Meng who had a price of $100,000 on her head, was taken to Taiping prison to await trial at Ipoh Assizes on August 29th, 1952.

Special Branch did not want Lee Meng's duties as courier mentioned in court, for they still hoped that Chin Peng might believe she had been arrested purely by chance. They wanted to guard the usefulness of the other CTs along the route, so when Lee Meng was brought to trial at Ipoh Assizes she was charged with having possessed a hand-grenade, for which the mandatory penalty was death. The charge was a curious one for there was no suggestion that she had had a grenade when arrested, but it was alleged that she had had one when in the jungle; no mention was made of any other activities. Because the local people were not considered responsible enough or sufficiently literate to supply juries, she was tried by the antiquated 'assessor system', under which the trial was heard before a judge aided by two assessors who would, in place of a jury, arrive at a verdict after hearing the evidence. There was, however, one peculiar anomaly, for whereas no British judge can reverse the decision of a jury, he was able under the Emergency Regulations to order a retrial if he did not agree with his assessors.

Dressed in blue slacks with a green and white checked blouse, Lee Meng faced a British judge, Mr Justice Thompson.* Both assessors were Asians – an Indian and a Chinese. Though the prosecution admitted Lee Meng had not been carrying a grenade when arrested, they insisted that she had had one between 1948 and 1951 in Ipoh. Lee Meng's defence was that in 1948 she had gone to live with her sister in Singapore and had remained there until 1950. She denied she had ever lived in the jungle. Photographs were produced showing her in CT uniform, carrying a rifle and grenade, but Lee Meng said the photographs were not of her. Nine surrendered CTs identified Lee Meng as a jungle leader. Lee Meng's defence lawyers said the men were committing perjury in the hope of receiving free pardons. In brief, Lee Meng's defence was a denial of everything.

To the horror of Special Branch men discreetly watching from the public gallery, the Indian and Chinese assessors found Lee Meng not guilty. Mr Justice Thompson, however, thought otherwise. 'How as reasonable men they came to that opinion I have no means of knowing,' he commented. 'I disagree with their opinions and order a retrial.'

Ten days later Lee Meng was retried before one Asian assessor and one European. After three days the Asian found Lee Meng not guilty, the European found her guilty. A different judge, Mr Justice Pretheroe, agreed with the European and sentenced her to death in a court-room drama that caught world attention, not so much because a pretty girl was on trial for her life, but because the two trials seemed to indicate a flaw in justice. Had Lee Meng by chance been caught a hundred miles away in Penang (or in Singapore or Malacca) she would have been tried

* Later to become Malaysia's first Lord President.

by a jury, and there, even if the judge had disagreed with their verdict, he would have had to respect it. (This had happened in Malacca where a judge disagreed violently with the jury's 'Not guilty' verdict against a well-known CT, but none the less had to acquit him.)

Lee Meng's appeal to the Malayan High Court was dismissed, but her lawyers lodged an appeal to the Judicial Committee of the Privy Council in London and Lee Meng returned to Taiping jail to wait until the case reached Downing Street.

Nine thousand miles away from Malaya, where the rainy season had just ended, newspaper boys were turning up their coat collars against the fog and crying the result of the FA Cup draw, when a Chinese barrister, Mrs P. G. Lim Lee, walked into No. 9 Downing Street. Mrs Lee, together with British barrister Dingle Foot, were playing out the second act in the drama of Lee Meng; it was on February 14, 1953, that the Judicial Committee of the Privy Council heard Lee Meng's appeal. Lords Porter, Asquith and Tucker were seated behind hillocks of law books as Foot and Mrs Lee urged their case; but despite more than two hours of impassioned pleas, the attempts to get the case re-opened failed.

Almost immediately a petition for mercy was addressed to the Sultan of Perak. Hundreds signed it – including fifty members of Parliament; but this was nothing to what happened a few days later, for on February 19 the Hungarian government offered to release a Briton, Edgar Sanders, who was serving thirteen years in Budapest for alleged spying, in exchange for Lee Meng.*

---

* Sanders, a 48-year-old British businessman, had been sentenced in 1950 as an alleged 'saboteur and spy'. He worked for the US Telegraph Company in Budapest, and his American chief, Robert Vogeler, was sentenced to fifteen years, but the US government had obtained Vogeler's release in 1951.

The Cabinet was divided. Eden was in favour of the exchange, but Churchill told the Commons, 'There is no question of bartering a human life or deflecting the course of justice or mercy in Malaya for the sake of securing the release of a British subject unjustly imprisoned in Hungary.'

Churchill's reference to 'the course of justice or mercy' was interpreted as meaning that he would not decide on a course of action until the result of the clemency petitions to the Sultan became known, but meanwhile the public clamour to exchange Sanders for Lee Meng grew. Thousands of names were added to the petition already in the Sultan's hands, and it would seem that Churchill and Eden were privately in favour of an eventual exchange. Mrs Winifred Sanders, the wife of the imprisoned Briton, cabled Churchill personally, 'Please do all possible to release my husband, father of my three girls.' For Mrs Sanders, the Hungarian exchange plan was the first indication that her husband was still alive, and as she said with some logic, 'I want my husband back as any woman would and the Communists obviously want the girl. Surely there can be no reason why such an exchange should not be offered.'

The emotional clamour, however, clouded one important issue. All the pleas for mercy or exchange ignored the question of whether or not Lee Meng was a brutal murderess. True, the retrial had left an uneasy feeling that justice had stumbled in Malaya, but so far as Lee Meng's guilt was concerned, it was conveniently forgotten in the hysteria that she had elected not to give evidence at her trial. She said she had been living in Singapore, but she called no witnesses to support her story, no shopkeeper, no neighbour who might have been expected to have met her. These were points entirely disregarded by her champions in London. Nor did they mention that after her conviction, Lee Meng, speaking from the dock, called the

CTs who had given evidence against her 'dead surrendered devils'. It was a curious phrase for an innocent woman to use.

In any event, the petition succeeded. On March 9 the Sultan, on the advice of the Council (and after two hours of deliberations) commuted the death sentence to penal servitude for life. The world-wide publicity no doubt helped to spare Lee Meng's life, for five other women CTs whose cases had not attracted any attention had already been executed.

The way was open for the Hungarian exchange; but now Churchill decided against it, after receiving from Special Branch in Kuala Lumpur a dossier showing just how important a CT Lee Meng had been. Her mother had been banished for Communist activities; Lee Meng was a member of the Perak State Committee – certainly one of the top twenty Communists in Malaya. There could be no doubt, insisted Special Branch, that to let Lee Meng go free would risk an upsurge of terrorism throughout Malaya. The Communists would see such action as evidence of weakness. In the Commons Churchill was pressed to arrange the exchange, but, backed by this new information, announced that, 'The government after earnest consideration have decided that they cannot entertain the proposals made by the Hungarian government.' Despite cries of 'Shame!' and persistent questioning by the Opposition, Churchill refused to be drawn into argument. As the *Daily Telegraph* commented in agreeing with Churchill: 'Only a heart of stone could feel no sympathy for Mr Sanders's fate or for his wife's anguished appeals,' but added: 'The real issue is this. Many worthy Britons still live behind the Iron Curtain. If we agreed to the Hungarian proposal, the precarious liberty of these people would see endless profit in imprisoning them ... until such time as they could be turned to account.'*

So the file on Lee Meng – the girl whom Special Branch had been trailing since the day the courier was abducted in Singapore – was finally closed.

16 THE NEW CITIZENS

As the drama of Lee Meng was being played out – but before its climax in London – the tide was already turning in Malaya. During the first six months of 1952, the monthly average of CT incidents had fallen to 428, as against 507 in the previous year. Attacks against estates and mines dropped from 138 in February to 73 in July. Throughout the country one could sense that the atmosphere had changed dramatically. There might be dangers ahead, but to the average planter and miner it was now just a question of time before final victory, while to the Malays and Chinese anxiety and frustration were giving way to hope. To the squatters in their New Villages a new life had opened, backed by Templer's pragmatic optimism about the future of Malaya as an independent nation and the promise of almost immediate citizenship to hundreds of thousands of Chinese.

Templer's priorities had as much to do with this heady feeling as the reduced number of incidents, for he never forgot that this was a civilians' war and was showing the greatest precipience in the field of politics; he had not only galvanized a lumbering administration, but he had such charm and shrewdness that he quickly improved relations between the government and the Malay Sultans. And it was Templer who, after the Kuala Lumpur municipal elections, perceived the significance of Tunku Abdul

---

* Sanders was released in August, 1953, after serving less than four years of his sentence.

Rahman's victory – that this was the man to watch, to cultivate. As John Gullick wrote: 'Nothing in Templer's professional career as a soldier was likely to make him a more far-sighted and liberal colonial governor than the professionals. He was the man who, so it was said, had sacked Adenauer from his Burgomastership in liberated Germany. Yet in Malaya he avoided the typical pitfalls of British colonial policy, i.e., moving too slowly and backing a loser in the independence stakes.'

Templer now turned his mind to one problem very close to his heart: a new citizenship code for the hundreds of thousands of Chinese to whom Malaya was home, and who had contributed so much to the wealth of the country. Templer saw this as the single most significant multi-racial step on the way to independence.

The groundwork had been well prepared, particularly by Malcolm MacDonald, who had at the beginning of the war formed the unofficial Communities Liaison Committee, where leaders of the different races had met monthly through all the years of strife in an effort to thrash out political and racial programmes acceptable to all. At times both Malays and Chinese threatened to walk out on each other, yet in the end they each made concessions. Finally they found a formula for citizenship; it would be granted automatically to men and women of immigrant origin who had been born in Malaya, and to the children of *one* parent who had been born in the country.

By now the Tunku enthusiastically shared Templer's hopes. So, naturally, did the Chinese. In the end, however, this was one decision which would rest with the Sultans. Even after the citizenship code was agreed to by all the political parties, and then had the approval of the Legislature, it would have to be put before the Sultans who in the summer of 1952 held their annual 'Rulers' Conference' in Kuala Lumpur. Of course the British had the power to bulldoze any measure past any opposition, but

Thompson suggested to Templer with some firmness that, for the sake of future relations, this was one decision which must not be forced on the Sultans, for as he put it, 'After all, this is their country and they are the sovereigns.'

In fact, after lobbying by Templer, the Sultans agreed readily – for they were astute enough to realize that without a harmonious multi-racial society, Malaya might have to wait years for independence. And so from midnight on September 14, 1952, 1,200,000 Chinese – sixty per cent of the Chinese in Malaya – and 180,000 Indians became Malayan citizens. Many others were able to apply for citizenship under the new law which had substantially relaxed the conditions. The next morning long queues formed outside government offices in all major towns to bring proof of their eligibility, and then to register.

In Kuala Lumpur the queues goggled at an extraordinary sight outside the registration office. A car drew up and out of it stepped a tall dark-haired Englishwoman, with an amah and two small children, a boy and a girl. Their names were Master and Miss Thompson. Bob's wife Merryn had been born in Malaya where her father, Sir Alec Newboult, had been Chief Secretary. As the children of one parent born in Malaya the Thompson toddlers automatically became the country's first white Malayan citizens.

Templer now turned his attention to a problem which had for long thwarted the security forces: the Aborigines. Thousands of Abos in deep jungle were being coerced by CTs to grow food and act as guides and spies. These simple people were not necessarily pro-Communist, but they were shy of *every* stranger who stumbled on their lonely camps, and because of this were easy prey to the Communists.

The government had earlier brought some thousands out of the jungle into areas nearer towns in an effort to deprive CTs of their help, but the experiment had proved a dismal failure. Unused to civilization, the Abos contracted diseases like measles, normally shrugged off by towns-people, but from which Abos could die. Others literally pined away, so it was decided to send them back to the jungle, where it was hoped that British patrols could keep in contact.

Templer now decided that to do this effectively he needed a strategically placed string of jungle forts in the Abos' tribal and hunting grounds, particularly as Chin Peng after his October 1951 Directive had built several large rest camps and bases in Abo country from which the Communist leader hoped eventually to launch major operations. These were virtually impossible to find - indeed on one occasion five battalions of troops spent six unsuccessful weeks in deep jungle trying to locate a known CT base.

With jungle forts British troops would be able to remain for long periods in remote Aborigine areas. Manned by twenty or so specially trained police, Templer hoped they would serve not only as bases but as advance intelligence posts when the Aborigines gradually lost their fears – not only of CTs but of white men.

Among the first to build a fort, which would be supplied by air drop, was Sergeant Monty Gay, an ex-Palestine policeman who was sent up the Pahang river with a platoon of Malays to a point twelve miles from Kuala Lipis, the capital of Pahang, and told, in effect, 'Build a fort.' He did. He looked around, saw the bamboo clumps along the banks of the river, set the Malays to work. In 32 days the Fort was complete, with barracks, however crudely built, a lock-up, home-made chairs, tables, wardrobes, all con-structed from the branches of trees and split bamboo. The jungle outpost was christened Kuala Medang station, and it had cost Monty Gay exactly twenty-five cents – for nails.

Kuala Medang was the first of fifteen forts that were

built in the next few months, and it was at one of them
that Arthur Young, the Chief of Police, was ambushed in
the autumn of 1952. Young spent much of his time travelling to remote spots, usually with an armoured escort,
though he felt that 'this procession of an armoured car
followed by me in a saloon with an armoured Land-Rover
bringing up the rear seemed anything but secure, and did
no more than indicate that I was the meat in the sandwich.'

On one occasion the 'bread' in the sandwich suffered
more than the 'meat', for in an ambush near Kuantan on
the east coast, the officer in front of Young had his nose
shot off while the one behind received a bullet in the back
of the neck. Young was unscathed.

On November 25 Young took a helicopter to the isolated
Legap Fort, which had been set up to help the Sakai deep
in the Perak jungle. As he walked in Young noted that his
host, Police-Lieutenant John Middleditch, had inscribed
over the entrance a quotation from the Old Testament:
'Enter ye the stronghold, ye prisoners of hope.'

They did – and sat down for lunch. Within ten minutes
the luncheon party was under intensive fire from CTs who
had doubtless been attracted by the helicopter. Young
remembers that he was actually lifting a forkful of stewed
beef to his mouth as the first bullet ripped through the
wall inches above his head. He grabbed a gun and 'fired
a few rounds in anger – the only ones in my life.'

Young had done wonders for the police force. The old
animosities were being eroded in the new concept of a
force that was regarded by the public as the spearhead of
the attack. This was largely due to the determination of
Templer and Young to increase the size of Special Branch.
'I considered the priority of this need so high,' Young
noted at the time, 'that one-fifth of all the senior ranks in
the Force were employed in Special Branch.'

Without doubt Templer relied greatly on the calm,

unruffled Arthur Young, perhaps because, though Young admired Templer greatly, he was quite unafraid of him. Inevitably they had their differences, for at times Templer could go too far. He did so at a meeting of the War Council (at which Young was not present). Annoyed for some reason by the police, Templer referred to them as 'disloyal'. Unfortunately the word found its way into the official minutes and Young's reaction was immediate. 'I saw the police, whose morale I was striving to build up, subjected to undeserved criticism.'

Not the man to take an insult lying down, Young went to his desk and wrote an indignant letter to Templer. The word, he said, was unjustified, false and he entirely repudiated the accusation.

The next day Young received an urgent summons to King's House. As he entered Templer's office, there was no sign of the usual grin of welcome and he was not even asked to take a seat.

Templer, 'with an unpleasant twist to his lips and a very acid tone in his voice', said abruptly, 'Arthur, you wrote to me. And I don't like it.'

Very politely, and standing stiffly to attention, Young replied, 'I didn't think you would, sir.'

There was a long silence which Templer seemed deter- mined not to break. Finally Young said, 'I'm here to speak for a very fine force, and if I may say so, I've done exactly what you'd have done had you been in my place.'

As Young noted: 'Still no comment. He fixed me with a piercing stare whilst I looked at him equally full in the eyes.' Young was quite prepared to return to London by the next plane rather than submit, but at length Templer opened the side drawer of his desk, stuck his feet in it – the sure sign that he was relaxed – and said, 'Arthur, I apologize.' And indeed Templer even insisted on making the apology public at the next meeting of the War Council.

Mostly, however, Young's brushes with the General

provided light relief, as when Young discovered that Templer had calmly appropriated a number of the highly attractive blue police 'dress' sarongs used on formal occasions at the depot. It seemed that on one of Templer's visits to the depot – he was always popping in to see Young – the sarongs had caught his eye, and he had promptly sent an aide to collect a few to adorn his servants at King's House. The depot officers, Young remembers, 'were horrified at this unworthy use of their beloved regalia but in face of HE's request there was nothing they could do. Young thought otherwise. He immediately asked the aide concerned to present his compliments to Templer and request that the police uniforms 'which His Excellency had *borrowed*' should be returned to the depot. 'They were,' Young remembers, 'without a word.'

Templer had also made great strides with his plans to arm the Chinese Home Guards. More than seventy New Villages were already protected by armed Chinese. Others were patrolling areas assigned to them, so relieving the police and army of static duties.

Handing over these responsibilities was, as Harry Miller wrote, 'a risk because of two dangers: that their weapons might find their way to the Communists, or the Communists would consider Home Guard-defended villages as "soft" targets and attack them. As far as Templer was concerned the risk involved was less important than the need to instil an offensive spirit into villagers and to make them determined to defend home and family.'

Only rarely did the Chinese Home Guards fail – though they did on one occasion, at Kulai New Village, a 'show village' twelve miles from Johore of which Templer was particularly proud. One night CTs calmly arrived at the gates of the village, demanded entrance, and the Home Guards were so overawed that they let them in. There was no fighting as the CTs collected twenty shotguns and ammunition and then returned to the jungle.

Templer learned of the incident during the night. He got up, ordered his helicopter, paced the gardens of King's House until it was ready and set off for Kulai. A grey and pink dawn was streaking the sky when Templer landed on the village badminton court. And in the words of Peter Rice of the police, who was investigating the incident, 'he played hell with the villagers saying that he had trusted them and they were nothing better than a bunch of cowards.' A stoic Chinese translated his words – until he came to Templer's next remark. From then, the confrontation descended to pure farce.

'You're a lot of bastards,' shouted Templer; and Rice, who spoke Chinese, listened carefully as the translator announced without emotion: 'His Excellency informs you that he knows that none of your mothers and fathers were married when you were born.'

Templer waited, then, pointing a finger at the astonished villagers to show who was the 'tuan', he added, 'You may be bastards, but you'll find out that I can be a bigger one.' Missing the point of the threat completely, the translator said politely, 'His Excellency does admit, however, that this father was also not married to his mother.'

But it was typical of Templer that he immediately sent the Home Guards twenty new shotguns.

Of course during all this time the murders and terrorism were continuing, though the number of incidents was dropping; but everyone who looks back on 1952 remembers not the tragedy and terror, but the new feeling of invigoration in Malaya, and particularly the fact that Templer seemed to be so much occupied with forward thinking, with the *future* of the country. Just before Peter Lucy left with Tommy in the summer of 1952 to start a new life planting sisal in Kenya he met Templer and remembers him saying, 'I could win this war in three months if I could get two-thirds of the people on my side.' And Peter's reaction was, 'He's getting them – it may take time, but he's getting them.'

If there were some who Templer felt were not pulling their weight – particularly Europeans – he could be withering. On the day when (as it happened) the Perak Derby was being run at Ipoh and a golf tournament was being held at Johore Bahru, he was invited to address a Rotarian audience in Kuala Lumpur. To the businessmen expecting the usual polite after-lunch speech, he said bluntly, 'You see today how the Communists work. They seldom go to the races. They seldom go to dinner parties or cocktail parties. And they don't play golf.'

Nothing seemed too small to escape Templer's attention; he read every letter reaching King's House, including one which he showed to Bob Thompson in which a writer complained that he was charged ten cents for a cup of water in hospital. 'Sounds true to me,' he said, and turning to an ADC, added tersely, 'Fix it!' On one of his secret visits to Desmond Palmer's Special Branch hideout, Templer suggested that every dentist in Malaya should be contacted. 'Every CT we catch seems to have *some* gold teeth,' he said. 'There must be records of their dental history.' It proved invaluable advice.

More and more Templer was becoming interested in the country's social services. A second batch of student teachers had been flown to England; he was deeply involved in rural industrial development, in granting loans to local co-operative societies. When he was short of cash and there was none forthcoming from London, he borrowed it locally himself. After a request for $4 million for American carbines had been turned down by Churchill, Templer arranged a dinner with the Sultan of Brunei and asked him bluntly, 'Will you lend it to me?' He added shrewdly, 'I can only offer you four per cent, but you have my word the loan will be repaid.' He got the money.

When it was evident that Voice aircraft flying low over the jungle with their recorded messages were being successful against CT waverers, Templer spent the best part of three days learning a long message in Mandarin which he recorded.

It was at this time that Thompson introduced Templer to C. C. Too of Psychological Warfare, and Templer was fascinated by Too's latest exploit, for the ebullient Chinese had conceived the idea of putting on a theatrical company tour composed of surrendered CTs who were rehearsing a grisly play called *Bloody Revenge*. Too was convinced (rightly) that if the play were shown in the villages and kampongs, it would have a profound effect on any men who might be toying with the idea of joining the opposite camp.

The Malayan Chinese Association provided funds for a mobile stage and curtains. General Electric Company built a mobile lighting system; the scenery was painted by a local artist. Writers were drawn from the more intelligent CTs who had been indoctrinated by listening to plays. CTs acted the roles of squatters, farmers, tappers, even police, in a simple story showing the victimization of a small group of people by Communism, their resistance and (of course) eventual victory.

Templer went to listen to a rehearsal before the play had its premier at a village near Ipoh – where the actors were escorted by armed guards, and the entire village turned out. The play was such a success that it was finally broadcast on Radio Malaya.

Emboldened by this publicity, twelve other surrendered CTs – two of whom had been actors before the war – started their own company and toured Malaya for three months in *New Life*, the story of a peasant family whose son joined the CTs – and changed his mind just before the final curtain came down.

17 THE FLIGHT TO EXILE

Just as 1951 was Chin Peng's peak year of success, so 1952 became the most successful 'killing year' for the security forces. In all Chin Peng lost 1,502 men, including four major leaders in the space of a few months.

The first of the quartet to be killed was known as 'Manap the Jap'. The squint-eyed son of a Malay mother and a Japanese father, Manap had become Commander of the 10th (Malay) Regiment after Abdullah vanished into comparative obscurity. He had a price of $75,000 on his head. Early one Sunday morning in May 1952 he was walking down a jungle trail on the edge of a rubber estate near Kuantan in East Pahang. A Sten gun was cradled in his arm, and he was alone. Round the corner came a Gurkha patrol with 23-year-old rifleman Bahaudur Raj scouting ahead. Suddenly he saw a Sten gun twelve yards away. He fired instantly; a body seemed to move into a firing position so Raj fired another burst from the hip. Only then did he discover that the CT had fallen across a horizontal bough as he died, making it look as though he was getting ready to fire. It was all over in ten seconds. The body was taken to Kuantan mortuary for identification; the assistant took one look at the squint-eyed corpse on the marble slab and cried, 'It's Manap!' The two men had been to school together.

Less than two months later Chin Peng lost another key commander, 'The Bearded Terror of Kajang'. It was the Kajang gang which had caused so much trouble to Peter Lucy, and its leader was killed after a classic example of police and army co-operation. Special Branch intercepted two courier messages in code. One was cunningly concealed in a tube of toothpaste, the other inside a durian.

From the two messages Special Branch discovered the identity of a Min Yuen man obviously in contact with the Bearded Terror. They picked him up, fed and clothed him, promised him a reward – and eventually he talked. It was now a simple matter for Special Branch to give troops of the Suffolk Regiment, which had been operating in the area for three years, an accurate description of the Bearded Terror's hideout – a comfortable shed in a Forest Reserve fifteen miles from Kajang, which he shared with his mistress, his deputy commander, and a bodyguard of two.

At 2.30 p.m. on July 6, after a good lunch, the four CTs and one woman were sprawled on the floor of the hut drinking coffee. The radio was blaring. A stock of food, including fresh tomatoes, lettuces and tinned goods lined the walls. Without warning three young Englishmen, all under twenty, walked into the camp. Lieutenant Raymond Hands, Privates K. Baker and W. Wynant, all of the Suffolks and all national servicemen, were scouting ahead of their platoon when they stumbled on the hut. The soldiers opened fire instantly. The CTs fled, but as the Bearded Terror and his mistress raced across the jungle track the young lieutenant killed them both.

The three soldiers returned to the hut. The radio was still playing, and the coffee in the cups was still hot. 'It seemed a pity to waste it,' said Hands modestly, 'so we drank it.'

The third man was beheaded. This was 'Shorty' Kuk a member of the Central Committee with a price of $200,000 on his head. 'Shorty' was twenty-nine and the mastermind behind murders, ambushes and train derailments in the Malacca-Johore area. He met his death near Jerantut in Pahang after an abortive journey to meet Chin Peng. When finally Shorty Kuk arrived at the rendezvous, Chin Peng had gone, but he had left a stay-behind party to wait for Shorty and give him instructions written in code in a small notebook with shiny red covers. Almost as an afterthought, Chin Peng left Shorty Kuk some less important documents – including a government leaflet with Shorty Kuk's photograph on it and the announcement of the $200,000 reward.

Shorty Kuk, who had a bodyguard of two men and his mistress, stuffed the red notebook into one of two personal haversacks and set off back to Johore. However, he made one error. He was so proud of the price on his head that he could not forbear to show the leaflet to his bodyguards. Two days later the driver of the Sakai Express heading for Jerantut was startled by the sight of two men and a woman by the side of the track. Two were waving frantically for the train to stop. The third was holding up a dripping human head. The driver stopped the train and the three CTs announced calmly that this was the notorious Shorty Kuk. After reading the reward leaflet, they had shot him during his sleep and decapitated him in order to produce his head as proof in the hope of collecting the reward. They also brought Ah Kuk's two personal haversacks filled with documents. The driver took them to the nearest police station, where a reproving Malay policeman ordered them to wrap up the head in brown paper.

News of Shorty Kuk's death was kept secret for several months so that Bob Thompson on the Planning Staff could study the papers found in his haversacks, for these proved to be the most important haul of the war. There was the little red book (the code of which had already been broken), which contained Chin Peng's policy and military plans. Other notes detailed examples of CT difficulties in getting food; there were orders to make more use of Aborigines (which led Templer to increase the number of jungle forts). There were specific instances of growing bitterness between the CTs and the Min Yuen, who were disgruntled because CTs took their food and fled to the safety of the jungle, leaving the Min Yuen to bear the brunt of government attacks.

The fourth man surrendered. Ming Lee was born in the Johore town of Segamat, and had over the years built up an image of a dedicated tough Communist. All attempts by Colonel Richard Miers and the South Wales Borderers to capture him had failed. In fact Ming Lee had just evaded their latest trap and Miers was trying to write an explanatory report to HQ, when the door burst open and a Special Branch officer blurted out, 'Ming Lee has surrendered.'

An astounded Miers ran to Special Branch headquarters – and there was a wizened, half-starved little man with protruding yellow teeth wolfing a plate of curry. Miers recognized him instantly, and before he spoke caught himself thinking, 'But how could such an insignificant-looking creature have caused us so much trouble, have tied down hundreds of soldiers and police and dominated the lives of thousands of civilians?' Miers found the answer in a pair of black eyes, keen, bright, darting round the room, yet not shifty; indeed, they indicated a sense of humour.

Ming Lee looked up from his plate, saw Miers, stood up, saluted and – without a trace of arrogance but with no obsequiousness either – said, 'You have given us a hard time lately, Colonel.' Then he returned to his curry.

A puzzled Miers was asking himself why, after evading capture, Ming Lee had suddenly decided to surrender. The CT finished his curry, wiped his mouth with his hand, and then astonished Miers with the casual information, 'I've given up working for those Communist people. They're no good. And you are winning anyway.'

Miers remembers feeling almost breathless at the sheer practical philosophy of the man, who showed no signs of shame, antagonism or fear of possible punishment. And he was even more astounded when Ming Lee was taken outside to be photographed with British and Malay officers –

a photo which Miers knew would make invaluable propaganda. Ming Lee obviously appreciated this, and since he was to be the central figure he was determined the photograph should be a good one. As Miers watched, 'he fussed about like a prima donna, adjusting his chair to the light, getting up to view the group from the camera end and then making suggestions for improvement. Perhaps the Brigadier would kindly move in a bit to the left? Ming Lee acting as master of ceremonies at a photograph of his own surrender was absurdly funny.' Only then did Ming Lee take his seat, lean forward and bare his yellow teeth into a smile as the camera clicked.

Looking at this man with the eyes of a soldier, Miers might have been excused for thinking 'It was, to me, confirmation that no European can really hope to understand the mind of a Chinese who has been steeped in the creed of Communist terrorism.' But if Miers could not understand the Chinaman's reasoning, could Ming Lee ever hope to understand the workings of a European mind? After a spell in a Government Rehabilitation Centre, Ming Lee became a free man; then the man who had once been the terror of Segamat returned there and got a job almost immediately – as groundsman at the Segamat cricket club.

All this was part of a dramatically changed pattern, which led to an entirely new surge of optimism in Malaya. The increased security forces, the new weapons, the first helicopters, were there for everyone to see, and they produced in almost everyone a new spirit of aggression, whereas on the other hand diehard CTs who a year previously would have carried out successful ambushes now began to falter, perhaps because the self-confidence of Malayans came at a time when there was bound to be a loss of confidence among CTs, who in the four years of the war had lost 6,500 killed, captured or surrendered (to say nothing of those eliminated by jungle disease).

Even in the one area where security forces could hardly make a dent, the toughest CT failed twice in a week to lay a successful ambush. This was the district around the Johore village of Yong Peng ('Eternal Peace') where some of the most vicious CTs in all Malaya were operating. Communism was so open that several planters, to their annoyance, received daily copies of the local underground Communist newspaper. With an uneasy laugh the planters referred to Yong Peng as 'one-third Red, one-third pink, one-third afraid'.

The CT leader was Goh Peng Tun, operational commander of the Seventh Independent Platoon of the Johore Regiment. Goh had perfected ambushes so successfully that Chin Peng circulated details of his methods. It was he who had perpetrated the outrage against Ah Fung on the Voules Estate at the beginning of the Emergency; he who first produced the swinging sandbag filled with iron spikes; and it was Goh who, in an ambush on the main road, impaled the first British soldier on pointed stakes hidden just where the CT knew the man would jump out of his armoured vehicle. In two years Goh had, according to official sources, been responsible for twenty-three deaths, including a police lieutenant, two special constables, and a Fijian major (whose watch he had looted). Goh was the embodiment of CT terrorism.

In July he laid an ambush that failed – but only by the narrowest of margins – in which two men had miraculous escapes. They were Major Ian Tedford of the Cameronians and Charles Morgan, assistant manager of the 9,000-acre Voultes Rubber Estate, 120 miles north of Singapore. Tedford and his troops were operating from Voules, and he and Morgan had been spending the day in Johore Bahru. It was midnight when they set off in Tedford's green Morris Oxford saloon for the estate – Tedford driving through the damp-smelling night, his right arm clutching a pistol, while Morgan, with head and shoulders out of the passenger seat, was 'cuddling a carbine'. Tedford also had a carbine next to him on the driving seat.

The first sixty-three miles were easy for they followed the *Straits Times* delivery van, but when they reached Yong Peng with its bamboo-walled thatched huts, Malay police warned them that telephone lines four miles to the north were down – and to the CT-conscious *Straits Times* van driver that meant a possible ambush, so he wisely decided to spend the night in Yong Peng. Tedford, however, had to attend muster parade in a few hours so he pushed on warily, the car's headlights cutting a beam into the blackness. It was at the fourth mile, where steep banks on either side of the road made perfect ambush conditions, that they expected trouble; but none came, and by the time they were eleven miles north of Yong Peng, it seemed as though the danger was past.

'We were doing sixty and screaming over a rise,' Tedford remembers, when the lights picked out a tree across the road. As Tedford yelled 'Ambush!' and jammed on the brakes, the car slewed round on the wet road, hitting the tree.

Machine-gun and rifle fire spattered from every side. As the windscreen shattered, Morgan dived out for one side of the road, Tedford for the other. Tedford grabbed his carbine and dived into the lallang, but as he jumped a bullet tore into his left thigh and the carbine slipped from his fingers. Before he could grab it men were flashing torches in his face and heavy boot sank into his back. Other men came running and Tedford knew he had only one hope of living. He was covered in blood, and in a war where bullets were precious he had to feign death. A man grabbed him by the hair, twisted him on his back. Torches blinded him – torches which showed his blood-soaked clothes. Numb with shock, he kept his eyes open in the fixed stare of death, 'the irises rolled hard and upward to the left, almost under the lids.'

A man clicked a round into a carbine and a face loomed above Tedford as the CT raised the muzzle gently to the corner of Tedford's right eye and started to press it gently into the eye. Tedford never moved. Finally the man shouted 'Goh Peng Tun!' and as the leader arrived, said in Malay, '*Tintu mati*'. He was 'definitely dead'.

And then, so he thought, they would leave him. Instead four men dragged him on to the road and started to strip him. They took his watch, signet ring, wallet containing the best part of a month's pay, his shirt. Though in agonizing pain, Tedford knew that to flinch would have meant death.

The car was ransacked. Seats were gashed and Tedford dimly realized that stuffing was being ripped out and soaked in petrol to make an improvised fuse. One man poured petrol over the car. Still Tedford did not realize what was going to happen – until a whistle blew, half a dozen men rolled him from the lallang across the road, and finally pushed the 'body' beneath the petrol tank of the car he had been driving barely ten minutes previously.

With his last strength Tedford rolled clear seconds before the car blew up. Half naked, he lay there until the flames quietened. Goh had gone, and Tedford found that by grasping his wounded leg above the knee he could slowly hobble. Ten yards from the tree he saw the white of Morgan's shirt. The planter lay face down, stabbed three times through the chest, once through the small of the back.

Miraculously, both men lived. Police attracted by the flames reached the two men within a few minutes. With a bandage and bayonet Tedford tied a tourniquet round his thigh, twisting it to stem the blood. A policeman jabbed morphia into Morgan. After a seventy-five-minute drive they reached the nearest hospital in Kluang as dawn streaked the sky. Both men were out of hospital in a month.

A few days later Goh struck again – and for the second time was unsuccessful. This time he was outwitted by a boy of fourteen, Terence Edmett, the son of a planter at Nanyo Estate near the Johore river. Terence had learned to drive the estate's four-ton armoured car, and was so efficient that he usually drove his mother and father, allowing them to man the guns in the vehicle's two turrets.

When the armoured car set off in rain on a routine inspection tour, Terence was at the wheel. Mrs Edmett had her turret closed against the wet, but Terence's father had his head out of his turret.

As they approached a bend, Terence saw a vehicle, apparently broken down, blocking the road. 'I wondered what the driver was doing,' he remembers. 'Then as we got closer, there was a shot.' Mr Edmett ducked from the sniper's fire and Terence drove on slowly with bullets from a fern-covered bank pinking against the armour. Because of the position of the turrets, Mr Edmett could not tell young Terence what to do. 'I crossed my fingers and hoped he wouldn't lose his nerve.'

Terence had the choice of three courses of action: to stop and fight it out, to try and slew his vehicle round the one blocking the road, or to use the weight of his armoured car to push it out of the way.

He chose the last plan. Easing the armoured car into low gear, he slowly shoved it hard against the vehicle blocking the path, at which 'the bandits seemed to get frantic. A real fusillade broke out.' But the wet mud helped him, and somehow he pushed the decoy car into the ditch, while 'inside our vehicle, the noise from what seemed to be hundreds of bullets was terrific.' Terence drove his way past the ditched vehicle, round the bend 'and in a few minutes we were away.'

Fortunately for the Edmett family, there was no age limit for drivers on private estate roads.

Ambushes were not confined to roads. But though trains were still being derailed, the security forces were now so much on the offensive that CT platoons often did not have time to conclude an operation. Four times in the space of a few weeks the Sakai Express was derailed between Jerantut and Temerloh, each time with 'Puck' Puckridge and his wife Mollie on it; yet each time the CTs were driven off. As Mollie remembers, 'They didn't seem to have the same guts any more.' But then, the CTs were facing much tougher odds. The days when they could attack a lonely plantation, or mine a train knowing they would have time to retreat, had gone for ever. When on one occasion the Sakai Express was attacked by CTs barely five miles north of Puckridge's estate, Puckridge led the passengers in fighting off the attackers – for all the world like men in a covered wagon epic – until help rattled up the rails in the form of an armoured train driven by 44-year-old Albert Thamby, who had joined Malayan Railways at nineteen. One of the coaches was burning. Thamby swept the jungle fringe with machine-gun fire, killed four CTs, then, telling his crew to keep firing, he doubled up by the side of the train, reached the blazing coach, and managed to uncouple it before using his armoured train to pull the rest of the train to safety. A year previously every coach on that train would have been burned.

It was the same in another threatened railway area in Negri Sembilan, where troops of the Green Howards found an answer after seventeen trains had been derailed. They patrolled the fifty-mile stretch of line in two armoured petrol-driven 'locomotives' known as 'Whickham trollies'. Powered by Ford V-8 engines, they carried two machine-guns which could be fired from behind the armour.

As the CT losses mounted, the killer squads – now often leaderless – were retreating into deep jungle and the rate of incidents was dropping. Food control schemes were strangling their lifelines, and for the first time even members of the Central Committee found themselves short of food. Irene Lee's brilliant capture of Lee Meng had disrupted the CT communication network so that by the end of 1952 Chin Peng was finding it more and more difficult to make regular contact with his subordinates. Many of his top commanders had been killed. In the New Villages, over half a million Chinese slept for the most part undisturbed, guarded by their own armed Chinese comrades.

But above everything else, there was one aspect of British war plans which was deeply troubling Chin Peng. It was the emphasis placed on *government;* government, as Thompson said, that not only functioned, but was *seen* to function, so that 'the births, marriages and deaths still get registered'. For this, as much as anything else, was the key to the changing fortunes. It had to be backed up by force – but as the troops scored their victories the government had to be seen doing an honest job – and anybody, even the humblest tapper, could now see and appreciate this, and begin to hope for the future. When the tappers went on their conducted war tours, Thompson always made a point of taking them to the Employees Provident Fund building in which employers and employees paid fixed sums out of wages. There Thompson would produce the tapper's card. 'It was hard for a man to become a Communist,' Thompson remembers, 'when you showed him that he had several hundred dollars waiting for him, when he retired – and that there would be more to come.'

And this, of course, was due to the great decision in the early stages – that the war should be controlled by the civil government, for though Templer was a general, it was as a civilian that he ruled. Only now was the significance of this becoming apparent to the people of Malaya. As

Richard Clutterbuck* wrote. 'The decisive element in doing all these things in Malaya was the police force; counter-insurgency is a matter of restoring law and order, and law and order is a matter for policemen with the training and the lawful status for the task – not for part-time armed villagers. Security and intelligence were provided by the police, for whom the army was a support but not a substitute.'

These reasons, together with mounting CT losses, caused Chin Peng in the spring of 1953 to make a momentous decision. He decided to flee Malaya and direct the war from a jungle base a few miles inside 'neutral' Thailand. It was an admission of defeat.

It must have been a shattering blow to the morale of his followers, and Osman China, who attended the jungle conference where the news was announced, remembers the blank dismay with which it was greeted. 'It was the worst moment of the war for me,' he remembered later. 'The faces around me were incredulous. We had spent nearly five years in the jungle, but this was such terrible news that for the very first time it crossed my mind that perhaps we were going to lose the war.'

We have only scanty details of this jungle conference, but what captured documents later revealed was 'a sense of stupefaction so great that no one even tried to dissuade Chin Peng'. Indeed, it seems that in many ways the heart had gone out of 'the cause'. Perhaps it was partly because several old faces were missing. Lau Yew, Manap the Jap, The Bearded Terror, Shorty Kuk – all were dead; Lee Meng was in jail; Lam Swee was working for the British. Nothing bore any resemblance to the good old days when victory had seemed to be within the Communists' grasp; now even their leader was forced to leave his own country.

* *The Long, Long War.*

It is not difficult to imagine the questions the delegates must have been asking themselves, their doubts, their fears, their dismays, as Chin Peng announced that he was taking a 'staff' of eighty men, including guards, across the border. It included Abdullah CD, discredited on the battlefield, but as a Malay useful to prove the multi-racial character of Malayan Communism.

This was the last conference Chin Peng held on Malayan soil. Within a few days he set off on the long journey northwards. It was four months before he finally waded across the shallow Golok river and stepped on to the opposite bank – into the safe sanctuary of Thailand.

18 THE LAST MONTHS OF TEMPLER

By the middle of 1953, Templer had made up his mind that he wanted to leave Malaya within a few months. It was not tiredness that prompted this decision, but a very different emotion. He realized that as Malaya moved towards the final defeat of Communism, the problems facing a country on the verge of independence would become more and more political and 'I felt it would be better for the country if I left. I was in danger of becoming too much of a father figure – and that would be unwise as Malaya approached independence.'

In London for the Coronation of the Queen in the summer of 1953, Templer lunched privately with Churchill at No. 10. The Prime Minister used all his considerable powers of persuasion to induce him to stay and had Templer wanted to go merely for personal reasons, Churchill's insistence might well have prevailed. But Churchill had the vision to see that Templer was, in fact, right. For always at the back of Churchill's mind was the knowledge that when Malaya did achieve independence, she must remain in the Commonwealth. To him the strategic situation of Malaya, Singapore, the Strait of Malacca were of supreme importance, and he wanted – through the medium of the Commonwealth – to preserve some hold on the area.

Like Templer, he realized the importance of letting the political leaders of the country have a clear field, without the presence of a man whom thousands of Malayans had invested with something of the awesome qualities of a god. So Churchill agreed, though he did ask Templer to remain for another year. This Templer was quite willing to do, for he still had many new ideas to put into practice.

On his return to Malaya, Templer invited MacDonald to dine, when almost casually he announced, 'I think I'm going to leave Malaya.'

MacDonald turned to him and said, 'But this isn't the right time. You *must* finish your job.'

'I've nearly finished it,' Templer said. 'The military war's nearly over. Only the political one remains and I'm not sure I'm any good at that.'

MacDonald, who had not always seen eye to eye with Templer, remembers going to bed that night and thinking. 'It takes a big man to talk like Templer did.'

Templer *was* a big man – and now he set about what he called 'tidying up the loose ends'. Soon he was discussing a revolutionary idea with Bob Thompson of the Planning Staff. In essence it was simple: why not group the surrendered CTs into a special force? Why not turn the poachers into gamekeepers?

Always intrigued by the mentality of surrendered Communists, Thompson felt they needed to 'belong' to some organization in place of the Communism they had renounced; he believed they tended to turn to other ex-CTs for guidance in the new world into which they had just emerged. They needed old comrades to proffer advice on the most elementary problems, such as how to behave to the British. It took some a long time to relax, to discover that the British were more tolerant than the CT commanders had been; Thompson also realized that in a strange way they could only justify their escape from Communism by being personally involved in the struggle against it – which was why time after time they begged to lead patrols back into the jungle to attack their former comrades.

So the Special Operational Volunteer Force (SOVF) was born in the summer of 1953, consisting of 180 ex-Communists grouped into twelve platoons of fifteen men each. Each man volunteered for eighteen months, lived in police compounds and received similar salaries to the lowest-ranking policeman. If they proved satisfactory they would be discharged unconditionally into civilian life.

Among the strangest members of SOVF in its early days were six married couples. The government took some care not to publicize the fact that it was using women; that in fact women could prove invaluable members of this new group and were often more adroit and ruthless than the men.

Templer was soon visiting the SOVF training centre at Sungei Buloh, twenty miles from Kuala Lumpur. Watching the first men being marched round the parade ground, he told the assembled army officers, 'To hell with the drill, you can say they're not as smart as they might be, but we don't mind about that. There's something entirely new in the idea of recruiting surrendered terrorists into the security forces. We must give them our trust no less than our weapons.'

Thompson also had a hand in another of the many new ideas which flowed from Templer. Since more and more CTs *were* surrendering, why not make it easier for them? Templer agreed, though Thompson did sound a word of warning, for he believed strongly that a surrender offer 'must be both attractive and fair but not too lenient or vague. It should be remembered that an offer can easily be improved later, as circumstances may require, but it is not easy to reduce the terms of an offer without prejudicing the government's good faith.'

So a formula was carefully worked out, after which millions of Safe Conduct Passes were scattered over the jungle. Signed by Templer, the passes promised 'Good treatment, food, cigarettes and medical attention if required.' The message added:

> Many of you who are now still fighting for Communist leaders in the jungles of Malaya are not hardened criminals, but youths who were tricked or intimidated into following the wrong path. There is no hope in Communism. I would rather you lived to serve the common interests of the people of Malaya than died like wild beasts in the jungle. I therefore call upon you to hide your arms and equipment, and report to the nearest police or military officer or Government official. I guarantee that you will not be ill-treated in any way. I have also given orders that a reward is to be paid to any member of the public who helps you to escape from the clutches of the Communist leaders.

Special Branch now had virtually complete lists of Chin Peng's army; it knew most of the areas frequented by particular units, and the newly-formed SOVF, together with hunter-killer platoons, had reached a peak of efficiency. In the first five years of the war 6,304 CTs had been killed, captured or surrendered, against 2,848 civilians murdered and 1,563 security forces killed.

All this led Templer to another brilliant plan which he had long harboured in the back of his mind. In any area free from CT incidents, and where the people had shown themselves helpful to the police, he proposed to remove every irksome restriction – rationing, curfews, police checks, movement of food – and call the region a 'White Area'. From one day to the next the population would be hauled right out of the war.

Choosing the first White Area posed several problems, for Templer realized the experiment would fail if any region receiving its freedom (with all the attendant publicity) was then infiltrated and reverted to being a CT area.

One way of helping to prevent this was to choose an area with only three land flanks, the fourth being the sea, and Templer had in mind one in particular – the beautiful, prosperous coastal strip of Malacca. No CTs could infiltrate from the sea. And it had another advantage. North of Malacca was a second possible White Area, also with its back to the sea. If Templer could proclaim first one and then the second area White it would only be a matter of time before the strip between the two 'pimples' (Templer's word) became White too.

'The only thing,' Templer remembers, 'is that I had to be absolutely certain that the people would never let the Communists go back, so before I declared Malacca White, I made life absolute hell for them.' The bewildered inhabitants, knowing nothing of their planned 'liberation', were subjected to every legal indignity the Planning Staff could devise. Food rationing was intensified, spot checks became daily occurrences, a new curfew was imposed, while troops rounded up the few remaining CTs and secured the perimeter. Soon the people of Malacca were among the most miserable in Malaya – which was exactly what Templer wanted, for he knew that when Malacca became a White Area, the people would be so overjoyed that every man and woman would be an Intelligence agent for the government, and that any CT who dared to move into the region would be reported immediately by people horrified at the thought of reverting to a life of restrictions.

Templer was absolutely right in this assessment. On September 5, a 221-square-mile stretch of Malacca was declared a 'White Area' and 160,000 people suddenly found themselves out of the war for the first time in five years. When Brigadier Mark Henniker of the Royal Engineers drove through the area he found 'the first effect was electrical. The people demonstrated their joy with happy faces and Union Jacks.'

Templer had made it clear that people in a White Area had not only to earn their liberty, but that once White, good behaviour had to be maintained.

'It's the job of every one to keep Communists out,' he told Malacca leaders. 'Refuse them supplies. Report their presence at once to the police if they do come back.' In fact one shotgun did disappear before the end of September – an event with an interesting sequel, for indignant villagers begged the police not to interfere and within three days the missing shotgun was quietly returned.

As well as establishing the first 'White Area', Templer was making other changes. The huge rewards for killing CTs were withdrawn, though large bounties would still be paid for capturing them alive. Soon the 17D regulation giving the government power of mass detention was abolished – in all 29,828 people had been detained since its introduction during the first months of the war.

One loyal colleague of Templer's had left Malaya during this period. After fifteen months Colonel Arthur Young, the Commissioner of Police, returned to London. His original agreement had been for a year, but Templer had insisted on his remaining longer, and Young had done a truly magnificent job. He had taken a force of divided men and welded it into one with a strength of 70,000, high in morale, splendid in ability. And he did one last service, not generally recognized, before leaving Malaya. He quietly fought Templer's choice of a successor. Templer had his eye on an aggressive senior officer who Young felt would not continue the work in the spirit he had created, for Young never forgot that the war could only be won if Malaya had the finest Special Branch in the world. And he knew just the man to succeed him.

So, 'for some time I had been guiding Templer away

from his own selection of my successor because I already had a candidate in mind: he was a junior to many of his brother officers and was not at headquarters. In anticipation of events, I arranged his transfer and his duties so that he would be well poised when the time came. HE insisted on seeing a short list, but eventually he warmly agreed with my own recommendation.'

So Young was able to hand over the force to 'Bill' Carbonell, a brilliant member of the Special Branch, and a man 'in whom I know the Force would have complete trust and confidence.'

Among his other activities, Templer started a drive to recruit more nurses to work in the New Villages; and this led indirectly to a romance between a Special Branch man destined very soon to organize one of the biggest surrender operations of the war and a young nurse who answered one of the advertisements which Templer caused to be published in England. She was a pretty dark-haired girl called Lucie Card of the St John's Ambulance Brigade, who came from Godstone in Surrey. She answered the advertisement, enrolled, and within weeks was driving a van nearly a thousand miles a month, often with only a Chinese assistant who in CT areas crouched on the floor surrounded by shaking, tinkling bottles. Lucie felt it was safer that way. CTs might have stopped the van had it been driven by a man.

After barely three months in Malaya, Lucie was suddenly faced with a moment of decision she had been subconsciously dreading for weeks. She was driving towards a kampong near Manong, where the twisting mountain road dipped as it reached a broad river. It was perfect ambush country. And there, as she swept round the corner, was an armed Chinese.

As she braked, terrified, she saw he was alone. There were certainly none of the usual ambush signs she had been told to expect, no fallen trees, no sudden emerging figures. In fact the man looked rather pathetic. And then a curious thing happened. The man must have been waiting for the St John's van, for as soon as he saw it he threw his gun in the lallang and raised his arms above his head; for one wild moment Lucie thought she was going to accept a CT surrender. Then she saw that the man's shirt was drenched in blood. He was little more than a boy – Lucie guessed his age at less than twenty – and in halting English he asked for help. But when Lucie said she would drive him to hospital, he shook his head violently and started to make for the jungle.

It was then that Lucie had to make her decision. 'Of course there was no decision really,' she remembers. 'I had to do something.' Aiding a known Communist might be wrong, but Lucie opened the back of the van and made signs to the Chinese on the floor to keep quiet as she took out rolls of bandages and tape. She realized she was trembling – until she started bathing an ugly bullet shoulder wound with antiseptic. When she had finished bandaging it Lucie hesitated before taking out a handful of sulphanilamide tablets. Silently she handed them over. The man had so far not said a word but now he thrust his right hand into the pocket of his frayed khaki shorts and brought out two dollar bills. 'For the pills,' he said. Then he picked up his gun and loped off into the jungle.

All the way back to base Lucie was tortured. The man could have been a murderer – they were all murderers, she had been told. Once he had put his gun down surely she and the driver could have overpowered him. She thought of other things she might have done. He had looked so trusting – and so very young – that it would have been a simple matter to inject a big dose of morphine and put him out. She was still troubled when she reached the Nurses' Home at Batu Gajah.

That night the monthly dance brightened up the Batu

Gajah Club – an event nobody in the district would dream of missing, particularly this month as a party of the Royal West Kents had moved into the area. It was exhausting, for there were fourteen women to a hundred men ('and every man,' Lucie noted in her diary, 'in excellent training for gaining his objective'.) She found herself dancing with a slim man in civilian clothes. He had sharp features, straight fair hair and the bluest eyes she had ever seen. No, he said, he was not a soldier, he was a Special Branch officer. Born in Scotland, name of David Storrier. He spoke in monosyllables. Just visiting the area, he added vaguely. 'Did he like Malaya?' she asked. 'Fine,' he answered, 'though I miss my fiancée. She's back home in Dundee.'

Storrier, who was twenty-nine and an ex-RAF rear gunner, told her he had been a policeman in Palestine before transferring to Malaya in 1948. Though he did not talk much, Lucie had an almost overwhelming desire to tell him about the CT she had helped – until he mentioned quite casually that he hoped she guarded her drugs carefully. 'We raided a CT camp the other day and found a bottle of Red Cross pills,' he added. 'They must have stolen them from a kampong. Makes your blood boil.' Lucie said nothing.

As the dance ended and they all trooped out to their cars, buckling on their guns, she remembers him saying, 'It'd be nice to have a party without having your hall table littered with guns.' Lucie also remembers feeling vaguely disturbed, a tinge of regret that he was engaged. He was different from the others and it would have been pleasant to know him better. 'See you.' He waved as he jumped into his car. 'See you,' she echoed – without for a split second imagining what would happen at one momentous later meeting.

This was at Jerantut in Pahang, not far from the Puckridge estate. For several weeks Storrier had been stationed there with one object in mind – to find Osman China, known to be somewhere in the area; and on New Year's Eve, 1953, he was standing by the Pahang river, watching the swirling, chocolate-coloured water thrashing against the banks, tearing away lumps of ochre clay, smashing against the flat ferry that was the only link between the west and the port of Kuantan on the east coast.

As Storrier turned back from the river's edge, with its wooden hut where normally bananas and Coco-Cola were sold, he was thinking of New Year's Eve in his home town of Dundee, and thinking too that this would be his last bachelor New Year's Eve, which meant the last he would spend in the dubious comfort of the run-down Jerantut rest house which was his home, and which had no running water, but only a Shanghai jar and dipper.

For, after months of letters and cables between Malaya and Scotland, he had at last persuaded his boyhood sweetheart to come out and marry him. Her passage had been booked, he had sent her the money and the banns had been read once in Kuala Lumpur. But Malaya was so far away from Scotland, it was now so long since they had met that, despite his repeated appeals for her to come, sometimes Storrier could hardly remember what she looked like, how she behaved.

When he reached the Jerantut rest house a mud-spattered car stood under the big square porch. Storrier shook off the rain, walked into the main long, high, blue-painted room, where fans were wheezing over the semi-circular bar with its big refrigerator in one corner. A few Java sparrows fluttered in and out of the air gap at the top of the walls. The rattan chairs and tables with their dog-eared magazines had been pushed round the edges of the room, the carpets rolled up, and the bandstand (with a bird's nest high over the piano) spruced for the New Year's Eve dance – which this year would be attended by the officers of the King's African Rifles, soggily encamped in tents behind.

At the far end of the room sat a woman drinking tea, and David Storrier recognized her immediately. She was Lucie Card, the nurse he had first met in Batu Gajah. They had met briefly on several occasions since that day and he had always enjoyed her company, so that when she announced that she was on her way to Kuantan and had been held up by the impassable river, David was delighted. Lucie had managed to get one of the four bedrooms at the rest house, and David remembers that almost without thinking he cried, 'Well, I'm sorry for your sake, but delighted for mine. Can I take you to the dance?'

Lucie Card also remembers that night – how the rain stopped just before sunset, leaving in its wake an almost uncanny silence, broken only by the dripping leaves of the papaya trees outside her window, the time between each drip gradually becoming longer like the slow, measured plonk-plonk of a tap with a loose washer.

The dance (in slow tempo to prevent excessive sweating) was a great success, and Lucie was welcomed with open arms by the women-starved officers of the KAR – especially as there were only two women at the dance. But soon after midnight, Lucie and David strolled outside. Behind them lay the jungle; in front the wet moon shone on the padang. In her diary Lucie wrote: 'The night had burst into a frenzy of jungle sounds from the tall trees that rose to a hundred feet or more and in which everything from cicadas to tree frogs, from grasshoppers to mosquitoes, joined in a hundred different noises, together with the piping of weird birds. It was as though animals and insects were trying to produce a symphony. I could hear cymbals, a sound like a double bass (from the frogs) and even one animal which made a noise almost like a trumpet.'

Neither could remember ever having spent a happier evening, but it was not until David Storrier had gone to bed and was tossing and turning under his mosquito net that a shattering thought struck him. 'Suddenly I knew for certain that I was in love with the girl. This was nothing to do with a childhood sweetheart, this was a feeling I had never experienced before.'

The next morning they had breakfast together, 'then I took a large gulp and asked Lucie to marry me.' To David Storrier's astonishment, Lucie did not seem surprised. His Scottish reserve had led him to expect some display of emotions, but 'Lucie smiled and after only a moment of hesitation she agreed.' She had been in love with him for months, she admitted, but had never dared to think of it because he was engaged.

Storrier explained about his fiancée – a situation into which men and women could drift so easily: how he and the girl in Scotland had been friends since schooldays, how their respective parents were in fact more interested than their son and daughter in the marriage. It was an old story – and after David had cabled his fiancée not to come out, and finally her understanding letter arrived, he detected a feeling of relief in it. (Though David's father, balked of his dream of uniting the two families, wrote from Paradise Road, Dundee, that if he had been the girl, he would have sued for breach of promise.)

Several problems had to be faced, among them the fact that the banns had already been posted in Kuala Lumpur. 'I just didn't have the nerve to go and tell the priest to change the name,' David confesses, so he had a new set of banns, this time bearing Lucie's name, posted in Ipoh.

As Templer prepared to leave Malaya in mid-1954, he could look back on more than two decisive years in which the rate of incidents had fallen from five hundred a month to less than a hundred, in which the 1952 average of twenty-eight murders a month had dropped to seven a month in 1953. 'The Malayan Communist Party,' he said, 'still has firm control of its rank and file but incidents showing aggressive leadership and fighting morale are declining.'

But to Templer there was one other battle which had been won even more decisively – the battle of the hearts and minds. 'Templer's broom [and] the Emergency,' wrote Harry Miller, 'gave the impetus needed to break down the barriers of prejudice, tradition, and vested interests. The theme in the country is "Malayanization" – of Chinese, Europeans, Indians, Eurasians and other races, who look upon the Federation as their real home and the object of their loyalty. This was the most complex of all Templer's problems.'

With dynamism Templer had implemented the Briggs Plan, consolidated the framework for democratic government, raised the morale of people who until his arrival had barely realized what the war was all about. By fighting for the hearts and minds of the people he had stimulated in them a will to win, so that by now the beginning of the end of the war was in sight. He had seen laws passed giving citizenship to more than a million Chinese; he had persuaded the Sultans to open the Malayan Civil Service to include a proportion of non-Malay Asians. And – of vital importance – he had inaugurated a vast programme of primary education – *Malayan* education. This was a staggering achievement, for there had never been such a thing as free primary education in Malaya. The various races were educated in their own communal school; they had no common language, pupils grew up in a plural society, which inevitably worked against Templer's dreams of a multi-racial society.

With one stroke Templer changed this. Seizing the golden opportunity presented by the resettlement of the squatters, he insisted that every New Village must have its *Malayan* school, and the building of new primary schools in other towns and villages – where the curriculum was in

Malay – became a number one priority. More than anything else, Templer's school programme helped to quell
the fears of men like Harry Miller who felt that with
political emergence there was also an uneasy fear that,
'Unless a united Malayan nation is achieved before the
British government hands self-government to the country
a much more terrible Emergency of racial strife may break
out.'

Before he left, on May 30, 1954, Templer announced
one last item of historic news. In a country that had never
known a national franchise, Templer was able to give
Malaya the firm promise that by mid-1955 the country
would hold its first national elections for the Federal
Legislative Council. In place of a Council consisting over-
whelmingly of members nominated by the British government, it would consist of 52 elected and only 46 nominated
members, giving Malayan politicians a majority vote, 'thus
setting the gate open to Parliament in a self-governing
country'.

It was the last gesture of a brilliant, magnanimous soldier
who had astonished many doubters by becoming an even
greater statesman; a man who knew that it was always
more difficult to win the peace than the war. Of course,
being Templer, he had to make his parting shot, and he
warned those who assembled to say farewell that there
would still be hard, tough days ahead.

'In fact,' said Field Marshal Sir Gerald Templer, KG,
GCB, GCMG, KBE, DSO, 'I'll shoot the bastard who
says this Emergency is over.'

Phase Three
THE ROAD TO VICTORY
1954–60

19 THE POLITICAL WAR OPENS

The war against Communism which General Boucher had confidently predicted would be won 'after the rains' was now six years old; and though the early signs of defeat no longer existed, there were certainly no signs of early victory. Yet it was in the next three years that the path to victory would be hewn, for this was the period of Communist decline. With the departure of Templer (and the creation of an instant legend) the war was 'under new management'. The days of a Supremo had ended. Donald MacGillivray, who had been Templer's Deputy High Commissioner, became High Commissioner, but without Templer's all-embracing powers, while the post of Deputy lapsed. Lt-Gen. Sir Geoffrey Bourne became Director of Operations in command of all troops and police – but in matters of finance and high policy was subject to MacGillivray's authority. It was a logical step as the country prepared for major political advances which would knock more props from under Chin Peng.

It had needed Templer to break the back of the Communists; but since that back had been broken, the very absence of a 'dictator figure' gave encouragement to the people of Malaya, for MacDonald's early warning to Lyttelton that 'it's political advancement that will solve these problems, not bullets' still held.

As the war entered its seventh year in June 1954, the second reading of the Federal Elections Bill, providing for general elections early in 1955 was passed by the Legislative Council. More 'White Areas' had been declared, and CT units were being increasingly harried, not only with guns but, as morale sank lower and lower, by Voice aircraft flying overhead, and extolling through loudspeakers the comforts of home life, with particular stress on women, food and cigarettes.

One of the strengths of Voice aircraft lay in the fact that even the toughest CT commander could not be sure whether or not his men were listening. The death penalty for picking up a leaflet might deter many CTs from reading them, but the Voice aircraft could not be ignored, so that ancient DC3s flying low with their recorded messages played an impressive part in inducing waverers to surrender. Soon they were supplemented by heavily armoured Voice trucks manned by Asians speaking several dialects, using amplified loudhailers that could be heard six miles away. After the planes or trucks came the leaflets (ninety-three million in 1953), all painting a pleasant picture of life outside the jungle, often with photographs of surrendered CTs.

It was now clear that Chin Peng realized he had been defeated in the field and was poised to launch a political offensive in which 'peace' on his terms could be turned into a resounding Communist victory. And since the accent was now on the political evolution of the country – and the dangers of a political offensive by Chin Peng – Robert Thompson was elevated to the post of Co-ordinating Officer for Security. It was a role in the Defence Department well suited to his talents and one of his first tasks was to encourage the Chinese to take a still more active role in the war. For many months he had been concerned by the fact that even though 38 per cent of the population consisted of overseas Chinese (compared with 0.5 per cent in North Vietnam and 10 per cent in South Vietnam), it was sometimes difficult to convince the Chinese in Malaya that their adopted country was unquestionably going to win the struggle, particularly in view of

Communist victories in Indo-China and the increasing power of Mao Tse-tung.

Thompson knew the Chinese temperament as well as any man in Malaya; he knew that far too many Chinese had never regarded this as 'their' war, and from his first-hand experience of guerrilla warfare in World War Two, he could understand how they must have felt; that, as he put it, 'terror, subversion and penetration . . . can in time breed war weariness, disillusions and loss of hope.' He found an ally in General Bourne, who also felt that 'we couldn't suddenly expect Chinese leaders to take effective interest in Emergency affairs without giving them responsibility.'

It was to take a long time to gain the whole-hearted support of the Chinese, but now at least a start was made. Malay and Chinese leaders were asked to sit on the War Executive Committee at all levels. Within two weeks five political and communal leaders were sitting on General Bourne's top committee; Malays, Chinese, Indians, planters, miners, became members of the State or District War Executive. 'It was,' as Harry Miller felt at the time, 'one of the really important stepping stones towards eventual victory.' For now the Malays and Chinese in particular felt they were 'part of the war', that they were being trusted with its prosecution, being asked to help. With the first national elections less than a year ahead, this was one of the most significant political moves of 1954.

At the same time Bourne decided on a major tactical change on the battle field. There were several reasons for this. The original Briggs-Templer plan had proved itself and had in the words of the official report 'made real progress over the past few years', but as the report stressed, two other factors were beginning to affect the Malayan situation. The first was 'the deterioration of the position of the French in Indo-China', for though the French defeat had nothing to do directly with the war in Malaya, the evidence of a major colonial power being overthrown by Communism was bound to give heart to any waverers. The second point was 'the increasingly delicate political situation'. The word 'delicate' did not imply any divergence of views between the Malayans and the British; but the British did feel that with the clamour for independence growing daily, it was imperative that the Malayan Emergency should be ended quickly.

The new offensive plan* had three main objects: first, SAS units would be deployed along the spinal mountain range to unseat CTs from jungle bases and win over the last remaining unfriendly Abos; secondly, army and police field forces would be used to 'dominate' known bandit areas, remaining in them; and thirdly, police and civil authorities would take over more responsibility for food control.

In many ways the second point of Bourne's plan was the most significant: that troops should remain in given areas where they could work closely with Special Branch. Special Branch had made it clear to Bourne that Communist domination in many area was in the hands of men who had been known locally even before the war started; they made their presence felt as personalities, whereas until now troops had frequently been moved from place to place without any thought of a continuing influence in a given area. But, as Harry Miller felt; 'Domination means that the people in the area slowly lost fear because of the continued presence of troops, that the troops got to know their terrain as intimately as the local Communists.'

Side by side with this, Bourne launched a major jungle food denial and domination scheme in Pahang. Called 'Operation Apollo', the Gurkhas and King's African Rifles aimed to crack the CT organization astride the main

* Seventh Report on the RAF in Malaya, Air Vice-Marshal F. R. W. Scherger, CBE, DSO, AFC.

Communist north-south route and it quickly proved to be one of the most successful strikes of all time. Special curfews, tougher rationing, restrictions on the sale of goods like medicine and cloth were imposed. In a matter of weeks CTs, denied food they had been getting easily from Min Yuen and Abo sources, were beginning to surrender. More than fifty dumps of food, clothing and equipment were found by Malay, Gurkha and British troops. Apart from those killed, twenty-three CTs surrendered. There was, however, one who could not be found. This was Osman China, and to Bob Thompson this elusive CT remained one of the major threats to security. With Chin Peng poised to open up a political front, his propaganda machine must somehow be muzzled, for though the CTs were now becoming more and more demoralized, Osman China still functioned as brilliantly as he had done in 1948. His propaganda office in the deep jungle of Pahang was distributing a nationwide news service for Chin Peng. It had to be stopped before any 'peace offensive' by Chin Peng went into high gear.

Bob Thompson paid a call on an old friend, Bill Carbonell, the Special Branch officer who had succeeded Arthur Young as Commissioner of Police. Both men had grown up together in the service of Malaya, and as Thompson expected, Carbonell – 'once in Special Branch, *always* in Special Branch' – immediately saw that this was no task for the jungle-bashing troops who had done so well in 'Operation Apollo'. Instead it called for a lone hand – a man of iron nerves, imagination, patience, and above all flair, plus an understanding of the Chinese mind amounting almost to sympathy.

The reason was simple, Osman China dead could be replaced. Indeed, he already had a brilliant assistant called Hor Leung, ready to step into his shoes. But Osman China alive could be one of the war's major victories, particularly if he could be bribed to persuade his comrades to surrender.

The man chosen to track down Osman China was David Storrier, the tall, thin, handsome Scot who the previous New Year's Eve had had a whirlwind romance with Lucie Card at Jerantut and had now married her.

It was Storrier – every inch the quiet, unassuming professional detective – who was to be the first man in Malaya to see Templer's daring (and criticized) plan of offering CTs enormous cash bribes bear fruit on a massive scale, for though bribes had of course been paid frequently, it was not until now that a hunted CT would reap a fortune in cold, hard, cash – a fortune far beyond the wildest dreams of the average man.

20 THE MAN WHO LOVED SHAKESPEARE

Osman China was one of the most brilliant propagandists in South-East Asia. A dedicated Communist, he shared the ability to think seriously along Party lines with a practical zeal that made him overcome obstacles before which others would have flinched. Even after years in the jungle, he was still supplying news services to a dozen Communist papers all over Malaya, which seemed to flourish despite the fact that troops would from time to time stumble on small and antiquated printing presses. Different newspapers circulated in their own states or areas. All bore resounding titles such as *Humanity News* in Perak, *The Beacon* in Johore, *True News* in the far north, *Battle News* in Pahang. As a secret government report put it: 'Their content is similar and is largely devoted to accounts of CT successes, the elimination of traitors, and accounts of rape, murder and theft by Security Forces.' More sinister was the fact that these last items 'are obviously printed under a central Bureau directive since the format seldom varies.' That bureau was run by Osman China.

When David Storrier was told of his new assignment he was delighted. While working in Pahang he had from time to time come across traces of Osman China, and in a curious way which he was unable to define, even to himself, he could not help admiring the man, who seemed genuinely to believe in what he was doing – and to be able to carry his plans through.

From the purely personal point of view Storrier was also pleased. After his marriage to Lucie she had continued in her nursing work, but now her contract had expired and she could join him, so they were able to arrive in Lipis, take over a small police house and start married life together for the first time.

Lucie loved Lipis, though it was hardly her idea of a state capital for it consisted of little more than a main road lined with shophouses leading to a T-junction dominated by the solid white police station, with a bank of symmetrically arranged stones spelling out its name next to a flagpole on the cropped green verge, a police board with small caves to protect (in theory anyway) notices from the rain, and rattan blinds guarding the arch-shaped windows of the charge-room from sudden blinding tropical storms.

But it was the Pahang river which fascinated Lucie most. The road leading to it was lined with red, yellow and white flowers or shrubs, and even the grass on the steep bank sloping from the road to the river below seemed greener than anywhere else. Steps led down to homemade wooden houseboats, their washing fluttering on lines, whose only physical connection with the land consisted of wobbling gangplanks hardly more than six inches wide. Papaya, banana, mango trees flourished on the steep drop between roadway and river, while a few strips of latex from rubber trees in the kampongs always lay drying on the road.

During the first weeks, Lucie was busy moving into her first house. In Lipis she bought a Florence oil cooking stove with a tin oven that fitted over the two burners. She bought a refrigerator, 'acquired' a dog, a cat and a pet cockerel. She was not allowed to have any servants, for all David Storrier's plans revolved round informers who would never have visited him had local servants been in evidence. (Lucie remembers how often when she was alone after dark 'I would see two little hands tapping at the window and know someone wanted David.')

CT morale in the area was bad, and several CTs surrendered. Many were starving and Storrier would cheerfully take them home for a meal. Some slept a night or two in the house and it was quite obvious to Lucie that something important was brewing in the area. David would disappear for days at a time and return exhausted, often covered with the peculiar pallor that denotes days spent in the jungle without seeing the sun. But there were happy interludes. Yeop Mahidin, who had operated so successfully in Temerloh, was now working in the area with Storrier and sometimes David would bring Yeop home for supper, stopping his Morris 1000 on the way at Fun Wah, a two-storeyed, tile-roofed Chinese shop on the riverside which sold everything from biscuits to beds – plus excellent Chinese food ready cooked to be taken home and really cheaper than cooking in the house.

Almost before Storrier had settled down on the trail of Osman China, he and Yeop Mahidin were involved in a charming incident 'of the sort', as David remembers, 'which made that rather grim life suddenly worth living'. It happened when Lipis was 'invaded' by eighteen pretty girls.

Even though Kuala Lipis was the state capital of Pahang, it was so forgotten at the end of the northbound road, which ceased abruptly on the outskirts of the town, that nobody could imagine visitors arriving on pleasure trips. Yet as Storrier walked down the steps of the police station to greet Lucie, the ancient four o'clock bus from Kuala

Lumpur came wheezing along the main street, turned left at the T-junction where Storrier stood, came to a halt – and out tumbled eighteen pretty, giggling Malay girls, dressed in their finest sarongs, some with frangipani blossoms in their hair, others carrying bunches of wild orchids.

The bus lumbered on, and as the girls stood in a shy knot in front of the car park near the police station Storrier asked a sergeant to find out what they wanted. The man returned with an incredulous look on his face. 'They want to see Yeop Mahidin – all of them,' he said.

Storrier knew where the fanatical keep-fit Yeop would be at four o'clock – playing tennis. He sent a message and a bewildered Yeop finished the set, jumped into his car, reached the police station - to be greeted by girls who laughed and waved as he climbed out, Yet Yeop had not the faintest idea who they were or what they wanted.

Finally one diminutive girl in a batik sarong presented Yeop with some flowers and asked him shyly, 'Don't you remember me?'

Yeop racked his brains – to no avail, until she said, 'I'm Siti. Don't you remember Temerloh – arresting me after that fight we had in the jungle, and then making me drunk in front of those British officers?'

Then it all flashed back – the wild struggle as he had caught her in the blinding rain in the jungle, the interrogation in Temerloh rest house.

'But what are you doing here?' Yeop looked at her, hardly able to reconcile this clean neat girl with the bedraggled creature he had brought out of the jungle.

Siti explained. The others had also been persuaded to surrender at different times by Yeop or the Vagabonds. They had all served their terms of rehabilitation ('The happiest three years of my life,' said Siti), and were on their way to Temerloh to start new lives. They had made the journey north to Lipis 'to say thank you for helping us'.

The south-bound bus had long since left. There was no accommodation in Lipis. But that, announced Siti, didn't matter. They would stay the night with Yeop and his wife.

'But we've only three rooms,' protested Yeop.

That was of no consequence either. The girls would sleep on the floor. 'When you found us, we were sleeping in the jungle,' one laughed. 'Anything's better than that.'

And stay the night they did. They had all taken cookery lessons in the rehabilitation centre and insisted in preparing a gargantuan meal for Yeop and his wife and the Storriers, after which they stayed up talking until two in the morning.

And all the time, as Yeop looks back on that night, he could not rid his mind of the thought that each one of those girls had been a near Communist when he first met her. What a vindication of his policy of 'making bad people into good citizens'. Had they been sent to prison, who knows what might have happened. The die-hard criminals with whom they would have shared cells, the inhumanity of warders, the bitterness, the frustration – all of this might easily have encouraged them to sympathize with Communism again.

'I felt that night,' Yeop remembers, 'that if I never did anything more for my country in all my life I had at least given it eighteen fine, honest citizens, and when the girls came to say goodbye the next morning I'm not ashamed to admit I had to choke back my tears.'

It took David Storrier only a few weeks to receive virtual proof that Osman China was on the verge of surrender. Agent after agent, calling by night at the modest house on the edge of Lipis, had provided fragments of news, small pieces of a jig-saw puzzle which, when fitted together, produced a picture of a small band of dedicated Communists at the end of their tether. Occasional surrenders would confirm the news that since the army had earlier cleared vast areas of food dumps and supply depots, pockets of CTs were now living off the jungle – and that meant semi-starvation, for Osman China and Hor Leung were not fighters but intellectual Communists, unable to cope with the jungle like ex-Force 136 men.

Storrier himself discovered several massive dumps. In one he had found hundreds of tins of Chinese vegetables, meat, medicines, stocks of paper and pencils – intended no doubt for Osman China, but which had never left the dump. In another Storrier had discovered thousands of yards of water-proofed tent material (which came in handy, for Storrier cut off a length before destroying the stocks and made a new hood for his Morris 1000).

Security Forces had by now also cut off one other CT lifeline – the Aborigines. Deep in the Abo jungle, SAS troops were manning jungle forts supplied once a month by airdrop – forts with names like Dixon, Shean and Tolanok – in the Abo country, protecting the timid Abos and guarding their vegetable gardens from predatory CTs.

But there was one problem. Nobody could pinpoint Osman China's camp; and it would be fatal to send in troops, who would shoot their way in if they did find the camp. For Storrier wanted Osman China and Hor Leung alive, together with their staff of writers. He knew they would be invaluable to men like Bob Thompson and C. C. Too. He had to be a patient until his first big breakthrough came in October.

Late one night a tap on the window warned him of visitors. They were four Aborigines, shy and frightened, dressed in scanty loincloths and with a dozen or more strings of tiny brightly-coloured beads looped over their shoulders. When they came diffidently into the house, he noticed they had small haversacks for their tobacco, flint and tinder slung over their backs. Two carried blowpipes much larger than themselves, and bamboo quivers for their arrows, no doubt poisoned.

They came from Kuala Medang Station, the fort built twelve miles away by a young ex-Palestine policeman for twenty-five cents. Storrier knew it well. It lay five miles or so from the main mountain range, in an area covered with innumerable tracks which had been used by Chin Peng when fighting the Japanese. The police in the fort there looked after ten scattered kampongs with a population of about fifteen hundred Aborigines. Quietly he asked how he could help.

Their information started Storrier tingling with excitement. They knew, they said, the whereabouts of three dispirited CTs who wanted to surrender and, after making sure they would be eligible for a reward, they offered to lead Storrier to them. The CTs insisted that Storrier must be alone, and the next night he returned with them.

For four days Storrier trekked through the jungle and swamp – at night bitten by insects, by day covered with the leeches which crawled up his clothes until they found flesh on which to fasten while they drank his blood.

There three CTs awaited him. They were covered with jungle sores; one had the enormous protruding belly that meant near starvation; another was suffering from beri-beri; the third clearly had malaria. They were members of Osman China's camp who had been sent out as couriers and whose absence had not yet given rise to suspicion. Storrier will never forget the night he spent with them in the local Abo chief's kongsi house, for if the CTs were to be believed, Osman China was wavering. Storrier asked how they could possibly know, since every camp had its quota of diehard Communists before whom none dared to voice their true thoughts. It was a feeling, they explained, an atmosphere. They had all worked together for nearly six years, and 'we just know that most of the camp would surrender if it wasn't so frightened.'

For a year, they said, Osman China and his followers had been living on bananas, tapioca, snake and elephant meat. In place of cigarettes they had been smoking cheroots made from papaya leaves. They had been without drugs for the jungle sores that covered their bodies. All were suffering from dysentery. Four had malaria. Even the wooden stocks of their rifles and tommy-guns had been eaten away by jungle rot. Seven times in the past twelve months they had escaped military ambush; on one occasion Osman China, who had fractured his leg in a jungle accident, had rolled into the jungle and escaped as his comrades fled.

Sitting talking to them in the smoky light of an oil-lamp after a meal of wild boar and fresh vegetables (far better than any available in Lipis), Storrier realized it was essential for the CTs to return to Osman China's camp immediately. With the prospect of large rewards dangling in front of them, they might be able to persuade Osman China that they would all be rich if he did surrender. According to the book, of course, Storrier should have taken the CTs into Lipis for 'processing' before sending them back to the jungle. This, however, would mean wasting at least eight days and would inevitably arouse suspicion in their camp. There was only one way: he must send them back and say nothing in Lipis. This he did, after telling them to report to the same Aborigines if or when they had news.

Storrier's plan all but worked – it certainly would have done but for cruel luck, for though Storrier could not know this, the returning CTs were highly successful and within a month Osman China had decided to surrender. As Storrier learned later, the three CTs found the camp near to disintegration when they returned, and in a week or so they were broaching the subject of possible surrender. Osman China hardly hesitated, and the camp staged a 'free speech meeting' – an extraordinary occasion, for this to Communists amounted to a heinous crime. Only half the CTs were fit enough to attend, but Osman China, who was a brilliant, persuasive speaker, put the facts before his ragged jungle audience. They were on the edge of starvation since the Abo food supplies had been cut off. It would be better, he argued, if each man made his own choice and set off on his own to join a better equipped CT unit, or – and Osman China made his meaning clear without using the word surrender – to make new lives for themselves. The majority sided with him; those who disagreed were stripped of their arms. Osman China was taking no chance of sharing the fate of Shorty Kuk.

That night he sent one of the CTs who had contacted Storrier with a message to the Abos. Unfortunately all but one of the Abos were away hunting, and the one who took the message became frightened. Perhaps the gentle Abos preferred to gather strength from companionship. This one promised to go to Storrier immediately but never went,* and Osman China's first bid to surrender came to nothing.

By now Christmas was approaching and David Storrier was taken to hospital for an operation for goitre. He was convalescing with Lucie on a rubber estate six miles up river from Lipis when, on the morning of December 28, 1954, the old-fashioned telephone rang. It was Yeop Mahidin calling from Lipis. Three Abos ('They seem to know you very well!') had come into Lipis looking for Storrier. Finding his house empty, they had gone to the police station. There they announced that Osman China wanted to surrender but would only do so to David Storrier.

'Keep them till I come!' Storrier yelled down the ancient telephone – his convalescence, his host, forgotten in the excitement. Within five minutes Storrier and Lucie were

* Not until later did Storrier interview the simple Abo, who told him unaccountably that 'I was afraid I might be punished for aiding a CT.'

in a sampan with an outboard motor, sprayed by the wash of brown water as the flimsy craft slid and bucked along the Pahang river.

In Lipis, Storrier called at the police station, picked up the three Aborigines and took them home, while he packed a few belongings – a carbine, pistol, some tinned rations, water-bottle, sheath knife, morphia, and syringe – just in case he was wounded in an ambush. Yet it seemed safe, for these were the Abos he had met before and they insisted that Osman China was already in their kampong, a small place called Ula Atok, ten miles south-west of Lipis.

Taking two Malay constables with him, Storrier set off. The way to Ulu Atok was not difficult though it took time, for to avoid the danger of walking into a trap Storrier deliberately took a roundabout route which meant a stiff climb above the jungle level. Storrier could hardly restrain his excitement and yet he remembers that 'the sense of victory was tinged with regret,' perhaps because Osman China was not a killer but a dedicated believer. 'I suppose that made a difference.'

The Abos willingly took him by the hill route, and, tired after the unaccustomed exertion, Storrier rested at the summit, and for a moment forgot the drama that lay ahead in the beauty of the scene, for Storrier had spent so much time *in* the never-ending monotony of the jungle that he had hardly realized the colour and beauty that flourished unseen high *above* the trees. It was a beautiful day, and as he looked down from the crest of the ridge, the jungle treetops were spread below him like a multi-coloured carpet of violent flowering creepers, clusters of tree-tulips, orchids, butterflies, birds of every hue darting in a world unknown and unseen from below.

He remembers that he felt very exhausted, but he pushed on in clammy heat and finally reached the kongsi of the headman under the shade of a giant banyan tree with roots hanging down from the upper branches like twisted, fossilized serpents. On the ground near the steps stood a food cupboard, its legs resting in rusty cigarette tins filled with water to stop the ants climbing up to the wire mesh doors.

The headman invited him into the long communal room. And there, as though Storrier had reached the end of a journey, stood Osman China; only thirty, he looked like a scarecrow in his tattered uniform. Emaciated, covered with sores, his hand trembled as he held it out and said, 'You must be Storrier. You've persuaded me to give up.' Then, in excellent English, he added with an attempt at a smile, 'I've brought eight of my friends out with me.'

Like a true Scot, Storrier was a great believer in the therapeutic value of whisky as a means of loosening tongues, of lessening tension. He uncorked a bottle of scotch and the nine CTs spluttered over the fiery liquid. Like many surrendering CTs, Osman China was more uninhibited and talkative in the first few hours (before his enthusiasm had waned). No doubt the 'shock treatment' helped – the plate of steaming curry, the whisky. At first Osman China looked at the food suspiciously, then he could no longer resist it and started to wolf it down.

They stayed the night in the kongsi, and the next morning Osman China led Storrier to his camp. As Storrier looked at it: 'I felt a sort of pity for the men who had been living in it like animals for month after month. It was easy to understand why they had come to the end of their dedication.' For no longer were these 'the good old days' when camps of a hundred CTs had been common, where Communists were housed in elaborate huts with parade grounds, with streams for bathing, with days occupied in physical training, drill, lectures, political discussions. All that had changed. All that faced Storrier, looking round the camp, was a collection of miserable huts perched on platforms, each one reeking with a stench that must have repelled the normally clean Chinese. He could imagine the nerve-racked life they must have led, always on the alert for enemy troops, always prepared for instant flight in a jungle rife with disease, hardship and hunger. Not for the first time, Storrier's feelings were tinged with a touch of admiration for their bravery.

'You look done in,' Storrier told the man who walked with a limp from the broken leg that had never been properly set in the jungle; and then added on the spur of the moment, 'You'd better come and stay with my wife and myself for a bit.'

So started a strange friendship between two men who until that moment had been sworn enemies. Storrier, of course, had gained a great moral victory in *not* killing the good-looking man who had gone into the jungle six years ago with a copy of Shakespeare under his arm. But when later he came to analyse that friendship, it was not the personalities that seemed to matter. To Storrier it all came back to the profound difference between the two guerrilla wars in which he had been so deeply involved – one jungle, one urban. In Palestine, it had been a Lenin-type urban war, sometimes with both sides shooting it out in the streets, so that as the British saw innocent women and children struck down they came to loathe their adversaries. And though it was true that the CTs had committed some unspeakable atrocities, the Mao-style jungle war was on the whole cleaner. For the most part it was one man against another, the hunter and the hunted, and Storrier remembers feeling that if he had had to kill Osman China (as he would have done if necessary) it would have been with the same regret that the big game hunter feels when he brings down a jungle adversary.

In Lipis Lucie provided her first meal for their strange new house guest. It included tinned sausages – and Osman China observed with a wry smile that they reminded him of dinner at Singapore's Victoria School where he had passed his Senior Cambridge Examination.

But it was after dinner – and also after Storrier had mentioned the rewards granted to men bringing out CTs – that Osman China said he believed he could persuade more waverers to surrender by employing a highly unusual 'surrender-by-mail' campaign. Because he had been running a 'news service', Osman China was one of the few CTs who knew many jungle letter routes, and he told Storrier that he felt his friend Hor Leung, a high-ranking member of the Pahang State Committee, 'might be persuaded to join us'. Osman China wrote to his old friend among others. The letter was handed to an Abo headman and after some delay Hor Leung wrote back: 'I would like your assistance in surrendering.'

So once again Storrier set off for the jungle, this time with Osman China and a force of eight men, including a radio operator. They set off by river at dawn in two sampans with small outboard motors and did not reach the Abo settlement, which was called Kuala Kenip, till late afternoon. There was only one kongsi house, where the headman made Storrier welcome, while the police quickly and skilfully made themselves bashas by knocking into the ground two upright forked poles, laying a ridge pole across and covering the frame with attap palm leaves.*

The next morning Osman China sent a rather quaint message to Hor Leung: 'I have arrived here with my boss. He's quite a good type. You needn't be afraid of him.' The letter was handed to an Aborigine and Storrier settled down, prepared for a long wait. To his astonishment, Hor Leung walked into the camp ten minutes later. He almost

---

* Attap not coconut because, unlike the coconut, the attap palm has no trunk and therefore no climbing is required. The fronds spread upwards and outwards from the base and it is a simple matter to cut fronds off, split them down the spine and lay over-lapping half-sections across the frame to make a completely weather-proof shelter.

fell on Osman China's neck and then, turning to Storrier, said laconically, 'Thanks for coming.'

Hor Leung was as remarkable in his way as Osman China. A chubby-faced smiling man who spoke hesitant English ('I haven't spoken to a European for several years,' he apologized), he was quite up-to-date on international Communism. To Storrier, watching the two men talking and laughing, it all smacked of an unreal dream, for they started discussing politics as though they were in their own homes, not in an Aborigine house ill-lit with an oil-lamp. Hor Leung calmly announced that there must be internal dissension in Moscow because of the assassination of Beria. He then started discussing Nehru's latest anti-colonial speeches, and when Storrier mentioned casually that he seemed to know many parts of the world, Hor Leung modestly said that at school he had always been good at geography.

'Very useful in the jungle,' said Osman China with a grin.

Much more important, Hor Leung now produced highly exciting information. He knew of three groups of CTs equally anxious to surrender, and if Storrier agreed, he would send messages to them. Storrier did agree.

In all, Storrier spent thirteen nights in the headman's longhouse as the CTs trickled in. He had radioed Lipis to freeze the area of all troop movements, and to stop spotter aircraft flying over the area; though he did ask for Voice aircraft (long recognized as peaceful by all CTs) to fly low over the district, announcing that Osman China and Hor Leung had surrendered.

For Storrier there was nothing to do but wait. The matter of surrenders was out of his hands, and so, in a way, this was his convalescence. He ate Abo food, spent the days fishing with the Abos or panning (unsuccessfully) for gold which was occasionally found in the small rivers. On the thirteenth day Storrier decided it was time to return to Lipis. In all, eighteen more CTs had given themselves up, making twenty in all. It was the biggest surrender operation so far in the war.

Storrier now had to find a way of taking his CTs back to Lipis. His two sampans could not possibly carry them, so he radioed to Lipis for a helicopter after setting the Abos to work clearing a patch of secondary jungle to make a landing zone. Storrier did one thing more. Before the helicopter arrived he arranged with the headman to call in every possible Abo to a vast jungle meeting. In front of the strange assembly clad in loincloths, each man with his blowpipe, each woman daubed with paint, Storrier paraded his twenty CTs – to prove that not one of them had been tortured into surrendering. He knew the Abos would pass the word to any other CTs in the area.

It was almost with a feeling of regret at leaving that Storrier watched the helicopter hover over the pad and finally come in to land, blowing up high clouds of dust. Hundreds of Abos had assembled and the CTs had to help police prevent them from running madly for the jungle – or on to the pad – before the blades had stopped turning. They had never seen anything like this before and were terrified. Storrier had to admit that 'it was worth the entire operation, just to see the expression on the Abos' faces as the helicopter came in to land.'

Back in Lipis, Osman China stayed for some time with the Storriers and proved invaluable. He sent messages to CTs that he was being well treated, and in all more than forty surrendered, with not a soldier operating in the area. Very soon Osman China was given freedom to move about Lipis – and would regularly return the Storriers' hospitality by taking them out to dinner. Later, under the auspices of C. C. Too, he went 'on tour' in rural areas addressing anti-Communist meetings in flawless Chinese or Malay.

Osman China received rewards totalling nearly $80,000 for persuading CTs to surrender, Hor Leung slightly less.

Payment of these huge cash sums – more than a tapper could hope to earn in a lifetime – made some members of the government uneasy, and they did not find it easy to approve. Yet they had to admit that Special Branch by now understood the CT mentality enough to believe that a big reward was the surest way to bait a trap.

Storrier had only one small and unimportant regret. Before leaving Lipis, Osman China wanted to present him with a gold fountain pen and pencil as a farewell gift 'to the man who was so kind to me'. Before accepting what might have been construed as a bribe, Storrier asked the Chief of Police if it would be in order to accept the gift. To his dismay, he was met with a firm 'No'. Osman China was so upset that he too asked for special permission, but it was refused.

There were, however, no heartburnings over the reward paid to the Abos who led Storrier to the first CTs. The money enabled them to acquire articles beyond their wildest dreams – though an incredulous Storrier tried in vain to stop them descending on Lipis where they bought refrigerators, gramophones and radios working off the mains, and which they then hauled back with pride to their jungle kampongs which had never known electricity.

21 THE CONFRONTATION

In many ways 1955 was the most significant year of the war. Though 25,000 British troops still squelched wearily in swamp or jungle patrols, though Special Branch was patiently drawing the net closer, though brutal murders continued, this was the year when the emphasis really switched from the bullet to the ballot. Of course the war went on, but it seemed that the atmosphere had changed.

It was most noticeable in Kuala Lumpur, with its opulent mosque and tailored travellers' palms. For over six years the Federal capital had been feeling the strain. No one trusted his neighbour. Important people kept their movements secret; shops closed at 6.00 p.m. instead of eleven. Half the restaurants had drawn their shutters. Fear of inflation and currency depreciation had ironically led to the only boom in Kuala Lumpur: the goldsmiths were doing a lucrative trade among people nervous of hoarding cash.

Then almost without warning things changed. To Dr Reid Tweedie, visiting the capital in the spring of 1955, 'It was a feeling hard to describe, as though someone had given the whole city a pep pill.' David and Lucie Storrier spent three days' leave in the capital and Lucie particularly remembers the night they had dinner at the Coliseum, for long the favourite bar and restaurant in Kuala Lumpur. The Coliseum was famous for its outside curry puffs – served in the mahogany-lined bar – and its 'sizzling steaks', for which the client was draped in a large bib and given a nearly red-hot iron plate on a wooden tray on which the steak was cooked in front of him.

'The difference,' Lucie remembers, 'was incredible. Half the planters round the bar hadn't bothered to bring their guns. They stayed drinking and singing till midnight. The last time we were there the place looked like an arsenal till five o'clock – and like a morgue by half past as everyone left for home before it got dark.'

Of course the capital was gripped by the excitement of the country's first general election, with politicians feverishly preparing for polling day in July. The fact that there was to be an election at all was in itself indicative of the increased confidence, for though the High Commissioner would still rule in the Queen's name and have the power of veto, this was the final step before independence, with much more power being handed over to the people of the country.

It was now that Tunku Abdul Rahman again showed his political shrewdness. The Tunku was determined to win the election because he knew that if he did so, he would be poised to lead the country when it was granted independence. As leader of the United Malays' National Organization, he realized that to make certain of winning the election he must enlarge his alliance with the Malayan Chinese Association (which had given him victory at the 1953 local elections) to include members of the Malayan Indian Congress Party. In other words, the 1952 Alliance Party must become the Triple Alliance. Quietly the Tunku set about winning over the minority Indian party by offering them certain seats on condition that they would not field candidates against him in others. Thus the Tunku was able to prepare for the election secure in the knowledge that the Triple Alliance Party would have a solid backing – especially as, sensing the war-weariness of the people, he included a proposed amnesty offer to Chin Peng in his election manifesto.

A month before the election, with the country increasingly gripped by political fever, Chin Peng dropped a bombsell. He offered to negotiate a peace settlement at a round-table conference. This was Chin Peng's first peace feeler, and it took the form of a letter posted in Haadyai, Southern Thailand, addressed to the United Planters' Association of Malaya 'for transmission to political and communal organizations'. In it he suggested that the various political parties should hold a conference to plan ways of ending the fighting.

Chin Peng did not add his name to this, the first of many letters he was to send. It was signed 'Ng Heng, a representative of the Supreme Command Headquarters of the Malayan Liberation Army'. By now Special Branch had complete lists of wanted CTs but none included this name, and it has been generally assumed that this was an alias for Chin Peng.

The Communist leader had chosen the moment astutely, knowing that most parties were making

independence and peace their main electioneering platforms, but the government – backed wholeheartedly by
Malayan political leaders – rejected the letter as 'a typical
Communist peace offensive' aimed at disrupting the elections, and 'a letter of defeat by the Communists'.

'We have seen these sudden shifts in Communist policy
before,' said a government statement, 'and we shall not
be misled by this one. Knowing the true purpose of the
Communist offer and the motives which underlie it, the
government rejects it absolutely and has no intention of
negotiating with the Communist terrorists. If the Communists genuinely wish to end the emergency, they can do
this today.'

On July 31, eighty-five per cent of the electorate went to
the polls. Though Malay nationalism was the dominant
political factor, the Tunku skilfully modified it to accept
the need for compromise with the Chinese and Indian
Communities. The result was a resounding victory for the
Triple Alliance party, which polled 818,000 votes and fifty
one out of fifty-two seats. So the portly, handsome, 43-
year-old Tunku, with his closely cropped Ronald Coleman
moustache and spectacles that slipped regularly down his
nose, became Malaya's first Chief Minister.

It had taken no small skill on his part to weld together
the Malay, Chinese and Indian parties, for trust between
the races did not grow easily. Since, however, the future
of the country was at stake, all races contributed to this
act of faith, and the foundations for an inter-racial state
were laid.

Malaya was now but one stage removed from independence, and a new phase of the war had opened in which
Malays would take a much greater share of the responsibility. In his first public statement the Tunku promised
that his first priority would be a 'swift ending' to the war
and that he would offer an amnesty 'at the right time and

with the advice of the experts'. He made it clear that his second priority was independence, though he was not going to 'rush into it'. He did, however, strongly criticize the fact that the High Commissioner still retained the power of veto, insisting that these powers must be made 'purely advisory' within two years or earlier if possible. 'If the High Commissioner vetos Bills passed by us,' he declared, 'we are not working for the people and we might as well walk out. Naturally we are not anxious to clash, but I cannot rest until this matter of veto powers is finally settled.'

Not all Malay leaders felt so strongly. When the fun-loving pro-British octogenarian Sultan of Johore celebrated his diamond jubilee a week later at Johore Bahru, the State capital, he gave a strongly-worded warning against premature independence.

'It's all very well to clamour for merdeka [freedom],' he declared, 'but where are your warships, your planes, your armies to withstand and repel aggression from outside?' After saying that he often wondered why the British people should continue to send their sons to be killed in Malaya, the Sultan declared: 'If I were British I would leave Malaya today. But if the British go today, someone else will come in tomorrow.'

The Sultan's speech so infuriated the Tunku and other members of the Federation Government attending the celebrations that they boycotted the state banquet to which they had been invited.

There was no veto or disagreement, however, when on September 9 the Tunku offered Chin Peng an amnesty so generous that he was even prepared to absolve CTs for murder. 'Those of you who come in and surrender will not be prosecuted for any offence connected with the Emergency which you have committed under Communist direction either before this date or in ignorance of this declaration,' the Tunku promised. Those who refused to give up their Communist beliefs could surrender and be repatriated to China.

Twelve million Amnesty Passes were showered on the jungle. In Chinese, Tamil and Malay, each leaflet guaranteed:

> The holder of this pass wishes to accept the general amnesty arrangement declared by the Federation Government. Instructions have been given to all security forces, police, military and government officers, to look after the holder of this pass carefully and treat him fairly. They will be held responsible for carrying out these instructions.

It does not seem that the Tunku expected dramatic results from the amnesty offer. Rather was he putting Chin Peng into the position of having to reply, to act. Meanwhile the government was content to wait. Three weeks later Chin Peng did reply with letters indicating that in all but name the CTs were beaten. He called for an immediate ceasefire and talks to end the war. Letters posted in the Perak village of Klian Intan, eleven miles south of the Thai border, were addressed to the Tunku, David Marshall, Singapore's Chief Minister, and several other prominent politicians. All were signed quaintly, 'Yours honestly, Chin Peng.' David Marshall's first reaction was: 'Let us be fair to Chin Peng, it's a very courteous letter.'

Chin Peng made three basic points: he wished to send an envoy to Kuala Lumpur; an immediate ceasefire should be arranged; and a meeting should take place between Tunku Abdul Rahman and Chin Peng as soon as possible. 'To avoid further losses of human lives and property,' wrote Chin Peng, 'and to enable the various political problems to be settled in a peaceful atmosphere, it is essential that the representatives concerned must first come to an agreement on complete ceasefire. We believe that if the British military authorities are sincere, a complete ceasefire can be realized early.'

Chin Peng's letter clearly showed that he recognized one thing: the Malayan nationalist movement had fallen into the hands of his opponents and he was trying to produce an equation which would end a useless revolution with some advantage to himself. The letter was significant enough to be published in full in Russia's Cominform Journal.

The Tunku's feelings were clear: obviously Chin Peng was deeply anxious about the future, especially now that the Alliance Government 'had knocked the props from under the MCP anti-colonial platform'. And he told close friends that he had no objection to meeting Chin Peng if that would speed the end of hostilities.

In the strange way that the evil of war always seems to produce some unexpected good, this offer of Chin Peng's was to have far-reaching effects on Malaya and do incalculable harm to the Communist cause; for there were two violently opposed reactions to it in Kuala Lumpur.

The politicians – who had promised to work for peace – felt that the meeting should take place, that Chin Peng would surrender and that even if the Communists were permitted to remain as a legal political party – well, they could be watched. The British were horrified at such a prospect. Special Branch was convinced that Chin Peng could never regain the initiative in a shooting war; they were equally convinced that the peace proposal was a typical manoeuvre on the part of a Communist leader determined in the long run to control the country by one means or another, and that 'they would be more dangerous outside the jungle than inside'.

With Special Branch against the meeting, the tension in Kuala Lumpur was highly charged and many leading politicians began to believe that the British were not over-anxious to end the war, since it had long ago been agreed that independence would only be granted *after* victory. As Harry Miller discovered, 'politically the British government suddenly became more unpopular. They were suspected of not wishing to give the country independence.'

In fact the British were in a dilemma, for if they prevented the Tunku from flexing his muscles and trying to end the war, they would be accused of 'Imperialism'. If on the other hand they agreed to the meeting, Chin Peng would without doubt exploit the move as a Communist victory.

And so, simply because the British *were* faced with a dilemma, a momentous decision was made, and it so happened that Bob Thomson played an important role in this owing to a curious factor unconnected with the war. The Tunku and Thompson were close friends because they shared one passion – the racecourse, which had been responsible for the Tunku taking twelve years to pass his law finals. Bob's wife Merryn also shared their enthusiasm, and of course she had known the Tunku well when her father was Chief Secretary. And so for a long time the Tunku and the Thompsons had been in the habit of meeting quietly, unofficially, and the Tunku had come to rely a great deal on Thompson, feeling that he was one man in the government with whom he could always talk off the record – and as Security Co-ordinating Officer, Bob Thompson had a great deal to talk about. The Tunku sounded Bob Thompson now.

Who actually devised the simple but courageous solution to the anti-British feeling will never be known, but after consultations with Whitehall, the British government, which had always insisted that independence could not be granted until the Communists had been beaten, swept away all the fears of Malay politicians with a new, bold declaration that Britain did not need to wait until the end of the war before giving independence. It no longer considered that 'the continuation of the Emergency' remained 'an obstacle to the Federation's advance to self-government'. Thompson regarded the solution as knocking years off the time Malaya would have had to wait for independence'. And ironically it was Chin Peng's letter that without doubt had hastened the date.

Now that the government was armed with this knowledge – for this was still another prop knocked from under Ching Peng – there seemed no reason why the preliminary talks should not take place. Somewhat naturally, Chin Peng had no forwarding address, but he asked the Tunku to give his reply in code over Radio Malaya, and the code message was relayed for several days, no doubt puzzling listeners who heard the incomprehensible items of broadcast information. To Chin Peng the message was loud and clear. The Tunku agreed to a preliminary meeting between Communist representatives and Mr. I. S. Wylie, Deputy Police Commissioner. Wylie had been parachuted into Malaya with Force 136 and had known Chin Peng well. He also knew the leader of Chin Peng's delegation – Chan Tien, also of Force 136, who had attended Communist conferences in Prague, London and Calcutta, and had taken part in the Victory Parade in London.

The preparatory commission met three times – in October and November at Klian Intan in an atmosphere that would have been regarded as comic opera had it not been of such serious import. Villages blocked the main street to catch a glimpse of Chin Peng's representatives, real CTs who were for the moment 'free'; the CTs were interviewed by the local Press, and Chan Tien was even able to order back numbers of the *Straits Times* containing articles about himself. But the talks *were* important, for they finally paved the way for Chin Peng to come out of the jungle and meet the Tunku for the first time since hostilities opened.

In the last ten days of December security forces received a sudden ceasefire order covering an area of four hundred square miles near the Thai border. To everyone 'in the know' the inference was obvious: at last Chin Peng, whom nobody had seen for years, wanted to make peace. The meeting was to be held in the English School at Baling, a town of 17,000 people twenty miles from the Thai frontier, and if on the face of it there seemed at last a real prospect of peace, Special Branch still had certain reservations; for they believed that if any concessions were made to Chin Peng it would be tantamount to losing the war. Their fears were not groundless, for talk of concessions was in the air; both sides badly wanted to end the war – the Communists because they knew they were being beaten, the Malays because the war would be an intolerable burden during their first years of independence. What made the impending meeting more dangerous was the fact that the Tunku as Chief Minister was able to insist that only Malayans should take part in the talks with Chin Peng. Special Branch was only too aware that the Tunku would certainly court unpopularity by allowing a long war to continue at a time when Chou En-lai was making concessions at Bandung and preaching the gospel of co-existence. Nor were Special Branch fears allayed by the Tunku's remark: 'I feel we are in a strong position. But when I am strong, that is when I feel there is room for leniency.' And, as many people argued, Chin Peng had only fought for his beliefs and would it not be easier to bury the past now that independence was all but reality? The idea was attractive, for as Professor Anthony Short puts it, 'There is, I believe, a refreshing quality of Asian tolerance which is willing to forget the past and unwilling to create unnecessary trouble, particularly on a matter of principle.'

In London, however, the mood was very different. The *Daily Mail* declared: 'A tiger will emerge from his lair in the Malayan jungle to talk of peace. The tiger is Chin Peng, leader of the CTs who for more than seven years have spread death, destruction and misery in a vain attempt to gain political power by force of arms. We may pray for peace in Malaya, but not peace at Chin Peng's price.' *The Manchester Guardian* was even more percipient: 'It is a delusion to think that the Communists in Malaya are coming to discuss surrender,' it said. 'Their coming is a move in their political manœuvres.'

Though the Tunku was no fool, Special Branch did feel that some politicians close to the Malay leader should be warned of the dangers ahead, and fortunately there was one man universally respected by all politicians because of his unique knowledge of the Chinese mind. This was C. C. Too of Psychological Warfare, who now produced a scintillating idea. Before some of the Tunku's advisers, Too staged an extraordinary secret 'dress rehearsal' of the forthcoming meeting at Baling.

It took place in Police Headquarters at Kuala Lumpur. Too played the part of Chin Peng, while the role of the Tunku was played by a British brigadier. Police had rigged up a conference table across which 'Chin Peng' and 'The Tunku' with their 'advisers' sat facing each other, with the questions and answers going backwards and forwards. Too knew exactly how Chin Peng's mind worked, and now he asked just the questions that Chin Peng would be certain to put to the Tunku at Baling.

For an entire day the 'Baling Talks' were staged – and from the outset it was obvious that the eloquent Too was beating and baffling the brigadier at every turn – and persuading the Tunku's dismayed advisers that without doubt the fears of Special Branch must be relayed to the Tunku.

Those arranging the talks faced another problem: someone would have to look after Chin Peng when he emerged from the jungle with, so to speak, diplomatic privileges. John Davis, Senior District Officer, Butterworth, was appointed Conducting Officer. Davis, however, was much more than a District Officer. A broad-shouldered man of forty-nine with twinkling blue eyes and a shock of unmanageable hair, he was, literally one of Chin Peng's closest friends, for in Force 136 he had spent two years with the Communist leader in the jungle before being deputed by Mountbatten to accept the Japanese surrender.

By Boxing Day all was ready in Baling. The one-storey school where the talks would be held lay behind the town, past the local doctor's house, on a slight rise, surrounded by gardens dotted with jacaranda and frangipani trees, with a huge mountain glowering across the other side of the valley. Troops had enclosed the school grounds behind a three-layered barbed wire fence, while in the largest building three partitioned rooms had been turned into a conference hall furnished with a long table with three seats on either side and places for interpreters at each end. Behind this room another building had been set aside for Chin Peng and his party to rest, eat and sleep.

The other members of the Tunku's 'team' were David Marshall, from Singapore, and Sir Chen Lock Tan, leader of the Malayan Chinese Association, Chin Peng would be accompanied by two members of his Politburo in Thailand – Chan Tien and Rashid Maideen, an inconspicuous Malay elevated to Central Committee rank to show the solidity of non-Chinese CTs.

The first meeting was scheduled for 2.15 p.m. on the 28th, and shortly after 8.00 a.m. Davis set off along a twisting eighteen-mile road to the remote tin-mining village of Klian Intan to meet Chin Peng. Here the country bordering the jungle had an almost eerie quality, for the top of a mountain had years previously been carved off by the Rahman Hydraulic Mines, leaving a moonscape of dozens of shades, with roads sliced into the sides where once the powerful hydraulic drills of the tin miners had thrust away all the soil, after which the rains had swilled down, turning the landscape into fantastic crumbled pillars amid the red and ochre cliffs.

Behind loomed the jungle and as Davis waited, surrounded by British troops camped on the flat summit of the hill, 'the thoughts of the past – of the good times Chin Peng and I had had together – kept racing through my mind.' Davis could not dislike the man. Indeed, he was eagerly awaiting the first glimpse of him, and when Chin Peng, dressed in a cream shirt (he regarded himself as a politician, not a soldier) emerged from the jungle fringe, David walked towards him. Both men smiled and as they shook hands both said the same words at the same time in Chinese: 'It's a long time since we last met.'

For half an hour before setting off for Baling Davis briefed Chin Peng and his aides (who included a cook, two secretaries and two couriers) on the mechanics of the meeting – the arrangements that had been made for food, sleeping quarters, the time-table of the conference. Then they drove down the moonscape in a jeep, changed into police trucks with hard seats, and set off in a convoy of six vehicles for Baling. There Chin Peng relaxed in the rest room where a new tube of toothpaste, a toothbrush and a cake of soap lay on every bed. The first thing Chin Peng demanded was 'Can we have some new singlets and underpants?' These arrived as his cook started a fire to prepare a meal.

At exactly 2.15, the Tunku and his party left their rest house, Chin Peng and his party left theirs, and both arrived at the makeshift conference room together.

The Tunku's terms were generous – any surrendered guerrillas willing to abandon Communism would be freed after a period of detention or, if they wished, repatriated to China. Chin Peng was prepared to disband his army, but insisted that the Communists must be recognized as a legal political party after Malaya's freedom.

'I'm not coming here,' he said, 'to urge questions of ideology, but if questions of peace are to be discussed, we are prepared to do so. However, the Malayan Communist

Party must enjoy equal status to fight by constitutional means.'

This was the trap which the Special Branch had most feared, for it was highly tempting for the political leader of a country on the verge of independence (and with an eye to votes) to accept such a proposition and conveniently forget the strife and subversion caused by Communism. The well-briefed Tunku refused, however, and the talks, which were held in English, were ironically doomed to failure partly because of the honesty of both leaders. It would have been easy for the Tunku, had he been more devious, to agree to Chin Peng's request while making a mental reservation to shadow all the Communist leaders as they returned to normal life, later arrest them and then, on the first flimsy pretext, declare the Communist Party illegal.

On the other hand, Chin Peng honestly stood his ground on his belief in Communism as a way of life. 'As a member of the Malayan Communist Party,' he argued, 'we believe in our ideology. We will never allow ourselves to be forced by others to give up this ideology. We wish to put our ideology to the people. In fact the main purpose in coming to these talks was to get recognition for the MCP.'

Chin Peng could not afford to be devious. He could not employ the old Communist trick of agreeing to dissolve the Party while deciding secretly to reassemble its members when the time was ripe for one very important reason: only if the Communist Party were recognized could Chin Peng claim that he had won the independence of Malaya. If he could 'prove' that, then he would be able to salvage victory out of defeat and be in a position to parade his conquering army through every street in Malaya on Independence Day as they had paraded after the surrender of Japan.

The first day's talks did not break up until after eight

that night, and the next morning the impasse continued
with Chin Peng finally saying, 'If you demand our surrender we would prefer to fight to the last man. I am not
telling a lie, I am telling the truth.'

Sadly Tunku, who had at one stage held out high hopes,
replied to the podgy Chin Peng,* as he pulled another
cigarette from his circular tin, 'If you want to have peace
in this country one side must give in – either we give in
to you, or you give in to us. I will never give in, so *you*
must give in, otherwise what has happened in China and
Korea and Indo-China will happen to us and Malaya is
too small to be divided by warring factions.'

Chin Peng's manners had until now been exemplary,
but suddenly he became angry and, pushing back his chair,
he stood up and cried in Mandarin, '*Chay Yang Hao*!'
which means in the Chinese colloquial, 'That suits us
fine.' At this the talks ended, and a possible third day's
meeting was abruptly cancelled.

It was a bitter disappointment to the Tunku, who had
genuinely hoped that he and Chin Peng could come to
terms, especially as he was able to give Chin Peng the
latest count of Communist casualty figures for 1955 – 245
surrenders, 362 killed, 56 captured, with 14,000 square
miles of Malaya now 'White'. Chin Peng, however, seemed
uninterested.

At least the Tunku was cured of a certain naïve streak
in his nature. 'When I was briefed by British experts I
always felt they were interested in making a bad case
against Communists,' he confessed sadly, 'but now Chin
Peng has taught me that Malaya and Communism can
never co-exist.'

There was an intriguing, if unimportant, epilogue to the
meeting, which goes to show the narrow margin that so
often separates enemies, or perhaps more, how easy it

---

* Davis thought his increased fat might be due to beri-beri.

would be for men to be friends if only governments and ideologies did not rule their actions.

It was too late for Chin Peng to return that night to the jungle, so John Davis escorted him back to the moonscape mountain where British troops hastily erected two tents – one for the CT leader, one for his conducting officer. Davis, however, spurned the second tent. 'Chin Peng is a friend – why on earth shouldn't we share a tent?' he asked. And so Davis and Chin Peng, one-time comrades in arms, now sworn enemies, slept in the same tent. Chinese food mysteriously appeared and the two men talked until the early hours of the morning. Davis found Chin Peng to be deeply upset. He had, he said, 'fully expected to win the war', and then added with an odd lack of logic, 'You British have let us down.'

'I always had a great deal of time for Chin Peng,' Davis remembers. 'He was by far the most intelligent of all the Communists, calm, polite, very friendly – in fact, almost like a British officer.'

The next morning Davis went with Chin Peng to the jungle fringe and when one of the bodyguard doubted the neutrality of British troops a hundred yards away, Davis offered to walk into the jungle 'just to show you that you won't be shot'. With Chin Peng he walked a quarter of a mile into the deep jungle, all the sun obscured by the heavy umbrella of trees, just as the two men had walked hundreds of times in the days of Force 136. Finally Chin Peng said, 'You'd better go back. I'll give you one of my men to escort you.'

It was at this moment – 10.30 a.m. – that John Davis uttered the last words he ever spoke to Chin Peng. 'What!' he exclaimed. 'Be escorted by a Communist in my own country! I'll go back alone.'

Chin Peng smiled faintly, the two men shook hands and Davis walked back to the sunlight. Within a couple of hours troops were taking down the barbed wire fence at

Baling, forty telecommunications men were dismantling their complicated apparatus, and by that afternoon the sleepy trading town under the shadow of the mountain had returned to normal.

22 'THE FAT ONE'

While the Tunku and Chin Peng were trying in vain to find a formula to end the war, Special Branch had decided that an all-out-effort must be made to break the Communist domination in one of the few remaining black spots in Malaya – Johore, still under the domination of Goh Peng Tun, the brutal murderer who had killed a Fijian major and nearly killed Ian Tedford of the Cameronians in a midnight ambush. Goh had to be found, and it was now that a fascinating larger-than-life character, straight from the pages of Simenon, was called upon to pit his wits against Goh. Evan Davies was a master in the technique of using double agents. He had been a policeman on the beat in London before being promoted to Special Branch, followed by a spell as a Commando during World War Two. He had two characteristics – an uncanny knowledge of how to infiltrate into the underworld, and a charm of manner (combined with impeccable manners) which immediately stamped him as being on equal terms with world figures. These he had met in great number, for until his arrival in Malaya he had been Churchill's personal bodyguard. Because of his benign countenance and portly figure, Churchill had christened Davies 'The Bishop'.

In Malaya Davies had been engaged in highly secret work against CTs, yet in a curious way he had become friends with many of them. The realistic Chinese felt they could trust Davies and soon found their own name for the portly gentleman with the moustache. The name was Fai Chai, 'The Fat One', and it became known, feared, yet respected, in every CT camp in Malaya. Davies was very proud of it, and of the phrase he was to hear time after time when contacting CTs: 'I hear, Fai Chai, that you deal straight.'

Now he packed his bags, together with a handsome stock of Hennesay XO brandy and several boxes of large Havana cigars (a habit he had picked up from Churchill), and set off in his cream two-seater sports car, driving with his usual dash and verve to Kluang in Johore, a sullen township of 35,000 people gripped like a vice by the Communist machine.

Kluang lay about sixty miles north of the Johore Strait. It was an ugly, predominantly Chinese town, which together with Yong Peng, thirteen miles to the west, had one of the most unsavoury reputations in the country. Virtually every family had a relative in the jungle, and had long since been cowed into abjectly serving them, occasionally for sympathetic reasons, more often from fear. Early in the war Goh, who was completely fearless, had marched into the town, singled out a man who had helped the police, taken him to the jungle fringe, and pegged him down in the hot sun to be eaten by ants. To make his suffering worse he added his own touch of refinement: he brought the man's pregnant wife and sliced open her stomach in front of the captive husband. Since then Kluang had offered him no resistance, despite the presence of several British regiments, including the South Wales Borderers under Colonel Richard Miers who had their neat camp (with its inevitable signpost 'To Cardiff 9,031 miles') on the edge of the town.

When Davies moved into a house inside the perimeter ring, he knew that even Special Branch – to say nothing of his domestic staff – could easily have been subverted, so the first thing he did was to transfer every Special Branch man in the area and replace them with men of his own choice. Next he dismissed every house servant and imported a Punjabi Sikh from India called David who was never allowed out except when Davies took him for the occasional week-end in 'safe' Singapore.

Evan Davies was a law unto himself, and without doubt some of the acting ability of his brother Rupert – who had played Simenon's Inspector Maigret – had rubbed off on him. Colonel Miers never forgot their first meeting at Kluang in the map-lined room where the daily District War Executive Committee met under the chairmanship of the Administrative Officer (as District Officers had been renamed). He happened to be Ian Mendel, who had been transferred from Temerloh, where he had worked with Yeop Mahidin.

One seat was empty at the long bare table. A few moments later, as Miers remembers, 'out of the window I saw a smart, open coupé dash in through the gates, skid round the corner and with a scrunch of flying gravel jerk to an abrupt halt. The door of the car flew open and out shot a dark-haired buoyant figure of a man clutching a fat briefcase under his arm. He bounded across the small grass lawn and, all in one movement, opened the door of our room, sat down, and began mopping his brow, "Sorry I'm late," he said good-naturedly.'

Miers was to work almost daily with Evan Davies as they followed the trail of Goh, and over his excellent brandy Evan initiated the Colonel into the fascinating jargon of Special Branch – words like 'cut outs' instead of go-between, 'sources' for informers, so that Miers had a 'feeling of coming out of a different world, a strange, dark, but rather exciting place'. And Miers, being a good soldier, had the sense to tell his men that 'it was this world on which we in the battalion were largely dependent for our success, for without good information we were unlikely to achieve much.'

Fortunately for Davies, Colonel Miers realized that if a Special Branch man were to be successful, he must work in secret, and Miers was quite aware that before long many strange men and women were visiting Evan Davies's house.

Davies made a start by opening a thousand blank files and telling his Special Branch men to fill them with 'people not numbers'. He wanted every item of information about the past lives of CT sympathizers. His men scoured South Johore for school photographs, teachers' names, nicknames, spending, eating, lovemaking habits, until Evan began to feel that he had a list of people who were alive, people with fears, hates, loyalties, he could understand.

One man in particular stood out as a possible contact. Known as the Raven because he wore his black hair long, he had fought with the British against the Japanese and was now leader of a jungle platoon close to Goh, and was charged with keeping him supplied with food and money.

The Raven had two daughters, and his wife who lived in Kluang was expecting a third child. The files seemed to indicate that she was one of the countless thousands of passive Chinese women who remained loyal and obedient to their husbands, though possibly uninterested in their politics. Davies decided to meet her. A Chinese Special Branch man disguised as a clerk called on her, drove her off in the wrong direction, doubled back, and finally deposited her on one of the eight different paths leading to Davies's house.

When she entered the room Davies was astounded. She was young, extremely beautiful, and very pregnant. For fully two minutes the two stood facing each other in silence in the hot room humming with mosquitoes. Davies deliberately looked at her bulging stomach and after a moment, still saying nothing, she nodded. Davies, who had a remarkable ability to think like a Chinese, remembers, 'She knew my unspoken question, and when she nodded it was to tell me that the Raven was the father of the unborn child.'

'You have two daughters,' said Davies. 'This one must

be a boy – I'm sure it will be. That would make the Raven happy, wouldn't it?'

She hesitated, then asked, 'I know that you are Fai Chai and that you deal straight. What do you want?'

Davies now made a remarkable proposal. He wanted nothing, he said. He didn't believe in demanding promises. 'But I do want you to have a son,' he told her. 'I'm going to send you to the best hospital in Singapore at my expense, and I would like to be the godfather.'

This he did. He spirited her out of Kluang, and in Singapore a boy – luckily for Davies – was born. A month later a slip of paper in a bamboo tube sailed through the open window of Davies's dining-room. It said simply, 'I have a son and I thank you for your kindness. I can be of help.'

Davies was never interested in surrenders. He wanted men who when joining his side would stay on in the jungle. 'This,' as he says, 'is how you get the big stuff.' The Raven was now committed – yet one false move could ruin everything. The Communist network in Kluang was so tight that if a man unexpectedly bought a cheap ball-point pen the Communists would hear about it – and demand where the money had come from.

Finally Davies hit on an ingenious method of getting messages to the Raven. He concocted a letter to Goh, ostensibly from the Raven's wife. Its contents were rather embarrassing: she wished to bear another child and asked if arrangements could be made for her to meet her husband so that they could enjoy their conjugal rights.

After the usual delay the Raven's wife received a pompous letter from Goh himself. The gist was that she could meet her husband for ten minutes once a fortnight behind a certain tree on a rubber estate.*

* With some relish Evan Davies recalls that the poor Raven was so terrified at these jungle meetings that he was never able to perform his husbandly duties.

From that moment the messages started to flow. Davies realized that this would not lead him immediately to Goh. This was only phase one, but he knew what he wanted from the Raven: a time, a place where Davies could lay an ambush, kill every single man in the Raven's platoon, then send the Raven back into the jungle with Chinese Special Branch detectives taking the places of the dead CTs. That way Davies would control an entire Communist cell.

He waited patiently for the next message, and it came in a manner that startled even the urbane Davies; for the Raven made a 'personal appearance' in the most dramatic circumstances, as Davies was giving a formal dinner-party for two brigadiers and their wives at his house. Since Kluang was considered dangerous, army wives were obliged to remain in Singapore unless invited to private houses which the police could guarantee as safe; so occasionally Davies would invite the wives up for a weekend and their husbands would move in. On this evening the officers were in their 'best blues', the ladies in long frocks, and David, the Sikh servant, was being assisted by two extra butlers, who as usual had been picked up by Evan Davies's Special Branch men.

For Davies it was a welcome break in the weeks of patient dealing with the Raven. He led a lonely life, for he knew that he must control a CT cell before he could hope to reach Goh, yet he had to keep the very existence of his plans to himself.

On this night, however, it was all forgotten – until the temporary butlers started serving. One was a handsome young Chinese with long black hair, and Davies instinctively realized who he was and that this meeting had been arranged for an important reason. He slipped out of the room for a moment, and sure enough on his pillow was a rolled slip. The Raven had come so that Davies could take a good look at him, said the message, for the Raven's entire branch would come out of the jungle for food in two days. The Raven would lead the party wearing a white handkerchief round his forehead. After detailing the time and place, the message ended, 'Please don't shoot me.'

Davies returned to the table – in the midst of an acrimonious discussion of the way 'the coppers' refused to give the army a break.

'All right,' said Evan, 'I'll *give* you a break. I can guarantee you six kills the day after tomorrow on a rubber estate four miles out of Kluang.' And as the Raven started serving the ice-cream and mangosteens, Evan added casually, 'There are only two stipulations. Every man must be a crack shot, and nobody must open fire till I've fired.'

He hoped the Raven got the message.

Two days later Davies rose at 3.30 a.m. and led a patrol together with six Chinese detectives to the ambush spot on the rubber estate. Communist spies were so efficient that Davies had to be in position before the tappers arrived – and after reaching the appointed place everyone stood up to their necks in a nearby river to rid themselves of the smell of sweat. No one could smoke, eat or drink. When in position, the last man, armed with a rake, levelled the lallang leading to the place where they lay, for the tappers could be working within two or three yards of them. When the tappers did arrive they suspected nothing – Davies knew that because tappers had a simple warning code they could flash across a ten-thousand-acre estate in seconds. Instead of giving the normal single knock with their tapping knives, they would give three taps – and the warning would be relayed.

Shortly after dawn, the Raven appeared, a white scarf tied round his head, leading a file of six men silhouetted against the grey light. Davies had arranged that his target would be number two in the file. After he fired the troops would blast at the rest of the CTs, excluding the one with the white scarf.

There was no drama about it – just an exercise in accuracy and speed. At the precise moment Evan Davies dropped the second CT. Almost simultaneously, the air was filled with noise and smoke. The troops ran out, the tappers scattered, and within ten minutes the CT uniforms had been stripped from the corpses and donned by the six Chinese Special Branch men. A few minutes later the Raven was leading them back into the jungle, and the troops were picking up the bodies.

One British soldier was hurt slightly in the leg. And one CT was wounded instead of being killed; and so, after his uniform had been taken, he was dressed in a detective's clothes. Both men were whisked to hospital, where the two enemies were placed side by side in the same ward. They were there, with Davies and an interpreter talking to the CT, when in bustled the ward sister.

'Now then,' Davies remembers her saying fussily, 'you must let these two boys get some sleep. They've obviously had a very busy morning.'

There was a grisly postscript the next day. Special Branch had by now photographic records of virtually every CT, but one of those killed in the ambush was unknown. Two shots through the neck had severed his head, and Evan Davies realized that the only man who could identify him was the CT who had been wounded in the ambush instead of killed and who was now in hospital.

Evan wrapped the head in a brown paper parcel and made his way to the hospital. When he asked the Chinese to identify the head, however, the patient nearly jumped out of bed in terror. Shaking with fear, he explained that all Chinese believed that if they looked on a severed head the spirit of the dead man would haunt them.

The persuasive Davies, in his most mellifluous voice, asked, 'Well, if you can't *see* he was beheaded, would that be all right?' The Chinese after some doubts eventually

agreed, whereupon the bulky Davies got down on the
floor, lay on his back by the bed of the wounded Chinese
and lifted the head up just far enough for it to be identified
but without showing his neck.

Once identified, Davies returned to his office and
dumped the parcel on his desk for a few moments. When
he returned the door was jammed and only after pressure
could he prise it open. Inside on the floor in a faint was
Miss Allborough, his secretary. She had opened the parcel
imagining it contained papers to file.

Now of course, Davies controlled a CT cell, and the Raven
even had an army radio engineer so that Davies could
keep in contact, using an ecclesiastical code. (Davies,
remembering his days with Churchill, was referred to as
the Bishop, and if they wanted to meet or send messages,
the Raven would ask, 'Tell me, Bishop, what hymn shall
we be singing at the next service?' Davies would reply with
a number indicating a village or map reference.)

The Raven had by now been elected a district committee member, and this should have brought him closer to
his quarry; unfortunately Goh suddenly moved north of
Kluang, and it was left to Evan Davies to force him to
return south, nearer the Raven. This he did with typical
ingenuity. First, Davies leaked the fact that the RAF was
going to stage a series of massive bombing raids in North
Johore, concentrating on the area where Goh was known
to be lurking. Now this, as Davies well knew, would never
intimidate a man like Goh. However, as the news of the
projected raids was leaked to Goh's followers, Davies collected nearly a hundred Special Branch Chinese and hid
them in a New Village north of Kluang. Next, with the
connivance of the RAF, a spectacular raid was launched.
The bombs were deliberately dropped over jungle, for the
RAF had been given no specific target areas.

When the bombers returned – but only then – Davies

sent in his hundred Special Branch men, disguised as CTs. A more sorry-looking collection of pitiful war victims it would be hard to imagine, for every one was a jungle bombing casualty – bandaged, bleeding, on crutches. (Davies had even found one ex-policeman whose arm had been amputated.) Davies called them his 'Ketchup Brigade', and as he knew it would, the news of the 'disaster to Communism' quickly reached Goh. He took the hint and moved south.

This was good news, but even so, and despite the dozens of informers working for him, matters were not made any easier when Davies lost one of his most useful agents.

The man was a member of the Min Yuen living in Kluang and Davies nicknamed him 'Charlie Boy' because his smile was a little too easy. He was 'a bit too smooth', and wore a flashy ring with the word 'Forever' engraved in English. Davies was not even sure how much he could trust Charlie Boy, though, as he remembers, 'When dealing with double agents you don't have to worry. Just let a man think he's in the know, but don't feed him too much.' Still, Charlie Boy did bring in valuable information for which Davies paid him, though never in cash. Sternly he always insisted on banking reward money, for the Chinese could never resist spending and every Communist in Kluang would know the next day. There was no secrecy in all Asia, let alone in Kluang.

Charlie Boy was feeding Davies with news of a woman CT believed to be a mistress of Goh, but she was getting suspicious and Davies had decided it was hopeless to try and convert her. She was so dedicated that she had to be killed and Davies decided to shoot her himself. Charlie Boy arranged to meet the woman on the edge of a rubber plantation where Davies would be hiding – and as Charlie Boy told Davies, 'I have great faith in you as a marksman.'

His faith was possibly bolstered by the fact that if they could eliminate the woman – possibly draw Goh out –

Charlie Boy would be eligible for a big reward. Evan Davies borrowed a new Belgian rifle from Colonel Miers, crept out to the rendezvous at first light – and was successful. Davies picked off the woman, Charlie Boy was unhurt, and Davies promptly banked his reward.

A week later Davies received a message from Charlie Boy in one of the numerous cigarette tins which he left on the approach road to his house. When they met Charlie Boy said he had been 'blown'. Somebody had seen him talking to the woman, and though it might take time for the news to reach Goh, Charlie Boy felt he should leave Malaya.

Davis agreed. A blown double agent was a liability, whereas forged passports and plane tickets could always be obtained in twenty-four hours. Charlie Boy was told he could leave in three days. His money would be given to him on the plane.

But Charlie Boy had one apologetic request. He had – and Davies remembers his smooth smile – run up a few debts. Only about a hundred dollars, but honour demanded that he repay them. With some misgivings, Davies let him have the money; it was only a trifle of the sum due to him.

The night before Charlie Boy was due to leave for Hong Kong with his wife, Evan Davies had just poured his first Hennessy XO after an excellent dinner and was turning to the latest airmail copy of *The Times* when the phone rang. There had been an 'incident' and Davies remembers, 'I knew before I jumped into my car that something had happened to Charlie Boy.'

It had indeed. Charlie Boy had lied to Davies. He had no debts. He had spent the hundred dollars on a farewell Chinese dinner for his friends. And that was the kind of secret that could never be kept in Kluang.

As Davies reconstructed events later, Charlie Boy had been sitting at the head of the table with ten guests when the door opened and Goh entered, accused Charlie Boy of the death of 'his sister', and pronounced sentence while Charlie Boy sat there. There was no fighting, no scuffling. Goh sliced off Charlie Boy's head with a parang.

By the time Davies arrived, every guest had long since departed. But Charlie Boy's headless corpse was slumped over a chair and his head was stuck in the middle of the Chinese food and empty 'Green spot' lemonade bottles. He was, Davies noted, wearing his best set of teeth, which he normally used only for weddings and funerals. And he was still smiling.

Slowly the net was drawing closer round Goh, who cannot have had the faintest idea that the Raven was working for Evan Davies. Yet Goh had an almost uncanny instinct for scenting danger. Time after time the Raven found the whereabouts of the CT leader, but each time Goh had changed his camp site. Now the Raven found the approximate site of a new camp – plus the vital news that Goh was absent for a few days. Since almost every attack on a CT camp demanded different methods, because of varying terrain, defences and so on – Goh's absence seemed to offer a perfect opportunity for a patrol to try and discover its exact location. After four days in the swamp, the troops ran out of food and when supplies were dropped a shred of parachute remained in a treetop. Goh spotted it – and promptly changed camps. After that Davies ordered a 'freeze' on the entire area until the Raven could discover the whereabouts of Goh's new camp. After some weeks the Raven found it – or rather its location, for it had been built for Goh who was expected in ten days.

The troops still faced the problem of not knowing what sort of jungle they would meet in the final attack. Scrub, rubber, belukar, swamp? It would make a vital difference in planning the assault. Colonel Miers felt that he must persuade Evan Davies to let a picked patrol 'have a look round' in the area which had been 'frozen' by the Special Branch man.

Miers could not, of course, know that Davies was running a complete CT unit in the jungle, but he did realize that he would have to handle the Special Branch man carefully. He called on Davies after dinner, to find him comfortably installed on a rattan long chair with a large cigar and a glass of brandy, studiously reading the latest batch of *The Times*. Davies's Sikh brought Miers an equally large brandy, whereupon ('It seemed a propitious moment to make my request') Miers asked permission to send a patrol into the frozen area, explaining why.

'The trouble with you soldiers,' grumbled Davies, who knew the Borderers had not yet killed a CT, 'is that you'd stoop to anything to break your duck. If I let you go into the area, and you see even one miserable little CT, you'd certainly shoot him and that would blow the whole thing.'

Miers meekly promised that he would not dream of doing such a thing and finally Davies agreed to let a picked patrol go in on the understanding that they would shoot only in self-defence. Remembering the tell-tale shred of parachute, he added, 'For God's sake ask your men not to leave their visiting card behind this time.'

For three days a patrol waded knee deep in swamp in the most appalling conditions. They could not smoke, light fires, wash or shave with soap. Their food consisted of 'Compo' rations which fitted into one half of a mess tin – small packets of tea, sugar, salt, corned beef, sardines, cheese, jam and tasteless biscuits: any cooking had to be done on a Tommy cooker, a round screw-topped tin containing eight hexamine tablets and a small frame which opened into a stand. One tablet generated enough heat to brew tea or cook a simple meal.

After three days the patrol returned to base in triumph – with a sketch map of Goh's elaborate new headquarters. But the plan and information made one thing clear: the camp could never be assaulted from the land. It was sited in swamp, guarded against surprise attack by a carpet of dry palm fronds 'which snapped with a noise like a pistol if trodden upon'. No man could approach that camp by stealth. Nor could it be rushed, for the CTs had dragged into position thorn trees and hedges of prickly pear to make an impenetrable wall round the group of buildings. At least half a dozen perimeter sentry-posts surrounded the wooden bashas, of which one in the centre, up against a tree, was larger than the rest.

To Miers, who had a great deal of experience of air support in Burma, one course seemed obvious: wait until Evan Davies told him Goh was in camp and then 'bomb it to smithereens'.

Launching a major RAF bombing attack, however, cost a great deal of money – and perhaps it was as well that Miers, when persuading the RAF, did not know that in the last resort everything would depend on the word of a Communist running a cell in the jungle. Fortunately Miers could only tell the RAF that one of the top Special Branch men was supplying him with the information – and when the name of Evan Davies was mentioned, no more questions were asked. Having agreed, the RAF now went into top gear. For the first time in the war they planned to use a radar beam projected from a beacon on a hill five thousand yards from the camp. This would guide Lincoln bombers straight to the target area – a rectangle 700 by 400 yards, on which they would drop 90,000 lbs of bombs.

For several days impatient crews and troops stood by – until the morning of February 20, 1956 when Evan Davies bustled into Miers's room and the Colonel knew immediately that the moment had arrived. He remembers, 'That was clear by Evan's air of high excitement, and indeed by his shirt which always worked its way out of his blue shorts when matters got tense until, if the news was really hot, a wide gap would appear between the two to reveal a large expanse of jolly white belly wobbling and creasing in tune with its master's animated story.'

Goh had arrived in the new camp, with most of his platoon; they expected to remain there for three days. Aircraft as far afield as Singapore and Penang were bombed up, helicopters with support troops were readied, and at dawn the next morning Evan Davies and Miers stood on a hillock outside the Officers' Mess at Kluang. Spread out towards the horizon was an unbroken sea of plantation and jungle, broken only by two hump-like hills, caught in the rising sun. Under one of these lay the CT camp.

By ten o'clock that morning Goh's camp was awake and bustling. Secure in their defences, one platoon was attending a literary class on the communal 'bed platform' of Number One Section. In the next hut, by the parade ground with its Red Flag, several men were resting. Three cooks were busy preparing the midday meal. They had nothing to fear, they went about their chores quietly, and when the drone of aircraft interrupted the jungle silence Goh estimated that they were flying at five thousand feet. But nobody worried because the CTs knew their camp was invisible from the air. The planes, they presumed, were merely passing overhead, and so the CTs took no precautions.

Then, without even the preliminary circling that usually preceded a bombing attack, the planes suddenly dropped their load. Some CTs casually watching the aircraft failed to realize what was happening. One called out, 'They're releasing miniature planes.' Another cried, 'They're dropping men.' Every man, including Goh, remained standing. The more excited ones stood on their beds to get a better view. 'They never thought of scattering and taking cover,' said the vivid official CT account of the raid, written by one of Goh's lieutenants who escaped.*

A 'mighty explosion' followed. (In fact this was the combined explosion of scores of bombs being dropped almost simultaneously.) 'Never in the past have we experienced this type of bomber.' In the panic none knew who was killed, for as the bombers flew off like a skein of geese the survivors saw a smaller plane drop Red marker balloons, after which two squadrons of Canberra jets tore into the targets. The CTs admitted that, 'almost all the Comrades were casualties, either dead or wounded. Comrade X, although he was seriously injured, immediately rallied the survivors and led them to safety. Fifteen minutes later a second wave of aircraft arrived. They dropped more bombs and strafed the area with machine-gun fire. It can be seen how ferociously determined the enemy were.'

Naturally the report did not mention Goh by name, nor did it mention that Hor Lung, the Regional Commander of Johore,† had been at the camp and had escaped. He was 'Comrade X'.

As soon as the raid was over, Miers went in with the first troops. The tangled vegetation was so dense that orders had to be given by bugle as Miers fought his way through the oily, waist-deep swamp until he reached the camp. Even he could hardly believe the sight that met his eyes. Not one roof, not a wall, remained intact. On the long platform serving as a communal bed were the bodies of the five men who had been attending the literary class. Two or three corpses floated nearby in the dirty swamp water. In all, Miers counted fourteen bodies. Some distance from the others, near the biggest basha, lay the

---

* 'The Tragedy of the Air Raid Incident of 21st February'. This document was recovered many months later.
† No relation to Hor Leung, who surrendered to David Storrier.

mangled bodies of a man and a woman. The man was Goh. On his wrist was the watch looted from the dead Fijian major.

The captured CT document analysing the causes of the tragedy pointed with unerring logic to the Raven. 'We must harbour an intense, smouldering hatred of all traitors and be resolute in keeping a sharp look-out for signs of their activities,' it warned. But the Communists never caught the Raven. Within hours, Evan Davies had supplied him and his family (including the godson) with travelling documents under false names. They were spirited to Singapore that same night, and under heavy guard boarded a ship for an undisclosed destination where the Raven was able to set himself up in business with the reward he had earned.

23 THE INDEPENDENT NATION

Plans for Malaya's constitutional development were now gathering momentum. As Evan Davies trailed Goh Peng Tun in the jungle, a major conference in London agreed that full independence should be granted to the country by August 31, 1957. Equally important, the Malayan government would in the interim period become responsible for finance, internal defence and security. This in-between period, with a gradual withdrawal of British personnel in Malaya, had to be delicately merged with the final independence plans 'so that,' in the words of the conference report, 'as well as reflecting the distribution of responsibility between HM Government and Malayan Ministers during that period, they will be capable of being continued into that stage of full self-government with the minimum of administration and other disturbances.' Britain was not going to risk another French-type Indo-China fiasco.

Tunku Abdul Rahman now became Minister for Internal Defence and Security in addition to his duties as Chief Minister. Soon a new Malayan Army HQ sprang up at Kuala Lumpur. The country's regular army of 9,000 was buttressed by a small Malayan Air Force and Navy. General Bourne's Operations Committee was dissolved, and the Tunku became Chairman of a new Emergency Operations Council, meaning in effect that Bourne had now become an adviser (though it says much for the Tunku that he left the fighting entirely to the experts).

For the British, there were inevitably moments tinged with sadness, particularly when overnight the British Advisers to the Sultans were abolished as a 'logical step towards independence'; and so many gallant men who had fought stubbornly for nearly ten years to beat the menace of Communism found themselves out of jobs.

This move was felt more deeply by the British than any other aspect of Malayanization. It was proposed by the British and none disputed its merits. Yet since the first British Adviser was appointed in 1874 when a Sultan asked for British help in quelling internal disorders, the Adviser had been throughout the years a man apart, dedicated to a country he came to love more than his own, a man surrounded by pomp and glitter, a 'Prince Regent' in his own state. Now, by a stroke of the pen, he was nothing more than a character from an old Somerset Maugham novel.

The approaching independence was by now beginning to cause divisions among the leaders of the Politburo in Thailand. The more aggressive members still wanted to continue the struggle by any means, regarding the current bad news as the kind of unfortunate temporary phase which could happen to any nation at war. But, they argued, the slightest sign of weakness would destroy morale. They had another point. With independence, Britain would no doubt limit the military and financial assistance she was pouring into Malaya – and Malaya without a Britain to assist her would be much easier to subvert to Communism.

Chin Peng was not of this school of thought. He was not a soldier anyway, and his politically attuned mind made him feel there were better prospects of success if he could achieve a cease-fire. He may have deluded himself that the Tunku would now relent and permit the Communist Party to have a legal status in the new Malaya. On the other hand, he may have hoped to repeat in Malaya the pattern of the fruitless Korean war peace talks. If, as in Panmunjon, Chin Peng could follow a cease-fire with long-drawn-out talks, this would give him a respite he badly needed. Protracted talks, with the Communists stalling every hope of reaching a solution, would also attract world attention, and might even induce Soviet Russia and China to give them the aid which they had been so tardy in sending.

The Chin Peng school of thought had its way, and consequently, at the end of March he sent a letter to Tunku Abdul Rahman asking him to resume negotiations. Chin Peng's offer was repeated on Radio Peking. The Tunku, however, could see exactly what Chin Peng was driving at, and turned down the suggestion in a broadcast. Talks could only be resumed, he said, on his terms, and with an agenda that would have to be agreed on beforehand.

He did, however, in a moment of magnanimity offer to spare Chin Peng's life. 'I have regard for an enemy like Chin Peng,' he admitted, 'who at Baling fought honestly for his aim – Communist domination of Malaya. I will save your life if you come to me. I am prepared to send you to China.'

To men like Bob Thompson, working quietly behind the scenes, peace feelers of this nature, together with Malaya's steady march towards independence indicated a new threat: that of subversion, the inevitable next step on the Communist agenda; and for a time - fortunately only for a few months – it brought into sharp focus one of the most brilliant theoreticians of the Malayan Communist Party.

This was Yeong Kwo, Deputy Secretary-General of the Party, who had not been in the limelight since he was resolutely opposed to terror tactics and had always urged the need to build a big underground organization. Born in 1917, Yeong Kwo had joined the Communist Party while at school in Penang. In 1941 he had been deported to China, but due to the Pacific War the ship had returned to Singapore and by 1946 he had become a member of the Central Executive Committee. Now he was balding, nearly forty, with uneven teeth, a pointed face, high forehead and the perpetual pasty look of a sick man.

Special Branch had almost caught Yeong Kwo on several occasions, especially when raiding innocuously-named groups like the 'National Independence League', and the 'Selangor Students' Union'. Yeong Kwo was interested only in subversion and infiltration – all the more so now the Malayan Communist Party had to face up to the fact that independence was being won not by the armed Communist revolution, but by the peaceful negotiations of elected political leaders; which meant that unless they were extremely adroit, the Communists would no longer be able to represent themselves as the champions of the Malayan people. Above all, it was now necessary for the Communists to extricate themselves from an embarrassing political position and from their military failure. Yeong Kwo was in no two minds as to how this should be done. 'Our tactics are to join with the Tunku in a common effort to get rid of the British,' he wrote. 'After there is a state of peace we can then immediately win over more support of the masses and go a step further by overthrowing the

Tunku's bourgeois dictatorship and changing it into a joint dictatorship of all races and strata.*

Yeong Kwo was known to be operating in the Kuala Lumpur area, but it was not until the middle of 1956 that the first positive clue to his whereabouts reached Special Branch. It came from a tapper who walked into a police station saying he had seen a suspicious Chinese bivouacked in the rubber near Semenyih, in South Selangor. (Morale had so improved that more and more tappers were bringing in casual information.) The tapper had been gathering twigs for his fire, he explained righteously, though Special Branch thought it more likely he had been stealing coagulated rubber.

The tapper got his reward and Special Branch started harassing the unknown CT. Finally troops of the Rifle Brigade were called in with information precise enough for a map reference. Burrell went ahead of a dawn patrol with a Special Branch man. In the dim light a shadowy form moved – just where they had been told a shadowy form would be. They fired, and the man collapsed. It was Yeong Kwo. As 'Darky' Burrell turned the body over he saw a scar on the man's jaw – where Yeong Kwo had been shot years previously by a soldier. But then came the really important find. Under the mosquito net draped over the CT's hammock, Special Branch found a virtual reference library of Communist plans, proving beyond doubt that Yeong Kwo – who had lived near Kuala Lumpur to keep his fingers on the political pulse – had in fact drawn up most of the plans to subjugate Malaya by subversion. The task of Communists, according to Yeong Kwo's documents, was 'to cover up and support an illegal struggle by means of open and lawful activities . . . but at heart we are no believers in legality and are not content with an open and legal struggle.'

* Legislative Council White Paper No. 23 of 1959.

By the end of 1956, nearly half of Malaya was 'White', and by 1957, Bob Thompson, whose brilliant work had so often remained anonymous, was made Deputy Secretary for Defence. This enabled him to direct his energies and skill to the most vital remaining problem before independence: that of preparing the country psychologically and of making sure that, with the approach of Merdeka (Independence) it did not lapse into a mood of indifference or, even worse, forgiveness. Thompson felt strongly that the war could have been lost at the Baling talks; he felt equally strongly that it could still be lost. He had always regarded his task as (in his own words) 'part intelligence, part countering subversion', and though the death of Yeong Kwo had robbed Chin Peng of his finest expert on subversion, this had by no means stopped entirely. Indeed it had taken a more subtle twist, one that was almost subliminal, skilfully directed to politicians and community leaders, so that many agreed with the attitude of one who said to Bob, 'When we get independence, we'll have beaten them and the Communists know it. Why not call it a day and make peace?'

This was dangerous thinking, and Thompson – together with C. C. Too and the invaluable Lam Swee – was kept busier than ever before directing a psychological war not only against the CTs but against any weakening in the resolve to continue the fight.

Thompson realized that to ordinary intelligent people the war must appear to have 'bogged down' at a time when, with the heady wine of independence about to be quaffed, Malayans wanted their independent country to be at peace, not war.

The Tunku was shrewd enough – and pro-British enough – to take this sort of criticism in his stride. He knew only too well that independence was not synonymous with safety; and he knew too that Malaya would still need the advice of Britons who had governed the country for decades. Indeed, at one of his quiet dinners with Bob Thompson, the Tunku turned to him and said, 'After independence, you go on putting things up to me in just the same way as the British do now – just tell me verbally the problems, and I'll see that you get the right answers.'

The Tunku was not so pleased when thirty-five Socialist MPs in London demanded that after Merdeka British troops should be withdrawn as 'their presence was incompatible with Malayan Independence'. This attitude, the Tunku felt, was part of a Communist strategy to encourage a similar 'End the War' demand in Malaya.

'It is as much the duty of the British people as of the Malayans themselves to meet and crush the Communist challenge,' he said. 'It is accepted by all the free world that the fight against the Communists in Malaya is not Malaya's concern alone. The Reds are trying to establish Communist dictatorship in South-East Asia – if they succeed, the whole of South-East Asia will be lost. Malaya is engaged not only in a life or death struggle, but also in a struggle to free this part of Asia from the Communist menace. If the British and other Commonwealth countries were to withdraw their support and leave Malaya to shoulder the burden alone, it would be necessary for this country to double her security forces and expenses in order to end the war.'

As August – and independence – approached, more and more areas were cleared of CTs. In June Trengganu became the first all-White state. In July, with only a month to go to independence, not a single person was killed by CTs for the first time since the start of the war.

By now there were barely two thousand active CTs left; a thousand in the north, five hundred in Johore, the rest being scattered over the country in small groups. Now, finally, these forces were split when in early August the White corridor in Pahang was extended through Selangor to include the Federal capital and stretched to the West Coast. Thus with a White belt cutting across the country, Chin Peng's forces in the north were completely isolated from those in the south.

August 31, 1957, might be said to have started the final phase of the war, for this was the day on which, after eighty-three years of British rule, Malaya became a sovereign independent state. The last vestiges of British control were handed over; Tunku Abdul Rahman, leader of the Alliance Party, became the Prime Minister, with Dato Abdul Razak, his Deputy Premier and Defence Minister.

Merdeka Day in Kuala Lumpur was held before representatives from thirty countries who watched the British flag being formally hauled down and the Malayan flag hoisted in its place; and who heard the Tunku in a warm tribute to Britain declare that Malaya had been 'blessed with a good administration forged and tempered to perfection by successive British administrators', and hope that 'this legacy left by the British would not suffer in efficiency and integrity in the years to come.'

After the parades, after the formal banquet, the pomp and ceremony, Bob Thompson returned home and it was this clear-thinking man who saw the real significance of what had happened, when he said to Merryn, 'Well – there's one thing that even Chin Peng can't disguise. He started a war to kick out the British Imperialists – and now there aren't any. We've not been kicked out – we've left, head high, and it's the British who gave Independence to Malaya, not Chin Peng.'

24 THE FINAL PUSH

Independent Malaya was still at war, for Independence did not mean an armistice – but now it was a subtly different war, for Chin Peng's jungle army, with no

"Imperialists" to fight, had became in effect outlaws in their own Malayan state. By September 1957, it totalled 1,830 men, of whom 470 were in Thailand, leaving only 1,360 CTs in Malaya. Yet the war had to be pressed forward with undiminished vigour. The responsibility for prosecuting the war was now vested in the hands of the elected government and all British troops remaining on Malayan soil came under it. They were led by General Sir James Cassels, who was appointed Director of Operations. Under an Anglo-Malayan Defence Pact, he was responsible directly to the Malayan government, and his task was to co-ordinate all war operations in the final mopping-up phase.

Three days after Independence the Tunku marked the historic date with a fresh amnesty offer which would last four months. Millions of leaflets incorporating safe conduct passes were showered on the jungle.

To the men reading them the future must have been bleak indeed, for while they languished on a diet of rats and frogs, more and more citizens of Malaya were literally out of the war. By now over 30,000 square miles – more than half the area of Malaya proper – had been declared 'White', with fences torn down, rationing abolished, restrictions removed. Only the hardiest, the most dedicated CTs, could withstand the temptations to surrender – and Chin Peng knew this.

There was indeed little the Communists could do now, though as J. H. Brimmell* put it, Chin Peng 'produced the hoary old Leninist line that Malaya's independence was not complete, as the country was tied by a defence agreement to Great Britain.'

For most people the war had virtually ended. And yet, for

* *Communism in S. E. Asia.*

many – faced with CTs more desperate for food and arms
than ever before – the killing did not stop.

Just before dawn on Boxing Day 1957, Staff Sergeant
William Harris of the 6th Battalion, the Malay Regiment,
set off in a Land-Rover with ten men to repair a broken-
down scout car which had been left on the roadside near
Mentakab in Pahang. Violence was on the wane and Bill
Harris, aged 38, had no hesitation in taking his fifteen-
year-old son Arnold for the ride. The boy and his father
rode with three men in the Land-Rover. The others followed in a breakdown wagon.

At a quarter to seven they were all in high spirits,
joking and laughing, with Arnold explaining how he would
assemble the aircraft carrier his father had given him for
Christmas. The road bent. A burst of fire shattered the
Land-Rover's windscreen. Two soldiers were killed
instantly as they leapt out. Another shot wounded Bill
Harris as he shouted to his son to get down. A few shotgun
pellets hit Arnold 'but I was so scared I didn't feel anything.' As his wounded father staggered on to the lallang
verge Arnold dimly realized that the firing had given way
to a gabble of voices, and looking up Arnold saw a dozen
or so Chinese CTs, all in uniform with red stars on their
peaked hats. Two started tearing the canvas roof off the
Land-Rover and looting the vehicle. Another asked Arnold
if he or his father carried a gun. Arnold shook his head,
then a short fat man helped him out of the Land-Rover
and laid him on the verge next to his wounded father. 'He
was very gentle,' Arnold remembers. 'He gave me two
aspirins.'

Eager hands searched his father and the bodies, stripping them of shirts, watches, boots, rifles, pistols, even his
father's camera, and as a parting gesture, one grabbed
Arnold's hat. Then they disappeared up the bank and into
the jungle lining the road.

Arnold's father was lying beside the Land-Rover. He

urged Arnold to drive it away. 'Never mind me,' he added, but when he realized that Arnold was determined to stay he asked him for water, telling him to try and find a stream.

There was no stream so Arnold grabbed the lid of a cardboard box and filled it with water from the Land-Rover's radiator. Carefully he pillowed his father in his arms and forced a trickle of water between his lips. Still with his father's head in his arms, Arnold waited for a car to pass. After what seemed like hours a black car packed with people came round the bend. The boy shouted but the driver refused to stop.

For a few moments Bill Harris seemed more comfortable, lying there with his eyes closed to the bodies surrounding him. But suddenly he opened them for the last time, smiled at his son, and said, 'I'm going, Arnold. Look after the family.'

Inevitably there were many continuing problems – and new circumstances raised new ones. Among these was the banishment to China of the last remnants of diehard captured CTs. For decades – long before the war – the few undesirable Chinese immigrants had been deported to Swatow, on the Chinese mainland near Hong Kong, but the number had increased enormously since the outbreak of war. Altogether more than 20,000 had been deported, and now the Chinese authorities in Swatow made it clear that no more would be allowed to land.

The Tunku asked Bob Thompson to see what he could do. By a convenient arrangement of some years' standing deportees normally left Port Swettenham on a Dutch boat which plied regularly to Swatow, and Thompson asked van Linden, the skipper, why the Chinese government was refusing to accept men who were after all their own countrymen.

'It's not the *government*!' exclaimed van Linden. 'It's the port authorities. They want something out of it, that's all.'

'What's the biggest luxury shortage in Red China?' asked Thompson.

'Motor-cars,' replied the Dutch skipper without hesitation.

'I thought you'd say that,' Bob agreed. 'Let's give the boys in Swatow three beautiful brand new cars every time we send a boatload of Commies out. That should keep them quiet.'

It did. The cars were accepted with relish – and no questions were asked by the Malayan Government.

Deportees raised another problem – shortage of tough detectives to act as guards to the CTs on the voyage. Van Linden refused absolutely (and rightly) to carry his human cargo unless there was an adequate guard. But as the war moved nearer to victory (and with an independent government anxious to watch the pennies) the police force was slowly being reduced to more normal numbers, and it was difficult to spare men tough enough to handle a boatload of Communists. This was why 'Two-Gun' Bill Stafford, the man who had shot Lau Yew in the first month of the war, reappeared on the scene. Stafford (who had also unearthed the war's biggest arms cache) was on the point of retiring. For some time he had been running a training school – and made no secret of the fact that he was bored. He wanted action, so when police headquarters asked him, 'Would you like a trip to Swatow?' Stafford jumped at the chance.

He would be detective in charge of 2,000 CTs being repatriated and the voyage would take eight days. It felt good, he remembers, to be (literally) back in harness again as he put on his black uniform and fastened his two holsters under his arms and set off on the 28-mile drive from Kuala Lumpur to Port Swettenham with two detectives and six Sikh policemen. As Stafford reached the long wooden pier – which stood in the water on stilts and was covered with wooden eaves against the sun – he had to pick his way over forms dozing gratefully in the shade. Small boats chugged across the harbour, sampans were deftly manipulated with one oar. On the quayside knots of men stood in contemplation.

A train puffed along the edge of the water, and pulled up by the vessel almost at the same moment as Stafford gained the bridge. He peered down on an astonishing sight. Guarded by scores of police, the train doors opened to disgorge 2,000 CTs – men, women, even some children, festooned with a few worldly possessions they had been able to bring with them: pots and pans, bicycles, parcels, tattered suit-cases, prams – and something else, unseen until each deportee had crossed the gangplank to the 'neutral' decks of the vessel taking them to a curious sort of freedom.

Then, as Stafford looked down, he saw one after another pull out hidden paper flags – of the kind children wave on royal occasions – bearing in blazing red the hammer and sickle. Soon, as a waving forest of white and red flags covered the decks below him, the CTs started crying slogans, but this was nothing to what happened a few moments later. Somebody must have spotted Stafford's face above the bridge rail and remembered his nickname, for suddenly he heard a yell, 'It's the Iron Broom!' It was followed by a series of furious threats.

To CTs, Stafford, whose methods sometimes caused raised eyebrows even in the force, was certainly one of the most hated men in Malaya, and it was not long after the ship had sailed before his chief Chinese detective (nicknamed 'One-Two-Three' by Stafford), came to Stafford's tiny cabin next to the chart-room and warned him bluntly, 'There's a definite plot against you, tuan. They're out to get you.'

Stafford's reaction was immediate. Though the CTs

might hate him, he had always been (like so many policemen) respected by the old lags he had arrested on criminal
charges. He had played fair with them. And he knew that
every boat-load of CT deportees leaving Port Swettenham
contained its quota of criminals, languishing handcuffed
in the makeshift cells. Telling One-Two-Three to follow
him, Stafford collected as many blankets as he could from
stores, two dozen cartons of cigarettes, all the spare food
he could find, and made his way to the hold. There, among
thirty desperadoes, he found some old 'friends'. Briefly he
outlined the Communist threats – then distributed blankets and cigarettes. The upshot was simple. He let two of
the toughest criminals out 'on parole', while a detective
remained ready to open the cells should assistance be
needed. It never was. The two criminals went straight to
the CTs and warned them that anybody molesting Two-
Gun Stafford would get his throat cut. They reached
Swatow without incident eight days later.

There were other problems – particularly in pockets of
hard resistance where fanatical CTs still dominated the
local population. Johore was the worst area, but there had
been an upsurge of violence farther north in the swamp
area of the Tengi river forty miles north-west of Kuala
Lumpur. It was appalling country, like jungle, only worse –
the leeches, the mosquitoes, the snakes, the towering trees
blotting out all sun, the spiky sword grass ten feet high,
the thick under-growth with its thorns – all with their
roots in a squelching slime of coffee-coloured water, sometimes five feet deep, and spotted with small peaty islands.
In here, in hideouts built under the vaulting roots of trees,
lived Ah Hoi, known to the police as 'The Baby Killer'
because, like Goh Peng Tun, he had once sliced open the
belly of a pregnant wife whose husband helped the police.
    In the spring of 1958 the ruthlessly efficient, unorthodox
SAS Regiment was called in to deal with Ah Hoi. The

commanding officer chosen for the task was a spectacular character – literally: Major Harry Thompson, seconded from the Royal Highland Fusiliers, stood six feet four inches, had a thatch of fierce red hair and a boxer's nose. He studied the problem, and decided to go into the heart of the swamp by parachute. That way they would leave no tracks.

The drop took place at seven o'clock on a February morning and thirty-seven men were out of the aircraft in eighteen seconds. Thirty-six reached the ground safely. One was caught in a tree and rescued by helicopter.

Thompson decided to follow the Tengi river. This, he guessed, must be the CTs' main highway, and even in the swamp, expert trackers of the SAS quickly found evidence that the CTs had been there. In places the Communists had had to cut their way through the spiky grass; at times the troops could see in shallow water the dent of a man's foot in the mud. At other times they found the shells of turtles which the CTs had eaten; and always when they reached a used camp, there was the stench of putrescent food, human dirt, rottenness, piles of refuse in the grey-brown ooze of mud.

For ten days the SAS, divided into two groups with radio contact, trudged on, their clothes torn to bits, their boots falling to pieces in the worst jungle in the world. They marched barefoot with leeches crawling over every man, already itching with prickly heat.

Each day followed a similar pattern. And each night, for the nights were the worst, the mosquitoes sang unceasingly. Though men covered themselves completely, it made no difference: the insects could bite through shirts and slacks. The men could not even have the solace of a last cigarette, for smoking was prohibited. After a bad night's sleep came breakfast – two sausages and a dozen or so beans, with biscuits and inevitable tea – and then, dishevelled, unshaven, scruffy and tired, they set off on the trail.

At times the entire unit would have to stop while men freed themselves from Malaya's most maddening jungle weed – 'Wait-a-bit' thorn which would become attached to a man's shirt, trail behind him for yards without his realizing it, until suddenly it pulled him up short. No amount of struggling helped a man to disengage himself. He had to take his clothes off to get rid of it.

At other times the rain pelted down, hissing and dripping off the tall, grim trees, often turning the swamp into a quagmire deep enough to reach men's shoulders. Still the SAS pressed on until one evening at dusk, after four weeks in the swamp, a sergeant called Sandilands saw three CTs seventy-five yards in front, across a stretch of water. Sandilands floated a log into the swamp, creeping behind it until he was in range. With his first shot he killed a CT. The others disappeared. Another CT was shot and his body was later discovered in a gruesome position – standing up, dead. After being fatally wounded, he had reached deep swamp and died while standing up to his neck in the thick slime.

Now the red-headed major was able to follow the wounded man's tracks, and start to squeeze Ah Hoi's gang between his two patrols. For twenty more days he pushed on, his legs a mass of ulcers from the thorns. There was no need for secrecy now, and powerful smoke signals were sent up. The men started two big fires, dampening them with piles of green leaves. As the pillars of smoke rose, two grenades were hurled in. In a matter of hours, the radio operator reported supply planes on the way. They made a trial run over the dropping zone, so low that troops could see the dispatchers waiting by the open doors. Then round they came again; the bundles fell out, seemed to float, then tiny parachutes slowed them down and in no time the men were sorting out new boots, clothes and food.

Three days later, a woman 'walked out of nothing. One moment there was no one,' Thompson remembers, 'the next she was standing in front of us.' She was tiny – barely four feet six inches tall, and her name was Ah Niet. Ah Hoi, she said, would never give up – but then Thompson told her that every camp had been pinpointed and if the CT refused to surrender he was going to lay on a saturation bombing attack. The woman returned into the swamp – and the next evening reappeared, once again like a wraith, and announced that she would bring out the entire platoon the following night. The British major would wait in a certain paddy field. Sure enough lights started to twinkle and out of the wilderness, using torches, came the CTs. One of them was an old little creature dressed in a woman's blue silk blouse and wearing a woman's hat.

'For heaven's sake, who's that?' asked the Major.

'That, sir,' he was told, 'is your baby killer.'

'I don't believe it,' the Major remembers saying – but it was, all five feet of Ah Hoi.

Some members of the platoon had at the last moment refused to come out, and Ah Niet, the woman, offered to lead a patrol to reach them. It must have been a remarkable sight as the tall major and the tiny woman set off together into the jungle. She was horrified at the noise made by Thompson's patrol. 'She was like a fish. She'd been swimming in and out of the jungle three hundred yards from a police post for years.'

When they got into the jungle swamp – with the patrol falling all over the place in the dark – Ah Niet begged for silence. Then, as the Major listened astounded, 'she made a whole lot of noises clucking like jungle grasshopper.' She was calling the CTs, and within forty-eight hours, the last in Ah Hoi's platoon had surrendered – three months to the day after Harry Thompson and his men had been dropped in the swamp.

Only one key man now remained in Johore and his name was Hor Lung, leader of the Johore Regional Committee and in many ways a remarkable man. He had escaped death in the massive bombing raid which had killed Goh Peng Tun. In fact the escape of Hor Lung, and even more his subsequent courage, provided still another instance of the astonishing fanaticism of dedicated CTs, for Hor Lung led the six men wounded in the raid through the ring of troops dropped by helicopter immediately after the bombing. With only one bag of medicines and bandages, he took them into deep jungle to spend three months recuperating. They had little in the way of food, and existed mostly on wild sago and bananas, slugs, occasional fish and snake meat, refusing to surrender – even though the most badly wounded must have known they would have been hospitalized and received lenient sentences as Surrendered Enemy Personnel.

Within three months the cool-headed Hor Lung had brought his men back to the edge of the jungle to start a vigorous offensive. By persuasion and intimidation he built up the remnants to platoon strength and settled down in a new base in the flat, swampy, mysterious country around Tasek Bera in southern Johore.

Forcing the meek Semelai Aborigines to provide him with jungle food, and getting substances like salt, sugar, tea and other luxuries from raids around Kluang and Yong Peng, Hor Lung grandiloquently named this 'The Common People District', and made several announcements to his commanders. He would establish a rear base into which he would eventually concentrate units scattered throughout Johore. They would be used as 'mobile squads'. The Aborigines would form the nucleus of a vast supply organization and act as forward spies. Once he considered the rear base safe from attack, Hor Lung promised to declare it a 'Liberated Area'. He would then set up a 'Peoples' Government' and invite 'the masses' to settle under his regime while the armed units concentrated on their protection.

By the spring of 1958 his dreams of setting up a Peoples' Government were fading. Despite the inaccessibility of his stronghold in Tasek Bera, he was finding it more and more difficult to manoeuvre as the war swung against the Communists. The government could now spare more troops, and though they could not mount an all-out offensive against the lake or swamp, they did eventually resettle the gentle Semelai Aborigines on whom Hor Lung had depended for help. The SAS Regiment, flushed with its earlier success, harassed him incessantly, destroying his food gardens, forcing him to move headquarters frequently. He issued new orders – units would move deeper into the swamp. They would store food, attack only by night. He commanded harshly and desperately, but now the confident, capable, 42-year-old Hor Lung was fighting a losing battle – and he knew it.

He must have realized that most of Malaya was 'White', and that even in the few black places like southern Johore CTs could no longer operate in groups of more than five to ten men. Every small CT unit was on its own. Many, including Hor Lung, had not heard from Chin Peng for months – and possibly were envious of his comfortable existence in Thailand. By the spring of 1958 the once proud Malayan Races' Liberation Army had dwindled to a mere 1,078 scattered fighters. All this must have passed through the twisted mind of this grim, implacable, chain-smoking Communist before he provided Malaya with its most startling surprise of the war.

Shortly after four o'clock on April 5, 1958, 28-year-old Police Constable Ahmad bin Wazir, father of four children, was drowsing as the afternoon sun drenched the

hamlet of Kampomg Tengah, a New Village of 850 people
two miles east of Segamat. He sat up as he saw a man
with closely cropped hair, wearing only underpants and
singlet, pass through the unguarded gate. The man walked
quietly up to the constable, and said in Malay, 'I'm a
terrorist. I want to surrender.'

The constable asked him his name but the man said he
would only disclose it to an officer and, as Constable
Ahmad remembers, 'I realized from his manner that he
was not a member of the rank and file.' Hor Lung spent
only a few minutes in the police post before being whisked
to Segamat headquarters. Only then did he reveal his
identity, and within a few hours he had been taken in a
private car to the home of a Special Branch officer, where
the highest ranking Communist still in Malaya explained
why he had surrendered. Military pressure had forced him
from the jungle base which was to be the capital of his
Liberated Area, so that he had lost contact with his units
and had finally been forced into the ignominious position
of having to forage for his own food. One other consideration had swayed him: he had always been haunted by the
fate of Shorty Kuk, and feared death at the hands of his
bodyguards, who were well aware that they could collect
a large reward if they murdered him. He did not deny
that he still believed in Communism.

Hardly anyone knew who the latest defector was – and
the secret was kept for four months as Hor Lung was
moved night after night from one police officer's home to
another, while they interrogated him and used him to plan
a landslide of surrenders.

It was the most brilliantly conceived surrender plan of
the war, and its success depended to a large degree on
the iron nerves of Hor Lung. These were no doubt
reinforced by the fact that he was offered a reward calculated on a sliding-scale basis which could escalate to a

figure beyond his wildest dreams, providing he could persuade sufficient followers to surrender.

The plan was based on the fact that, as the leading CT in Johore, Hor Lung had from time to time been in the habit of visiting every branch and committee in his area. Since the camps were frequently changed, Hor Lung would follow the usual CT practice of waiting at a jungle letter-box for a courier to guide him to secret camp.

Special Branch equipped him with the uniform of another surrendered CT (plus three red stars on his hat) and sent him back into the jungle, where he made for the nearest courier post. A military freeze was ordered over a vast area. (It would have been embarrassing if an unsuspecting soldier had killed Special Branch's most valuable asset.) So secret had been Hor Lung's defection that not a single CT knew their leader had surrendered, so now it seemed the most natural thing in the world when he suddenly turned up at a jungle post. Since independence had now been granted, it seemed equally normal for their most senior official to announce that, due to a change of plan, armed resistance was to cease. No doubt they believed Hor Lung – equally important they no doubt *wanted* to believe him. Most were relieved and delighted to leave the jungle after ten years.

Area by area, the jungle was swept clean and – still in the greatest secrecy – the surrendered CTs were taken into hiding. Special Branch faced only one problem: could Hor Lung stand the pace? He was chain-smoking, his nerve was slowly cracking – for one tiny leak could have meant his death each time he returned to the jungle, and each surrender increased the danger of a leak. When he reached the end of his endurance, Special Branch would give him a 'convalescent period', during which he would live with a Special Branch officer in his home, forget 'work', which would never be mentioned, but rest and smoke from the innumerable circular airtight tins of cigarettes placed at his side. After a week or two of this Hor Lung would be confident enough to set off and meet two or three more couriers and bring in yet more CTs.

To Special Branch the operation was also a fascinating example of the way in which Chin Peng's brilliant security network could be used against the Communists with deadly effect. Since CTs were taught not to pry into matters which did not concern them, and since the silence of a CT branch could mean that it was in danger of detection, nobody realized when an entire guerrilla unit walked out. Even if a courier failed to turn up, it could be ascribed to a dead letter-box; while as for Hor Lung, his movements were so secret anyway that nobody would have the remotest idea of his whereabouts – until, unexpectedly and unannounced, he would turn up and call a branch meeting. Not until the government, after four months, gleefully announced that Hor Lung had surrendered and brought out twenty-eight hard-core unit commanders together with another 132 men and women CTs did Chin Peng have even the faintest inkling of the catastrophe that had overwhelmed him.

It was the biggest mass surrender of the war, and by the end of August part of Johore was declared White, and towns like Kluang, Yong Peng and Segamat – each one the scene of violent death – were 'free' again.

The Tunku behaved magnificently during these four months – magnificently because to the people of Malaya, fed on routine announcements and communiqués, the Tunku was criticized for an apparent lack of action. Many politicians were tired of the war and prepared to relax the pressure, and the Tunku was, after all a politician in his first year of independent rule. However, he resisted all temptation even to hint at the spectacular secret victory until Hor Lung had finished his task.

Hor Lung was now eligible for an enormous reward, and with much heartburning he was paid just over

$400,000 – the equivalent of £50,000, causing Tunku Rahman to remark, 'He is now richer than any of us.'

Many people hated the idea, and agreed with the *Straits Times* when it asked: 'Are those rewards to terrorist leaders absolutely necessary? Every self-respecting stomach retches at the news . . . in the light of Hor Lung's statement [that] he is obviously an unrepentant Communist. He does not trouble to hide that.'

It was a powerful plea, yet with the war still draining $350,000 a day from the local Federal Treasury (apart from the cost to Britain), who could argue with the reply given by the Tunku when he was asked if he felt it right for Hor Lung to be so richly rewarded.

'We have to get results,' replied the Tunku. 'We cannot stick strongly to principles. If money can buy the end, we must use it.' He paused, then added thoughtfully, 'On principle, of course, Hor Lung should be hanged.'

So the last top-ranking Communist in Malaya was accounted for; within a few months his surrender was followed by mass surrenders from all over the country. By the end of 1958 there were only 250 CTs operating in Malaya, and General Cassels, independent Malaya's first Director of Operations, sacked himself by recommending that this post was now redundant. His recommendation was accepted and he left shortly after the turn of the year. At the same time Bob Thompson was appointed to the all-important post of Permanent Secretary of Defence.

There is little more to be said. In August 1959 the Tunku was re-elected as Premier, the Alliance Party gaining three-quarters of the seats in the Legislative Council. Obviously Malaya could not wait until the very last CT had been eliminated before declaring the 'Emergency' over, and by the end of 1959 Thompson felt the time was approaching when the few remaining CTs could be dealt with by the regular police supported by the Federation Army.

It was decided to end the 'Emergency' officially in the middle of 1960. Thompson initiated high-level talks with the Thai government for joint action in the border area.

The independant government had taken the war in its stride, for as the Tunku pointed out, 'During the last three years of the war, more roads were built, more jungle cleared, bridges and water systems constructed, schools and hospitals started, than had been done in the last three generations. We were not fighting the Communist terrorists with arms alone. We went a long way to win the hearts and minds of our people. We gave people more than the Communists could ever hope to give.'

Even Chin Peng had now to concede military defeat, and he issued a directive which admitted flatly that 'Any member of the Malayan Communist Party can apply for permission to leave the jungle if he is too old, sick, and anxious to get married or has a family outside that needs him.' Chin Peng's directive offered jungle fighters a 'severance pay' of $420 'which should last a man for a year', and advised CTs to settle down 'in a populated area'.

Within days of receiving the directive, the first CT had taken the $420 and surrendered – bringing with him a copy of the document. Within a week planes were dropping a million leaflets over Northern Malaya headed, 'Why don't *you* accept their offer?'

All restrictions were lifted except in the Thai border area, where a Border Security Council was formed to control the remnants of the much-vaunted Malayan Races' Liberation Army in remote regions in Perlis, Kedah, Perak and Kelantan – all that was left of the estimated 12,000 men and women who had passed through its ranks. Of these, 6,698 had been killed, 2,696 surrendered, 2,819 wounded and 1,286 captured. About a thousand more have died, deserted, or had been liquidated by their commanders.

The cost in lives to Malaya, and those who fought for it, had been heavy. The Security Forces had lost 1,865 killed, 2,560 wounded; 2,473 civilians had been murdered, 1,385 wounded and 810 were missing.

It was in its way one of the strangest wars in history, for to combat Mao Tse-tung's classic guerrilla tactics demanded new battle techniques without which it would have been impossible to bring the fight to the jungle lairs of the CTs. Success could never have been achieved without the backing of battalions of troops, squadrons of aircraft, radio communications. In twelve years, the original puny army had grown to 40,000 men; the police from 9,000 to 67,000; the Home Guard to 350,000. Aircraft dropped more than 525 million leaflets over the jungle. All these were needed in what Professor Short has described as 'the most significant defeat of guerrilla communism in Asia'; but it was also much more: a war in which Malayan Chinese played a heroic role as double agents in Special Branch; in which the police suffered 70 per cent of the total casualties; in which Malays in the special police squads killed more of the enemy then did the entire British army; a war which in the last resort was reduced to one of individuality – Irene Lee following the trail of Lee Meng, David Storrier patiently waiting for Osman China, Evan Davies stalking Goh Peng Tun, backed by men of vision who grasped the fundamental truth that Communism can only be beaten by winning the hearts and minds of the people – men like MacDonald, Gurney, Briggs, Templer, the Tunku, and last but not least, one man who saw the war through from start to finish – Bob Thompson.

And so, on July 31, 1960, the 'Emergency' finally ended – with the greatest victory parade Kuala Lumpur had ever seen, or is likely to see again. During the last week of July hundreds of thousands of Malayans streamed into the capital. Some walked, some rode bicycles, some took the buses which could now run freely, a few even trundled in on the Sakai Express. Every hotel room had long since been booked, but this made no difference. The Indians lay down in the gardens of the Sikh temple near Bandar Road and slept in the warm still night; the Malays dozed gratefully near the great red mosque in the heart of the city or the bright green padang between the Spotted Dog and the Moorish-style government buildings opposite. The Chinese – as usual – always seemed to have *some* relative where they could stay. Officials estimated that 20,000 men, women and children dossed down in the railway station alone – the ornate, flamboyant station unlike any other in the world. The Coliseum Bar had never done such business in its long and honourable history. At one time it almost ran out of whisky.

In streets decorated with bunting, the walls bearing huge placards of a benevolent, smiling Tunku, milling crowds let off fireworks for days on end – some consisting of long paper-covered bangers – as many as two hundred to one firework – on a string which could be suspended from a high building, so that when the bottom banger was touched off it automatically lit the one above, No machine-gun fire ever sounded more ominous. Street traders and hawkers did a roaring trade – particularly those selling satay, the succulent squares of meat on thin skewers cooked over charcoal and served with a hot sauce.

On the day of the great parade the crowds started lining the streets of the route before 4.00 a.m. Seats in the hastily-erected stands fetched astronomical prices on the black market; a corner of a packed window in a tenement with a view cost $10.

The victory parade took three hours to pass the main stands, with massed bands leading the way, followed by contingents from every branch of the service – everyone from Aborigines with blowpipes to men in armoured vehicles. Overhead Canberra jets roared.

Many old friends of Malaya returned for the celebrations, including the straight-backed man who had done more than any other to galvanize the country into action: General Templer. By chance he was seated on the dais next to Norman Cleaveland, the American chief of Pacific Tin. And it was left to this very pro-British American to pay one tribute to an absent – and perhaps forgotten – friend. As the last roll of drums faded, as the VIPs prepared to leave, Cleaveland looked at the placards of the Tunku smiling down from every corner, and turning to Templer said simply, in his direct American way, 'Pity no one thought of putting up a photo of Churchill. This country owes him a hell of a lot.'

POSTSCRIPT

Much has happened since the sun-drenched morning
when Bob Thompson dashed along the lonely jungle road
leading out of Sungei Siput as the first murders triggered
off a war that was to last twelve years; since the strange
midnight meeting between Dalley and the ill-fated Gent;
since the murder of Gurney; since the moment Templer
galvanized the country into new action. Some who fought
through that war went on to greater heights, some died,
some remained in the country they loved more than any
in the world.

Predictably, Bob Thompson had a distinguished career.
After remaining as Secretary for Defence until 1961, he
headed the British Advisory Mission to Vietnam and was
later knighted. He carved out a new career as the world's
greatest expert on counter-insurgency, and today lives in
an old, beautiful house in Somerset – which he leaves
regularly for Asia, as on the occasions when President
Nixon asked him to return to Vietnam.

General Templer became a Field Marshal, lives in a
quiet London street, and is still as straight-backed as on
the day he descended on Tanjong Malim. General Briggs,
who more than any other man helped to implement the
greatest social experiment in Asia, broke his health in
Malaya, and died only eleven months after retiring to his
home in Cyprus.

Almost all the cloak-and-dagger members of Special
Branch have settled by now for more humdrum lives. Evan
Davies returns to Malaya regularly as Security Chief to a
big international concern; while his old opponent Hor

Lung is the affluent capitalist owner (under another name) of a flourishing timber firm.

After Malayanization David Storrier returned with Lucie to live in a rambling country house near Godstone, Surrey, where Storrier now runs two highly profitable garages. His adversary Osman China applied to the *Strait Times* for a job as a reporter, but after being refused, left for Thailand and set up in business under another name.

Malaya's most glamorous woman detective, Irene Lee, became head of the Women's Police in the late 'fifties, but left the force in 1960 and quietly took a job as a secretary with an import firm in Singapore. Since then little has been heard of her – or of Lee Meng, the girl she so painstakingly trailed, and who remained in Taiping jail until 1964, when she was deported to China.

Yeop Mahidin, who led 26,000 kampong fighters, was given command of Malaya's expanding Territorial Army after the war, while C. C. Too became head of the government's Psychological Warfare Section. He is still there – with Lam Swee, who defected from the Johore jungle, still working in the next office.

Peter and Tommy Lucy live in England. Peter has become a London stockbroker, commuting from Sutton Valence, where he still shoots pheasants. Tommy is a member of Kent County Council. Ira Phelps died in retirement; so did 'Puck' Puckeridge; Norman Cleaveland still works with Pacific Tin and returns to Malaya regularly.

One man still insists on living in Malaya – in the White House high and lonely on the hill above Sungei Siput. To Dr Reid Tweedie, Malaya is 'home', and he still works as company director to several estates and still runs his 'Harley Street' clinic in the main street. It is as ramshackle as ever. And the good doctor still wraps up in the tropical heat against the cold he is terrified of catching.

Tweedie, like Malaya, is unchanged and unchanging. Of course he is older, and of course Malaya's cities now sprout new hotels, building developments and schools. The New Villages are old villages by now, respectable, growing, thriving. And yet, up the winding red path between the rubber only a few miles from the main road, Tweedie's house is the same as it was the day the war started. Indeed, the moment one leaves any main road the past comes out to engulf one – for where the jungle meets the road, where the giant ferns rise to a hundred feet, where the butterflies after the rain hover like a gaudy curtain across the steaming tarmac, where the monkeys cackle from above, and the snakes slither below, nothing has really changed and nothing ever will. The pitiless sun still blinds everything; the pelting rains still thrash against the rattan blinds or swell the ochre-coloured waters of the Pahang river; the ancient ferry at Jerantut is as unchanged as the country and its people. The Malay compounds along the banks, with their neat steps leading down to the water, are as timeless as the river itself.

There are dangers now, of course. Chin Peng still lurks north of the border, taking refuge not only in neutrality, but in the thought that if Mao Tse-tung had to wait thirty years in the 'Chinese jungle' before achieving victory he can do the same, for though the victory parade was held, no one can deny that the Emergency was not a self-contained war, one with a beginning, a middle and an end. It was a major defeat for Communism; but it was an episode in a continuing saga, whose next instalment may yet be to come, particularly if Chin Peng is able to exploit any outside conflict. After all, Lenin's chance was given to him by the Germans, Mao Tse-tung's by the Japanese. If the strife in Asia should bring a Communist government to the country where Chin Peng is waiting, his chance may come.

In the meantime Malaya – now part of the greater Malaysia – stands firmly on its own feet, proud, prosperous, multiracial, and still one of the most beautiful countries in the world, for there can be no change in the scenery where so much blood was shed and not in vain. The endless cathedral-like rows of rubber trees with the tappers there each dawn; the metallic sheen of the ponds sprouting with lilies in the tin-mining areas; and always behind, the jungle itself – the primordial jungle with its great straight trees blotting out the sun, the clumps of bamboo fifty feet high, the orchids and the tree tulips, the thick, spiky grass of the undergrowth, the hissing rains, the damp, wet belukar.

Even westwards over the mountains, where the cities and the money lie, every Chinatown from Ipoh to Johore Bahru is like the Chinatown of yesterday – the families with their bowls of rice squatting beneath the gaudy flags of washing jutting out on poles from the windows above; the endless shophouses still draped with their lacquered ducks, birds' nests, sharks' fins, and mounds of sweet, sticky condensed milk for the ever-increasing number of babies.

No, nothing has changed – except paradoxically everything – for freedom is everything; and though Malaya was never the slave state Chin Peng would have had the world believe, it is now independent. But the price of winning the world's first struggle against guerrilla Communism, of evolving a classic non-escalating formula for beating the tactics of Mao Tse-tung, was high and paid in blood, so it is not perhaps without point to remember that in the twelve-year war where liberty and independence were forged – and tempered with safety from aggression – more than 100,000 British army lads, together with rubber planters, tin miners, policemen and civil servants played their part, some of whom died in this fair and distant country for which they shed their blood.

BIBLIOGRAPHY

Books Consulted:

Brimmell, J.H., *Communism in S.E. Asia*, Oxford University Press, 1959
Campbell, Arthur, *Jungle Green*, Allen and Unwin, 1953; *Green Light*, Allen and Unwin, 1953
Chandos, Viscount, *Memories of Lord Chandos*, Bodley Head, 1952
Chapman, F. Spencer, *The Jungle is Neutral*, Chatto and Windus, 1949
Clutterbuck, Richard, *The Long, Long War*, Cassell, 1967
Crockett, Anthony, *Green Beret, Red Star*, Eyre and Spottiswoode, 1952
Griffiths, James, *Pages from Memory*, Dent, 1969
Gullick, J.M., *The Indigenous Political System of Western Malaya*, London School of Economics, 1965
Han Suyin, *And the Rain My Drink*, Jonathan Cape, 1956
Henniker, M.C.A., *Red Shadow Over Malaya*, Blackwood, 1955
Kennedy, J., *A History of Malaya*, Macmillan, 1962
Kirkup, James, *Tropic Temper*, Collins, 1963
Kitson, Frank, *Gangs and Counter Gangs*, Barrie and Rockliffe, 1960
MacDonald, James, *My Two Jungles*, Harrap, 1950
Miers, Richard, *Shoot to Kill*, Faber and Faber, 1959
Miller, Harry, *The Story of Malaya*, Faber and Faber, 1965; *Menace in Malaya*, Harrap, 1954
Moran, J.W.G., *The Camp Across the River*, Peter Davies, 1961
Mydens, Clark and Shelley, *The Violent Peace*, Atheneum, New York, 1970
O'Ballance, Edgar, *Malaya: The Communist Insurgent War*, Faber and Faber, 1966
Oldfield, J.B., *The Green Howards in Malaya*, Gale and Polden, 1953
Purcell, Victor, *Malaysia*, Thames and Hudson, 1965; *Malaya: Communist or Free?* Gollancz, 1954; *Memoirs of a Malayan Official*, Cassell, 1965
Pye, Lucien W., *Guerrilla Communism in Malaya*, Oxford University Press, 1956
Taber, P., *War of the Flea*, Paladin, 1970
Thompson, Sir Robert, *Defeating Communist Insurgency* Chatto and Windus, 1966

Documents Consulted:

Anatomy of Communist Propaganda, Malayan Government
Communist Banditry in Malaya, Malayan Government
The Federation of Malaya and Its Police 1786–1952, Malayan Government
Report of Police Mission to Malaya, March 1950, Malayan Government
The Communist Threat, Government of Malaysia Legislative White Paper No. 23, 1959
Unpublished papers, John Gullick
My Accusation, Lam Swee, Malayan Government
Malay Bandits under Abdullah CD, An Appreciation and Comments by Yeop Mahidin
Review of the Security Force Strategy in South Johore, J.B. Masefield, CPO Johore
Unpublished papers, Harry Miller
Report of the RAF in Malaya, 1954, Air Vice Marshal F.R.W. Scherger, CBE, DSO, AFC
Report of the International Seminar on Communism in Asia, June 19–25 1966, C.C. Too
Our Opinion of the Battle, Communist Party of Malaya
The Duties of a Sentry, Communist Party of Malaya
Military Weaknesses of the American Imperialists, Communist Party of Malaya
Manifesto of the Loi Tek Incident, Communist Party of Malaya
The October 1951 Directive, Communist Party of Malaya
Strategic Problems of the Malayan Revolutionary War, Chin Peng, 1949
The Tragedy of the Air Raid Incident of 21st February, Communist Party of Malaya.

All Orion/Phoenix titles are available at your local bookshop or from the following address:

Mail Order Department
Littlehampton Book Services
FREEPOST BR535
Worthing, West Sussex, BN13 3BR
telephone 01903 828503, *facsimile* 01903 828802
e-mail MailOrders@lbsltd.co.uk
(Please ensure that you include full postal address details)

Payment can be made either by credit/debit card (Visa, Mastercard, Access and Switch accepted) or by sending a £ Sterling cheque or postal order made payable to *Littlehampton Book Services*.
DO NOT SEND CASH OR CURRENCY.

Please add the following to cover postage and packing

UK and BFPO:
£1.50 for the first book, and 50p for each additional book to a maximum of £3.50

Overseas and Eire:
£2.50 for the first book plus £1.00 for the second book and 50p for each additional book ordered

---

BLOCK CAPITALS PLEASE

name of cardholder _____   *delivery address*
                     _____   *(if different from cardholder)*
address of cardholder _____
                                          _____
_____   _____
_____   _____
_____   _____
        postcode _____   *postcode* _____

[ ] I enclose my remittance for £_____

[ ] please debit my Mastercard/Visa/Access/Switch (delete as appropriate)

card number [ ][ ][ ][ ][ ][ ][ ][ ][ ][ ][ ][ ][ ][ ][ ][ ][ ][ ]

expiry date [ ][ ][ ][ ]   Switch issue no. [ ][ ]

signature _____

prices and availability are subject to change without notice